in detroit

Stephen Gifford Simmons
and the **Last Execution**
under **Michigan Law**

David G. Chardavoyne

Wayne State University Press   Detroit

GREAT LAKES BOOKS

A complete listing of the books in this series can be found at the back of this volume.

PHILIP P. MASON, Editor
Department of History, Wayne State University

DR. CHARLES K. HYDE, Associate Editor
Department of History, Wayne State University

Copyright © 2003 by Wayne State University Press,
Detroit, Michigan 48201. All rights are reserved.
No part of this book may be reproduced without formal permission.
Manufactured in the United States of America.
07 06 05 04 03   5 4 3 2 1

Library of Congress Cataloging-in-Publication Data

Chardavoyne, David G.
  A hanging in Detroit : Stephen Gifford Simmons and the last execution under
Michigan law / David G. Chardavoyne.
     p. cm. — (Great Lakes books)
Includes bibliographical references and index.
  ISBN 0-8143-3132-7 (alk. paper)—ISBN 0-8143-3133-5 (paper : alk. paper)
  1. Simmons, Stephen Gifford, 1780–1830.   2. Hanging—Michigan—
Detroit—History.   3. Capital punishment—Michigan—Detroit—History.
4. Detroit (Mich.)—History.   5. Detroit (Mich.)—Social conditions.
6. Detroit (Mich.)—Politics and government.   I. Title.   II. Series.
  HV8579.C33 2003
  364.66'09774'34—dc21

                                                                    2003002434

∞ The paper used in this publication meets the minimum requirements of the
American National Standard for Information Sciences—Permanence of Paper
for Printed Library Materials, ANSI Z39.48-1984.

THIS BOOK IS DEDICATED TO
KRIS, COLIN, AND MARK
FOR THEIR LOVE AND PATIENCE

contents

chapter 9

chapter 10

acknowledgments

I thank the dedicated staffs of the following institutions for their invaluable assistance: the National Archives, Washington, D.C.; the Burton Historical Collection at the Detroit Public Library; the Bentley Historical Library and the William Clements Library, both at the University of Michigan, Ann Arbor; the Library of Michigan and the State Archives of Michigan, both in the Michigan Historical Center, Lansing; the Michigan History Collection at the Farmington Public Library, Farmington Hills, Michigan; the Library of the New York Historical Association in Cooperstown, New York; the Guernsy Memorial Library in Norwich, Chenango County, New York; and the library of the Town of New Berlin, New York.

I also thank Mrs. Margery Facklam, United States District Court Judge Avern Cohn, and Wayne County Circuit Court Judge Arthur J. Lombard for their encouragement and help.

preface

On September 24, 1830, Stephen Gifford Simmons, who had been convicted of murdering his wife Levana in a jealous and drunken rage, met his death on the gallows in Detroit, then only a small village in the Territory of Michigan. This hanging was the last of the few public executions that took place in Michigan before the state abolished the death penalty in 1846. Simmons's trial and hanging are important not only because of their significance to the study of Michigan's early legal and territorial history, but also because of the current nationwide public debate over the death penalty.

In his exhaustively-researched and well-written account of Simmons's historic trial and execution, David Chardavoyne, a legal scholar, has given us an authoritative study of this important event. In some respects the title of Chardavoyne's book is misleading; he has given us more than a narrative of the trial and the hanging. From his extensive research into hitherto untapped historical sources, including court records, diaries, letters, census records, and rare legal documents, he has given us a portrait of Stephen Simmons as a farmer, a tavern keeper, and one of Michigan's early pioneers. Chardavoyne begins with Simmons's birth and early life in New York City during the American Revolution, then recounts Simmons's move to upstate New York and subsequent relocation to the Territory of Michigan in the 1820s.

In many ways Simmons was typical of the settlers who moved west to find homes and opportunities on the frontier. Like many of these settlers he lacked a formal education and had difficulty eking out a living. Simmons also engaged in the popular practice of investing his meager funds in land speculation at a time when Detroit and the surrounding area were opening up to settlers from New England, New York, and Europe. Unlike most of his neighbors, however, Simmons was constantly in trouble with the Territory's legal system.

There have been biographies of Michigan's early military, religious, and public leaders, including Anthony Wayne, Augustus B. Woodward, Lewis Cass, Father Gabriel Richard, and Henry Schoolcraft; Chardavoyne's work is one of the few that portray an ordinary settler and businessman.

A *Hanging in Detroit* gives us a detailed account of farming, tavern life, and travel in early Detroit and describes the social life of the period. The book thoroughly examines the extensive use and abuse of alcoholic beverages by many of Detroit's early settlers, including some of the town's prominent citizens, and scrutinizes Simmons's abusive treatment of his wife and family during his drunken episodes. In addition, the work offers a comprehensive discussion of Michigan's Territorial Court system that includes biographical sketches of the leading attorneys and judges in Detroit.

Another valuable aspect of Chardavoyne's study is the information he has gathered about a broad range of historical sources that document this early period in Michigan's history, many of which have seldom been consulted by historians. He has located forgotten records relating to the hanging and the events surrounding that incident, as well as dramatic eyewitness accounts of Simmons's behavior before the crowd gathered to witness his death, and used these materials to give us a mirror of life in Detroit during that period.

Such historians and writers as George Catlin, Silas Farmer, and Clarence Burton who have written about life in early Detroit have given superficial accounts of the Simmons hanging. Chardavoyne, however, has presented the first definitive study of the event and its significance in Michigan history.

Philip P. Mason
Distinguished Professor of History
Wayne State University
Detroit, Michigan

chapter 1

Introduction

If we would study with profit the history of our ancestors, we must never forget that the country of which we read was a very different country from that in which we live.

THOMAS MACAULAY, *History of England*

During the first fifty years of American rule in Michigan, the punishment for murder was death by hanging. But in that period—from 1796, when the British garrison finally evacuated Detroit, until 1846, when the State of Michigan's Legislature abolished capital punishment—only two people were executed under Michigan law.[1] The second and last such person was Stephen Gifford Simmons, a fifty-year-old tavern keeper and farmer who went to the gallows on September 24, 1830, for murdering his wife, Levana Simmons, in a drunken and jealous rage.[2]

Although the crime itself was sordid rather than scandalous, and although Stephen G. Simmons (as he invariably styled himself) was a man of few accomplishments in life, by the early twentieth century his death on the gallows had developed iconic status as one of the defining events of the time as Michigan began to change from a wild, underpopulated wilderness, known principally for its furs, to a thriving and civilized agricultural and manufacturing state powered by tens of thousands of settlers who had begun arriving from New York State and New England even as Simmons went to his death.

But Simmons's contemporaries do not seem to have perceived any significance in the story of Michigan's last hanging for many

years afterwards. There are only two contemporary written
accounts of the case, one in the city's newspaper and the other by
a visiting journalist. Nothing more was written until more than
fifty years later when three elderly men set out their reminiscences of the affair. There was silence once more until 1923,
when George B. Catlin, the librarian for the *Detroit News*, published *The Story of Detroit*, in which he retold old stories of the
city's history in an engaging and popular style. Unfortunately,
Mr. Catlin relied on the least reliable published source and added
more than a bit of his imagination in telling the Simmons story.
Nevertheless, he created a dramatic and colorful version of the
hanging of Stephen G. Simmons that has become unchallenged
history and the sole basis for every account written since 1923[3]:

> Owing to bad roads and the fear of lawless characters who
> sometimes robbed travelers found abroad at night, wayside
> taverns were kept at intervals of a few miles along every main
> line of travel. At the present site of Eloise County Hospital
> in Western Wayne County was one of these hostelries known
> as the Black Horse Tavern. In the city of Wayne was another,
> kept for several years by Stephen G. Simmons. Simmons was
> a man of massive build and of fine appearance. He was also a
> man of considerable education, but he became a hard drinker
> and when intoxicated he was quarrelsome and even danger-
> ous. He had picked quarrels and then mauled a number of
> men and had made many bitter enemies.
>
> He had a wife who was in feeble health, and two daughters.
> These women lived in terror of the husband and father because
> of his violent temper when drunk. One night he went to the
> room where his wife lay in bed, carrying a jug of whisky. He
> was in an ugly mood and insisted that his wife drink with him.
> She took several drinks, hoping to appease him, but he insisted
> that she take more. On her refusal he struck her a blow with
> his fist that killed her. Her terrified daughters witnessed the
> tragedy and tried in vain to restrain him.
>
> Seeing that his wife was dead, Simmons became gradually

sobered and very penitent. He was arrested, brought to
Detroit and tried for murder before Judges Solomon Sibley,
Henry Chipman and William Woodbridge, sitting en banc.
The prosecution was conducted by B. F. H. Witherell, while
George A. O'Keefe, a noted lawyer, defended him.

Simmons' guilt was plainly established by the testimony of
his own daughters. His general unpopularity undoubtedly had
some influence with the jury which convicted him in spite of
O'Keefe's eloquent plea for mercy on the ground that a
drunken man is not responsible for his acts.

The court sentenced Simmons to be hanged September
24, 1830. Simmons was given every protection of the law, but
it was so hard to find jurors that were not prejudiced against
him that over 300 talesmen were sworn and obtained their
dismissal on declaring that they believed Simmons should be
hanged. At the trial Simmons made a fine appearance as the
whisky was out of his system and he looked like a man of
superior mental as well as physical ability, as compared with
most of the men in the courtroom. But five years of turbulent
living and the testimony that during his drunken sprees he
had often beaten his wife and daughters settled the matter of
mercy for the offender.

The prospect of a public execution in Detroit caused a
great stir in all the adjoining territory. Thomas S. Knapp was
sheriff of Wayne County, but he balked at officiating as public hangman, flatly refusing to act in that capacity. There
was lively discussion of the matter in "Uncle Ben"
Woodworth's Steamboat Hotel. "Uncle Ben" held that the
law must be enforced or no man would respect it; that any
man who accepted a public office as judge or sheriff should
be willing to perform all the duties of his office, however
unpleasant. He was challenged on that statement and asked
if he would be willing to hang Simmons. "Uncle Ben" was
always ready to back up his own words and declared that if
he were appointed for that duty he would do it as a service
to the Territory for the upholding of the law.

Gov. Cass sent for him, and after talking the matter over, appointed him as acting sheriff in place of Knapp. Mr. Woodworth immediately began preparations for the execution, which he was determined to make as impressive as possible. He had a quadrangular grandstand of plank benches constructed about the jail yard, between the jail building and Gratiot Avenue, now Library Park. In the center, on the edge of Gratiot Avenue, a space was left for the scaffold, which was built of heavy timbers. On the day preceding the execution every road leading to Detroit showed a straggling stream of settlers from the surrounding country coming toward Detroit on horseback and on foot. That night the hotels were crowded and some of the people opened their homes to the visitors.

Next day the grandstand was packed with spectators two hours before the time set for the execution. Outside the ranks of benches stood a solid mass of people and back of them a row of men on horseback. "Uncle Ben" called out the regimental band to add to the impressiveness of the affair. Presently the heavy door of the jail swung open and he appeared walking arm and arm with Simmons, while a deputy walked on the other side of the condemned man. Simmons was bare-headed. He stood half a head taller than his conductors. His usually ruddy face was very pale, but he walked to the scaffold and mounted the steps leading to it with a firm step. He sat looking over the throng of witnesses while the death warrant was read, and then arose and delivered an able address in which he confessed his faults, warned all in his hearing to beware of strong drink and said that he had hoped for the mercy of the court and of the Governor.

Then in a strong baritone voice of excellent quality, he sang a familiar hymn of that period:

Show pity, Lord, O Lord, forgive,
Let a repenting rebel live;
Are not thy mercies full and free?
May not a sinner trust in Thee?

My crimes are great, but can't surpass
The power and glory of Thy grace,
Great God, Thy nature has no bound,
So let Thy pardoning love be found.

The scene produced a powerful impression upon the assembly. Many who had come to the jail yard eager to see justice done to a man they disliked began to feel themselves in a more forgiving mood, but only the Governor could halt the execution now, and no reprieve came at the last moment. The acting sheriff led Simmons to the trap beneath the beam of the scaffold. He had provided an unusually strong rope because Simmons weighed more than 250 pounds. The noose was adjusted and the executioner stepped to one side and pulled the lever which released the trap. Simmons shot through the opening and died almost instantly from the breaking of his neck.

The crowd hurried away from the scene to discuss the affair from beginning to end at the bars of various taverns, and as a result of this discussion there began to develop from that hour an aversion to capital punishment among the people of Michigan. They had not minded the hanging of a few Indians, but a white man, and one who could make the affair as gruesomely impressive as had Simmons, made it quite a different matter. Three men had been flogged that season at the public whipping post, but shortly after the execution of Simmons the act authorizing the whipping of small offenders was repealed and the whipping post, which had stood as a symbol of law in Detroit for 13 years, was routed from the ground and abolished forever.[4]

My initial plan was to retell Mr. Catlin's wonderfully dramatic story in my own words, supplemented by whatever small amount of additional material I could discover. However, as I found and reviewed the few eyewitness accounts, and as I discovered that various libraries and museums contained a large number of contemporary records and documents relating to the case and to Simmons's life, I had to recognize that, except for its bare outline, Mr. Catlin's account is largely a myth, although not entirely of his making. Although the relevant records are far from complete, and there are still many facts that can only be guessed at, it became clear to me that the story of the life, crime, and death of Stephen G. Simmons is more complex, but no less dramatic, than previous versions have suggested.

In writing what started out to be a short magazine article but ended up as this book, I have tried to answer basic questions that appealed to me as a lawyer: How did Stephen G. Simmons come to be placed on trial for murder and what happened at and after the trial? Why was Stephen G. Simmons hanged when other contemporary killers were barely punished at all? Both questions led me to investigate, as closely as I could, the life of the killer and the nature of the society or societies in which he lived. In the end, the reader will have to decide if I have been able to give a satisfactory answer to either question.

chapter 2

A Son of the Revolution

April 30, 1789, was a gala day in New York City, the most important day since the evacuation of the city by the British army
seven years earlier. In the former City Hall on Wall Street,
renamed Federal Hall when it became the seat of the federal government in 1785, General George Washington and John Adams
were to be sworn in as the first President and Vice President of
the United States under its newly ratified Constitution.[1] Stephen
Gifford Simmons, nine years old, had a front-row seat on the roof
of his family's tavern, a two-story, clapboard building with a steep
roof and attic dormers, which was directly across Nassau Street
from Federal Hall and nestled next to the Wall Street
Presbyterian Church.[2] From his perch, Stephen and the rest of
his family could see Washington and Adams walk out onto a
second-floor balcony overlooking Wall Street to take their oaths
of office. Later, as church bells rang throughout the city and can-
nons boomed from the Battery and from ships in the harbor,
Stephen could run along the streets, following the procession of
dignitaries to St. Paul's Chapel, where the new executive branch
held a service of thanksgiving.[3]

In truth, there is no evidence of how Stephen Simmons spent
that day, but it is highly unlikely that a boy of his age could
ignore the excitement and high drama taking place across the
street. Likewise, he could not avoid coming into contact with the
heroes of the Revolution who dominated the federal legislature
which, from 1785 to 1790, held its sessions at Federal Hall.
Imagine the feelings of the youngster as the legendary figures of
the great struggle for independence, in which his father and
brothers had served, stepped across Nassau Street and sauntered

into Simmons' Tavern for a bite or a dram during breaks in their legislative sessions. Although neither Washington nor Adams was much of a tavern-goer, Stephen would have seen and, perhaps spoken to, the likes of Secretaries of State John Jay and Thomas Jefferson, Treasury Secretary and Wall Street neighbor Alexander Hamilton, Secretary of War John Knox, Attorney General Edmund Randolph, Colonel Henry ("Light Horse Harry") Lee, and at least five signers of the Declaration of Independence in addition to Adams: Charles Carroll, Elbridge Gerry, Richard Henry Lee, Robert Morris, and Roger Sherman. The tavern was also a dining and meeting place for New York State and City officials such as Governor George Clinton and State Attorney General Aaron Burr. This must have been a heady clientele for the entire Simmons family, not just for its youngest son.

THE SIMMONS FAMILY OF OLD NEW YORK

Stephen's parents, John Simmons, Sr., and Catharine Dally Salter Simmons,[4] were issued a marriage license in New York City on December 21, 1758,[5] and were married later that month in New York City's Trinity Church.[6] It was the second marriage for Catharine in little more than two years. Born Catharine Dally (or Dalley), she had married William Salter in the same church on September 4, 1756.[7] When her husband died shortly thereafter, Catharine married John Simmons.

By the time of the Revolution, John and Catharine owned their well-known tavern at 63 Wall Street. Because of its location next to City Hall, Simmons' Tavern was a popular place for civic meetings both before and after the war.[8] For example, in February 1784 it was there that James Duane was installed as the first Mayor of New York City under American rule.[9] In 1787 there were 330 licensed taverns in New York City,[10] but Simmons' Tavern was one of the city's most popular establishments and its owner one of the city's most prominent tavern keepers.[11] As befitted the image of a convivial host of a jolly tavern, John Simmons was, at least in his later years, "a man of immense size"[12] whose obituary noted, among the plaudits, that he was "Said to be the most corpulent man in the United States."[13]

John and Catharine Simmons had five sons and a daughter who were alive when John made his will in August 1794. William was born in 1758 or 1759,[14] John Jr. in 1761, followed shortly by James and David. Their last two children, Stephen (born in 1780) and Catharine (born circa 1782), were twenty years younger than William and John Jr.[15] Although there are no accounts of their family life, by the criterion of given names the elder John and Catharine appear to have created a close family. Their children repeated those same names in their children so that the records are full of multiple instances of John Simmons's grandchildren named John, Catharine, William, David, and James. For example, Stephen and his wife, Levana Simmons, named three of their children Catharine, James, and David,[16] and they named another daughter Bathsheba after Stephen's aunt, the wife of his father's brother Thomas Simmons.[17] Stephen's mother, Catharine Dalley Salter Simmons, must have been a very strong influence on her sons because at least three of them, William, James, and Stephen, named a daughter after her.[18] However, it is telling that none of Stephen's siblings ever named a child after him even though his final disgrace did not occur until after all of his nephews and nieces were adults.

According to family stories, John Simmons, Sr., was born in Cuckfield, Sussex, England, and arrived in America as a young man. His will, written in 1794, stated that he still owned real estate "in Hanover Row, Portsmouth Common, England" at his death.[19] Despite or perhaps because of his English origin, John Simmons, Sr., and his sons John Jr. and William all served in the American forces in some manner. In the spring of 1776 John Sr. enlisted as a member of "the 2d Regt. of the New York Troops Commanded by Colonel James Clinton, Esqr.," a provisional Patriot organization formed in March 1776 and disbanded in

May of that year.[20] John Sr. was about forty at the time and, we can hope, not as rotund as he was later. John Jr., according to his pension application, served for two or three years with various New York infantry regiments, while William held the less arduous rank of army accountant.[21]

When the British army captured New York City in September 1776, not to leave until November 1783,[22] New Yorkers with Patriot leanings fled the city while Loyalist refugees from the countryside flooded in.[23] If the bitter animosities between Patriot and Loyalist were not enough incentive for New Yorkers to leave,[24] living conditions deteriorated quickly as the Americans established a land blockade around the city. Soon hunger, cold, and disease, including chronic smallpox,[25] set in, and any family that did not fear Patriot reprisals fled.

There is no direct evidence of when the Simmons family left the city, but indirect evidence makes it clear that they must have fled when, or soon after, the British arrived and that they did not return until the fighting was over. When the announcement of a provisional peace treaty reached America from London in March 1783, New York's exiles began to trickle back into the city to reclaim their homes and businesses.[26] As the time for the return of American sovereignty approached, one of the places those returned exiles gathered to plan the celebration was Simmons' Tavern. On November 18, 1793, one large group of New Yorkers "lately returned from a seven years' exile" named a committee "to meet tomorrow evening at Mr. Simmons' Tavern" in order to plan security and protocol for the reception of New York Governor George Clinton when he entered the city with the leading American troops on November 25.[27] That exile group advocated the deportation of any person who had remained in the city after the British arrived. They went so far as to exclude from all of their meetings all persons who remained or returned within the British lines, "whatever his political character may be."[28] It is unlikely that they would have been willing to meet at the Simmons Tavern if John and his family had remained in New York during the occupation.

The only evidence of where the Simmons family spent their exile is the baptismal record of John and Catharine's youngest son, Stephen Gifford Simmons. According to the records of Philadelphia's Christ Church, a "Gifford Stephen Simmonds," son of "John and Catharine Simmons," was baptized there on February 3, 1780, by the church's rector, Rev. William White.[29] Because of the flourish many writers of the time used to complete an "s," "Simmons" often appears as "Simmonds" in eighteenth-century records, while first and middle names were often reversed. There can be no doubt that this child was Stephen Gifford Simmons or that he was born in late January 1780. The family may have been living in that city, or they may have been taken in by John's brother and sister-in-law, Thomas and Bathsheba Simmons, in nearby Burlington County, New Jersey. Like New York, Philadelphia also suffered from chronic smallpox outbreaks during the war,[30] as well as yellow fever, and it may have been safer for the Simmons family to live in rural New Jersey. Indeed, Stephen's army record states that he was born in New Jersey,[31] and the fact that Stephen chose to name a daughter Bathsheba suggests that he must have had fond memories of his aunt. But there is really no conclusive evidence as to whether the family lived in Philadelphia or in the Jersey countryside during those turbulent years. All that can be said is that by November 1783 John was back in business at Wall and Nassau Streets where, on November 25, 1783, the date known in New York as Evacuation Day, the tavern was the site of a great public dinner given for Washington and his general officers.[32]

Returning citizens found New York City prostrate and the scars of the war and occupation still evident. Even Wall Street, the city's most fashionable neighborhood, was not immune. The Presbyterian church just to the west of Simmons Tavern still bore the signs of having been used as a barracks by the British. Trinity Church, at the junction of Wall Street and Broadway, was only a shell, a victim of the great fire that broke out as the British entered the city in 1776 and that destroyed the city from the Battery north, stopping just before it reached Wall Street. By

1788, however, the economy began to improve, and business was booming in 1793 when John Simmons decided to join "virtually every third American with money in his pockets" in speculating on frontier real estate.[33]

Among the New York politicians John Simmons came to know during or after the Revolution was "Judge" John Tayler. A Republican who was moderate enough to be a friend of arch-Federalist Alexander Hamilton, Tayler had served as a New York state assemblyman and senator as well as holding other state and local positions. Twenty years later, he would crown his career by being elected twice as Lieutenant Governor of New York (1811, 1813–17) and serving one year as Governor (1817).[34] In 1793, while Tayler was Recorder for Albany, where he had moved from New York City, he decided to invest in vast areas of virgin land west of Cooperstown, which were to be sold at auction by the State of New York. Tayler entered into a partnership with John Simmons and two other men, John I. Morgan and William Boyd, to purchase more than 43,000 acres along the Unadilla River in what would become, in 1798, Chenango County. John Simmons's share was nineteen lots totaling 4,850 acres, for which he paid just over twelve hundred pounds Sterling.[35]

The usual scheme of land speculators at that time, and at many other times in United States history, was to sell farm lots to an expected flood of optimistic immigrants and refugees from depleted farms in New England. But speculators in New York land in the mid-1790s, like Tayler and his associates, had missed the wave of pent-up demand moving west from New England to central New York after the Revolution. After the battle at Fallen Timbers in 1794 opened Ohio to settlement, the next wave heading west tended to bypass New York in favor of the warmer, more fertile, and cheaper lands in the Ohio Valley.[36] Moreover, the anticipated next wave of immigrants to the United States from Europe, particularly from England and France, never materialized. The wars between France and the rest of Europe that began in 1793 and lasted until 1815 ruined those plans. Money and men that the speculators expected to go into farming in the United

States went, instead, to fuel the armies of revolutionary France and its enemies. Many speculators who borrowed to buy land could not pay down their debts and were ruined.[37] But John Tayler, John Simmons, and their partners were able to withstand the crisis. Although almost none of John's 4,850 acres was sold before 1815, nor was any of the land he owned ever foreclosed for debt.

John did try to sell some of his frontier land. In April 1793, shortly after making his investment, John sent son John Jr. then thirty-one or thirty-two years old, to the Unadilla Valley. John and Catharine gave John Jr. and his second wife, Lucy, as joint tenants a lot containing 290 acres of rolling hill country and rich bottom-land along the Unadilla River, which John Jr. farmed for twenty years while acting as his father's sales agent.[38] In August 1795 John Jr. began advertising his father's other lots for sale in the only regional newspaper, the *Otsego Herald*, published in Cooperstown, New York, twenty miles to the east.[39]

The deed by which John Sr. and Catharine gave the 290 acres to John Jr. and his wife[40] is further evidence of their warm feelings for their children. Lucy Cunningham was John Jr.'s second wife, and the couple each brought three children to their union. John and Catharine accepted Lucy's children into the family and treated them like their own grandchildren. The deed itself declares that very reason for the transfer: "the natural love and affection which they hath and beareth unto John Simmons the younger at present of the City of New York and Lucy his wife and their children." The deed also provides that, even if Lucy were to remarry after John Jr.'s death, her three children, Robert, David, and Elizabeth Cunningham, were to inherit that property equally with John Jr.'s own three children, John, Samuel, and Elizabeth Simmons.

In sharp contrast to his brothers John Jr. and Stephen, who spent most of their lives as frontier farmers, William Simmons was a career federal bureaucrat in the nation's capital cities, New York, Philadelphia, and Washington, D.C., where the government moved in 1800.[41] Raised in New York, William learned the skills that qualified him to serve as an accountant for the

Continental Army during the Revolution. In the early part of his career William was an accountant for the War Department; later he held a similar position with the federal land sales agency.[42] In his early sixties William moved with his son, Charles Simmons, to Coshocton County, Ohio, where he died in 1825.[43]

John Simmons, Sr., died in New York City in August 1795 after almost thirty-seven years of marriage.[44] Because of his immense size, he could not be taken through the front door to be buried. Instead, "the pier between the door and the window of the house had to be torn out to allow the passage of his coffin." We do not know his age, but he was at least in his early sixties, an old man by the standards of the time. His widow Catharine was probably just as old but she was also either healthier or tougher; she survived her second husband by twenty or twenty-five years.[45]

When he made his will a year before his death, John made sure that all of his children would share in his estate, but he took particular care to provide security for his wife and for his two youngest children, Stephen and Catharine. John left his wife a life interest in "all my household furniture and plate" and in the residue of his estate (which would have included the tavern and his property in Chenango County) "for her support and to enable her to maintain and educate my two children, Stephen Gifford and Catharine, until they become of age." John also made specific bequests to his youngest offspring. Upon coming of age, Stephen was to receive thirty English Pounds in order "to buy a set of tools." John left to his daughter, Catharine, his "negro boy slave named Phill,"[46] his family Bible, and a gold mourning ring "that was given me by my mother, and which I desire may always remain with one of my posterity in remembrance of my mother." John also provided that, upon the death of his wife, his daughter was to receive the household furniture and plate. Finally, John provided that upon his wife's death, the residue of his estate, including the real estate, was to be divided equally among his children or their heirs.

John Sr.'s will gives us our first idea of the character of his sons, or at least how a fond father sized them up. He made a clear distinction among his older sons. Two, William and James, he appointed coexecutors with their mother. As for the other two, John Jr. and David, John Sr. noted that he had advanced money to both of them and that those advances should be deducted from their shares of the residue. The suggestion is that William and James were capable and reliable while John Jr. and David were decidedly less so. That evaluation of John Jr. might have been vindicated when, ten years later, the coexecutors had to bail him out when his farm on the Unadilla was sold for debt.[47] But John Jr. was then forty-five years old, and there are many reasons other than a youthful tendency to go into debt that could explain his money troubles.

John Sr.'s will also tells us something about how his father sized up Stephen at age fourteen. From descriptions made in 1830, he must have been an attractive young man: tall, well-built, and ruggedly handsome.[48] However, his father apparently did not think that Stephen was well suited to a sedentary life. John Sr. could have sent Stephen to Columbia or Princeton to become a minister or a lawyer. Alternatively, John could have made sure Stephen learned what was needed to become a clerk or a bookkeeper. The estate clearly had the wherewithal, and John clearly loved Stephen. Instead, John directed "that my executors shall pay out of the said residue of my estate, unto my son, Stephen Gifford, 30 pounds when he becomes of age to buy a set of tools."[49] At fourteen, it seems, Stephen, in his father's estimation, was better suited to the active life of a carpenter or mechanic.

A Lieutenant of the Light Dragoons

As often happens, Stephen followed a different career path from the one his father had anticipated. Not quite two years after John Simmons's death, on July 10, 1797, seventeen-year-old Stephen G. Simmons received a commission as a lieutenant of light dragoons in the United States Army.[50] We do not know if this was his choice or his family's, nor do we know if he simply applied for

a commission or benefitted from the influence of his brother
William at the War Department or of one of his father's tavern
customers. We can, however, guess that Stephen was motivated
by war stories told by his father or his brothers, and by serving a
pint or a meal to the many famous and honored veterans of the
Revolution who attended sessions of Congress and frequented his
family's tavern. For a teenager with that background and "a vigorous mind and an athletic frame,"[51] eager to experience grown-
up adventures, a military career was an obvious choice.

But the army that Stephen joined was, in numbers, morale,
and skill, a shadow of George Washington's Continental Army
during the Revolution or even of Anthony Wayne's Legion of
the West that in 1794, just three years earlier, had soundly
defeated the Ohio tribes at Fallen Timbers. In May 1796
Congress reduced the army's authorized strength from 5,414 officers and men to 3,3595[52] who were then scattered along the
nation's coasts and throughout the wilderness in units too small
to have any effective military role. Because of the difficulties of
communicating among units, the army became merely a collection of independent police forces controlled by their local post
commanders, too often unrestrained and self-serving tyrants.[53]
Soldiers lacked adequate housing, uniforms, or supplies. The gar-
den plots that many officers tilled often brought them more
money than their salaries did[54] and added nutrition to their soldiers' daily ration of one pound of beef, or three-quarters of a
pound of pork, and eighteen ounces of bread or flour.[55] Each soldier also received a gill (one-quarter pint) of rum, brandy, or
whiskey which killed the taste of the often rotten meat and
spoiled bread.[56] General Winfield Scott later remembered the
officers of that time as "swaggerers, dependents, decayed gentlemen and others fit for nothing else," who were "totally unfit for
any military purpose whatever." The older officers, usually veterans of the Revolution, were "sunk into either sloth, ignorance, or
habit of intemperate drinking."[57]

The abject state of the army was the result of Congressional
penny-pinching made palatable to the public by the fear of the

political and moral consequences of maintaining a professional military. As Samuel Adams wrote, "A standing army . . . is always dangerous to the liberties of the people" because of its tendency to become "a body distinct from the rest of the citizens."[58] In 1798 a group of citizens in Virginia expressed a common fear that reliance on a professional army would occasion "the oppression, the ruin, the *slavery* of the people."[59] So, if Congress could not do without an army entirely, it had popular support in keeping the army weak.

Given the appalling living conditions, low pay, and unpopularity, it is not surprising that, even though the reduction of force in 1796 reduced the authorized strength of the army's light dragoons to a mere eight officers and 126 enlisted men,[60] there were openings for new officers. Veterans of the Revolution grew too old for active service, while younger men quit in disgust or despair. One of those disenchanted young officers was Lieutenant Matthias Slough, Jr., of the light dragoons who had been promoted for bravery on the battlefield at Fallen Timbers in 1794 but who resigned his commission in early 1797.[61] Lieutenant Slough's resignation created a slot that Stephen filled a few months later when he put on the green coat, white breeches, high black boots, and plumed black helmet of a dragoon officer.

After three months of training at the army's central depot in Philadelphia, Lieutenant Simmons rode out in October 1797 in the company of another new cavalry officer, Cornet William Tharp, to join Van Rensselaer's Troop of Light Dragoons in eastern Tennessee. Stephen and Cornet Tharp took at least a month to travel from Philadelphia, along the rough trail that had already been hacked out of the forest between eastern Pennsylvania and Knoxville, capital of the new state of Tennessee.[62] However, by December, Stephen and Tharp had arrived in Powell's Valley (now the town of Powell) in the ridge country northwest of Knoxville, and they had settled in as the troop's junior lieutenant and cornet. Captain Van Rensselaer was not there to greet them because he was on an extended furlough to the family fiefdom near Albany, New York. In his absence the

company of three other officers and sixty-three enlisted cavalry-
men was commanded by Lieutenant James Vincent Ball, a veteran of three years' service, while seventeen year old Lieutenant
Simmons, with no experience at all, was second in command.

Knoxville and Knox County no longer needed the army for
protection from American Indian raids or an invasion from
Spanish Louisiana. With a population of about twelve thousand,
including about 2,500 slaves, Knox County was not part of the
wild frontier. Knoxville housed the state capital and Blount
College (now the University of Tennessee), it had a newspaper,
and large frame and stone mansions were replacing log cabins.
Instead, the purpose of the army in eastern Tennessee was to pro-
tect settlers traveling west on the Cumberland Trail and the
Tennessee River from bandits. Little more than a wagon track,
the trail ran northwest from Knoxville, through the Cumberland
Mountains, and then split, southeast to Nashville or north to
Kentucky, while the Tennessee River provided a water route into
central and western portions of the state. Both the trail and the
river attracted bands of armed robbers, and only the army provided settlers with organized protection from armed robbery.[63]

Stephen's assignments indicate that Van Rensselaer's Troop had
responsibility for security on the southern end of the trail and on
the waterways near Knoxville. Lieutenant Simmons spent his first
month or so at Powell's Valley, near where the Cumberland Trail
crossed Beaver Ridge, under the command of Lieutenant Ball.
However, during January 1798, Ball was sent to Knoxville, leaving
Stephen in charge of the troop, including the responsibility to prepare and sign the monthly muster roll.[64] In February Stephen was
sick, but he recovered quickly and, in March, he received his first
independent command. With Sergeant Clark, and fifteen privates,
Stephen was dispatched "on command" to Belle Cantonment,
now Bell Campground, a staging area for settlers a few miles west
of Powell. Stephen and his squad remained there until July when
they were sent to Mouth of Holston, where the Holston and
French Broad Rivers join to form the Tennessee River, another
gathering place for travelers heading west. By the end of August

1798, Stephen and his men were back at Powell's Valley where he remained through August 31, 1799.[65]

Thirty years later, one of Stephen's "nearest relatives" told Detroit's *North-Western Journal* that Stephen, "at an early age, became separated, by his own misconduct, from the circle of respectable connexions [sic]. Endowed with a vigorous mind and an athletic frame, capable of achieving an honorable independence, he had voluntarily thrown himself into the company of the abandoned of both sexes, and become a partner in all their enterprises, whether the objects were wealth or pleasure."[66] Although there is no evidence of how Stephen spent his off-duty hours in Tennessee, it is likely that his "misconduct" began there.

Although Knoxville was no longer on the frontier, it retained a taste for reckless living.[67] Whiskey drinking and tobacco chewing were near universal, and it would defy human nature if prostitution were not as well, although the most popular male pastime was tavern brawling. As one Tennessee historian noted:

> Whiskey drinking may have been responsible for some of the
> fights and brawls on the frontier, but apparently hundreds
> fought for the sheer love of combat. Although antagonists
> chiefly used fists, they often resorted to kicking, biting, and
> clawing. The nose and ears of an opponent were especially
> vulnerable to biting and clawing, and many a youth was
> scarred for life after such an encounter.[68]

Stephen was a very young man, separated from his family for the first time, by all accounts large and athletic, handsome and sociable. Exposed to the boredom and deprivation of army life and to a civilian world of drinking, violence, crime, and general mischief, it is likely Stephen did succumb to "the abandoned of both sexes."

Then, in August 1799, Stephen left his troop and returned to Philadelphia[69] where, on October 28, 1799, he was appointed paymaster of the army's newly formed regiment of light dragoons which was headquartered in Newark, New Jersey.[70] We do not know if Stephen was specifically chosen for the post and ordered to return east to take up his new post. Alternatively, after nearly two years in Tennessee, he may have simply taken a leave of absence to return home and appeared at army headquarters at a propitious moment when the second-in-command of the regiment, newly promoted Major Solomon Van Rensselaer, was looking for a likely candidate for the job. It is, of course, also possible that now Captain Ball used a well-known tactic of army commanders throughout the ages to rid himself of a troublesome subordinate by kicking him upstairs. Whatever the truth, Stephen was now a staff officer living in relative comfort among gentleman officers chosen for their impeccable Federalist political beliefs.

The light-dragoon regiment, including six new troops, was part of an increase in the army's authorized strength, from three thousand men to more than fifty thousand, resulting from fears that the revolutionary government of France intended to launch a trans-Atlantic invasion of the United States. Relations with our former ally were, in fact, strained by French seizures of American merchant ships and by a general unease about the excesses of the French revolution. At the same time, it was apparent to many people who considered the matter calmly, including President John Adams, that no French army of any size could cross the Atlantic without being intercepted and destroyed by England's Royal Navy.

Nevertheless, as it was about to adjourn in May 1798, Congress directed the President to raise a "provisional" army of ten thousand additional enlisted men, plus officers.[71] Two months later, Congress authorized President Adams to augment the regular army by a further thirty thousand men and officers by raising many new regiments including a regiment of light dragoons with a colonel, major, regimental staff, and six new troops in addition to the two already serving on the frontier.[72] In March 1799 Congress, in even greater panic, authorized the President to raise twenty-seven more regiments, including three of cavalry, in case of a war with, or imminent threat of invasion by, "some European prince, potentate, or State."[73]

President Adams was opposed to increasing the size of the army, but he could not refuse to do so openly. A moderate Federalist, Adams feared that raising more troops would only confirm in the voters' minds what the Republicans were warning: that the Federalists were anti-democratic royalists at heart who were plotting a *coup d'etat* led by the army. Adams temporized by appointing the aging George Washington to command the provisional army, but Washington refused to take the field. Instead, at Washington's insistence, the pompously militaristic Alexander Hamilton was appointed Inspector General and *de facto* commander of the provisional army.

Republican fears about Federalist motives were not without foundation. Hamilton seems, in fact, to have considered using his new command to influence domestic politics in some fashion. He filled the new regiments with Federalist officers, including Solomon Van Rensselaer whom he promoted to major and second-in-command of the regiment of light dragoons,[74] and he was careful to avoid appointing any officers who were not known to share his politics. The fact that Stephen was appointed regimental paymaster before he was twenty years old indicates that he was considered politically trustworthy.

Unfortunately for Hamilton's plans, and for Stephen's blossoming career, President Adams kept Hamilton's army toothless by quietly refraining from enlisting soldiers for the new regiments. As war fever subsided at the end of 1799, the provisional army consisted of the officers appointed by Hamilton and little else, leaving Stephen lacking a regiment to pay. It is not known what his actual regimental duties were, if any, although he may very well have participated in the great funeral parade held in Philadelphia on December 26, 1799, to mourn the death of George Washington:

> The day after Christmas, the official day of mourning in the
> capital, troops of light infantry and cavalry passed through the
> city to the slow military beat of muffled drums, in a grand
> solemn procession that began at Congress Hall and included a

host of federal and state leaders, city magistrates, Masons, and a riderless white horse with reversed boots in the stirrups.[75]

What else he may have done to pass the time is unknown, but it is likely that he continued developing the habits he had learned in Tennessee.[76]

Whatever Stephen's duties were as regimental paymaster, he did not perform them for very long. In February and May 1800 Congress repealed the laws creating Hamilton's paper army and reduced the light dragoons to their 1796 size of two troops.[77] Within months, Stephen was ordered back to Tennessee where he was present at the monthly muster of what was now Captain Ball's Troop of Light Dragoons on October 31, 1800.[78] However, something else must have happened because the muster roll for that day reported Lieutenant Simmons as "in arrest." A month later, on November 12, 1800, Stephen was "dismissed" from the army,[79] and Cornet Tharp was promoted to Lieutenant in his place.[80] Stephen was still on the troop's pay roster in January 1801,[81] but the words "in arrest" and "dismissed" leave no doubt that he left the army in disgrace. The use of term "dismissal" contrasts with the term used to indicate the separation from the Army his fellow officers, Major Van Rensselaer, Captain Ball, and Lieutenant Tharp, all of whom were "honorably discharged" on June 1, 1802,[82] the effective date of the act of Congress that abolished all federal cavalry.[83]

We do not know what Stephen did to cause the army to expel him under apparently dishonorable circumstances, but, given the generally low moral state of the officer corps, his offense must have been serious indeed. The fact that he served as regimental paymaster until just a month before he was dismissed suggests financial improprieties, but we cannot be sure.

A Chenango County Family

When Stephen left the army, he disappeared from the public record for almost fifteen tears. He was not counted in the 1810

United States census as a head of household in any state or in any other record available. There are several men named Stephen Simmons in the census, including one in Jefferson County, New York, who opened a tavern in Sacket's Harbor in 1806. But he was too old to be Stephen Gifford Simmons, and the others can be excluded as well.

If we do not know where he lived or how he earned a living, we can say that in about 1805, when he was twenty-five years old, Stephen married a woman named Levana. We know nothing about Levana before she became Stephen's wife: when or where she was born, where she lived before her marriage, her maiden name, or when, where, and why she married Stephen. It was difficult even to discover her given name. No account of the Simmons murder case has ever used Levana's given name but, instead, refer to her as Stephen's wife or as the children's mother. Levana's name is preserved only in several deeds recorded in Chenango County, New York, during the 1820s and in notes made by Clarence Burton regarding the criminal case file that he apparently discovered in the attic of the old Detroit City Hall but which has since disappeared again.[84]

There is some circumstantial evidence of when Levana Simmons was born, but it is inconclusive. During the murder trial, the *North-Western Journal* reported that Levana was thirty-nine years old at her death,[85] but census records indicate that she was a bit older. The returns of the 1830 U.S. census for Wayne County, Michigan, state that the household headed by Stephen G. Simmons included one woman between forty and fifty years old, but none aged between thirty and forty, and none more than fifty years old.[86] The returns for the 1820 U.S. census do not help narrow down her age because the returns for New Berlin, New York, state that the oldest female in the household fell within the interval of twenty-five to forty-five years of age.[87] Therefore, the best we can say on the present evidence is that Levana was between forty and fifty years old when she died in June 1830.

We can know or infer slightly more about Stephen and Levana's children. There were six living at the time of Stephen's and Levana's deaths in 1830, four of them female and two male:

Catharine, James, Ellen, David, Bathsheba, and Lavina.[88] Where they were born is unknown, but by analyzing census returns and court records, it is possible to approximate their birth years.[89] Catharine, the oldest Simmons daughter, was born between 1805 and 1810. In 1830 she and her two young children were living with her parents while she divorced her husband, one Fitzpatrick McCarty. James, the older son, was also born between 1805 and 1809. He was not living with his parents in 1830, although he may have been managing another family farm in Michigan. Daughter Ellen and son David were born between 1810 and 1812, and their sisters Bathsheba and Lavina between 1814 and 1818. The three daughters were listed in the 1830 census as part of their father's household. David was not, but he was at his parents' home on the night of his mother's murder.

FLOUNDERING ALONG

After John Sr.'s death, William took over management of the estate, acting as coexecutor with his brother James and their mother. James died in Philadelphia in 1809,[90] after which William and Catharine continued as "surviving coexecutors." Catharine apparently died after James but before May 1815. In that month William first executed a deed as the "sole surviving executor" of his father's estate when he sold Stephen all of lot sixty-nine in New Berlin, a total of 228 acres, for $1,824.[91] It is not known whether Stephen paid cash or, rather, like many buyers at that time, bought on credit.[92]

Chenango County, twenty miles west of Cooperstown, is even now, at the beginning of the twenty-first century, Leatherstocking country, composed as much of hills and woods as farmers' fields. Once outside of Norwich, the only town of any size, the landscape is a living illustration from *The Deerslayer* or *The Last of the Mohicans* painted by Howard Pyle or N. C. Wyeth. Steep, rounded hills, covered in forests of maple and oak, loom over small, green fields carved out, here and there, on their lower slopes or along the edges of the Unadilla and Chenango Rivers or the many creeks and streams that run through the county. At an altitude of more than 1200 feet above sea level, the Unadilla Valley has a short growing period, and farmers concentrate on forage crops such as corn and hay, or on such cold-weather crops as pumpkins, squash, carrots, and potatoes. Today dairy farming is the prime money crop, but in the early nineteenth century potash proved to be most families' most reliable cash crop. The residue of cremated hardwood trees, potash was valuable as a fertilizer and as an ingredient in soap, saltpeter, dyes, bleach, glass, and medicines. Although located near Binghampton and Cooperstown, Chenango County is still sparsely populated, working rural community and not a popular tourist destination.[93]

Lot sixty-nine in New Berlin Township is situated on rich bottomland along the west bank of the Unadilla, giving Stephen and his family as good a chance of prosperity as any farmer in the area. But according to one informal history of New Berlin written in 1876 by local resident John Hyde, Stephen and his brother John left their neighbors with the memory of two young neophyte farmers who were out of their depth: "Mr. John Simmons, and his brother Stephen, found that a city education was not adapted to the agricultural pursuits of backwoodsmen, however, they were both robust, strong young men, floundering along, clearing up their farms and raising crops as best they might."[94]

Although the author noted accurately that "Stephen G. Simmons sold his farm and moved west many years ago,"[95] there are enough problems with other details of Hyde's account of the Simmons family in New Berlin to make a reader cautious. For example, Hyde says that Stephen farmed lot seventy-eight in New Berlin Township, but there is no evidence that either John Sr. or Stephen ever owned a lot with that designation. Indeed, a nineteenth-century plat map of the township does not include a lot seventy-eight. Hyde also implies that John sold his lot soon after taking possession and making a few improvements. But John owned all or part of lot seventy-five for twenty-two years, from 1793 until 1815, except for a few months in 1806 when it was sold for debt and repurchased for him by his family. In his application for a pension as a veteran of the Revolution, John confirmed that he lived in Chenango County for twenty years.[96] John did sell portions of the lot, as Hyde noted, to Levi Blakeslee and Charles Harris, and the rest to one Augustus A. Anderson,[97] but those sales took place between 1812 and 1815, when John was more than fifty years old.

Conversely, Stephen owned no land in Chenango County until he bought lot sixty-nine on May 17, 1815, just eleven days after his brother John sold the last of his Chenango County property. It is possible that Stephen and his young family had been living with his brother, or that Stephen had been farming family land in the Unadilla Valley as a tenant, or that he was sent out to New Berlin that spring to replace John in managing the family lands. There is simply no evidence upon which to judge. In any case, Stephen was thirty-five years old when he purchased lot sixty-nine and forty-five when he left for Michigan. Hyde's descriptions of John and Stephen's experiences in New Berlin should, therefore, be taken for what they are: community memories set down more than fifty years after Stephen moved west and at a time when there were, according to Hyde, no members of the Simmons family left in New Berlin to provide accurate information.

Whatever Stephen's motive for buying lot sixty-nine, Chenango County records indicate that, soon after buying it, he sold about half of the lot to one Jack Bancroft for a modest profit,[98] and that he sold the rest of it, in August 1818, to a Stephen Goodrich, again for a small profit. Six months later, possibly in need of cash after a bad winter, Goodrich sold the 110 acres back to Stephen for seven hundred dollars less than the price he paid for it.[99] Stephen, Levana, and their family were, it appears, living on those 110 acres in New Berlin when the 1820 U.S. census was conducted.[100]

Stephen celebrated his fortieth birthday in early 1820. If he took stock of his progress, he would have had to recognize that in a society that emphasized the acquisition of wealth as the premier gauge of a man, he did not measure up. To support his wife and six young children, he had only his dubious skills as a farmer and 110 acres of land, worth perhaps a thousand dollars or less. He also lacked any civic distinction, the era's other measuring stick. Local records do not indicate that he ever held any public office or religious position in New Berlin. In sum, he was, by the standards of his time, a nonentity.

Imagine, then, his excitement when the news reached him that William was prepared to distribute the rest of John Sr.'s estate. His share of the estate's land would make him a major landowner in New Berlin and, perhaps, change his luck. William summoned the family to meet at his home in Washington, D.C., on April 20, 1820. There were several routes Stephen could have taken to get to Washington, including through New York or Philadelphia, but the easiest was to take a barge down the Susquehanna River to the Chesapeake Bay and then up the Potomac River to Washington. In the chill of April, the trip would not have been easy for a man who was no longer young, but the reward promised to make it worthwhile.

The signatures of the witnesses on the deeds that William Simmons executed to transfer the Chenango County lands to John Sr.'s descendants establish that, besides William and Stephen, the family conclave included three gentlemen from Philadelphia, David P. Simmons, William S. Simmons, and Condy Raguet. William S. Simmons was the son of Stephen's brother James who had died in Philadelphia in 1809. William S. shared his inheritance with his sister, Catharine S. Raguet, the wife of Condy Raguet. Stephen's brother John had sold the balance of his New Berlin property in May 1815 and moved to Dearborn County, Indiana, and was not represented at the meeting but did receive his share of the land. David P. Simmons received a full share of the estate, so he must have been either Stephen's older brother or the only surviving child.[101] Stephen's sister Catharine, who married George MacDaniel in Washington, D.C., in 1805, was not present or represented at the meeting, and she did not receive a share. If David P. was not her son, she must have died without leaving any children.

Stephen, after many years of rural life that had brought him little wealth and no distinction, may well have felt ill at ease among his more prosperous and urbane relatives. William Simmons was sixty years old and approaching the end of a successful career as a federal bureaucrat that extended back to the Revolution. He was the father of two sons, William H. and Charles W. Simmons, who were also government officials. The other Simmons men at the meeting in Washington, William S. Simmons and David P. Simmons were prosperous Philadelphia merchants, while in-law Condy Raguet was an equally impressive and interesting addition to the family. Born in Philadelphia in about 1784, he had already been a merchant sailor, a soldier, a banker, and a well-known writer on the economics of the currency and tariffs whose opinions influenced President Andrew Jackson. A few months after this gathering of the Simmons family, he became an attorney and a member of the Philadelphia Bar, and from 1822 to 1827 he would serve as the United States envoy and ambassador to Brazil.[102]

Whatever Stephen's feeling about his status in the family, he could console himself during his return trip to New Berlin that he carried a deed that added to his meager 110 acres another five hundred acres consisting of all of New Berlin's lots two and four. Although those lots were several miles from his other land on the Unadilla River, and were not next to each other, they did contain upland woods and pastures well situated along a stream.

Stephen cannot ever have intended to farm all three parcels himself. They were too far apart, and the effort would have been too great without grown sons or other relatives to help him. Instead, he may have looked at his new land, which had probably not yet been cleared and prepared for farming, with the calculating eye of a speculator, hoping to subdivide the lots and to sell the smaller parcels to newcomers to the valley. At the beginning and end of the winter of 1821–22 (in November 1821 and February 1822),[103] he did sell two small parcels, including thirty-two acres in lot sixty-nine, for a total of $520, but that money probably went to tide the family over the winter and to the next harvest. By 1825 there was still no wave of new settlers willing to pay high prices for small farms, so Stephen and Levana apparently decided to liquidate their Chenango County holdings and move to the Michigan Territory. In August 1825 they sold all of lot four and the remaining acres of their farm in lot sixty-nine, a total of 317 acres, to an immigrant who did appear on the scene, one Alexander Beatty, "late of the Kingdom of Ireland," for $1,463.66.[104]

Soon after making that sale, Stephen and Levana packed up the children and their belongings and became forerunners of the great tide of New Yorkers and New Englanders who would raise the population of the Michigan Territory from less than 15,000 in 1825 to 212,000 in 1840.[105] They arrived in Detroit in October 1825, and Stephen quickly bought a small lot to house the family while he looked around for a promising opportunity. By the time they sold the remainder of their New York land in 1828, they were firmly transplanted and recorded as "Stephen G. Simmons and Levana his wife of the Territory of Michigan."[106]

chapter 3

"A Country That Will Suit Your Mind"

Don't go to Michigan, that land of ills;
That word means ague, fever, and chills.

POPULAR 1820S SONG

My Eastern friends who wish to find
A Country that will suit your mind,
Where comforts are all near at hand,
Had better come to Michigan.

The Emigrant Song

THE GREAT MIGRATION

There is no direct evidence to explain the reasons that led
Stephen G. and Levana Simmons to move from Chenango
County to the Michigan Territory in the autumn of 1825.[1] Their
underlying reasons were probably no different from those of the
other families who emigrated to Michigan from New York and
New England between 1825 and 1840. Land in Chenango
County was becoming less productive, while Michigan offered an
abundance of cheap and fertile land, a milder climate, and,
because of the new Erie Canal, cheap and fast transportation to
the markets and port of New York City for their produce.

Although created by Congress in 1805, the Michigan
Territory did not initially attract many settlers, who preferred the
more accessible land available along the Ohio River. In 1810 the
white population of the territory was less than five thousand
French and American settlers, and by 1820 that number had
grown to no more than nine thousand, including the population
of the territory's western counties in what is now Wisconsin.[2]
When Stephen, Levana, and their children stepped off their ship
in that fall of 1825, Detroit had fewer than two thousand residents even though it was more than 120 years old and the only

31

substantial settlement in the territory. By contrast, little New Berlin had a population of 2,316 as early as 1820.[3]

"Little else than a military and fur-trading post,"[4] "a fort in the middle of a wilderness,"[5] Detroit in the early 1820s clung to the high banks on the American shore of the Detroit River, facing out to the water and generally turning its back to the vast inland forest. Until the end of that decade, the interior of Wayne County was essentially *terra incognita*. In 1820 the *Detroit Gazette* remarked: "It is truly a matter of astonishment that many of the citizens of Detroit, who have resided here for forty years and upwards, should be profoundly ignorant of the country twenty miles back from the river."[6] What the inhabitants did know was not encouraging. Detroit was surrounded on three sides by water: by the river and by two large swamps to the north and south. The Great Black Swamp to the south, "a shallow, muck-bottomed lake," covered four thousand square miles at the southwest end of Lake Erie between Cleveland and Toledo, making land travel between Ohio and Detroit nearly impossible.[7] The northern swamp made direct travel from Detroit to Pontiac in Oakland County dauntingly difficult except in the winter.

Federal surveyors had reported that Michigan was not habitable. What neither Detroiters nor surveyors discovered until well into the 1820s was that beyond the swamps were well-drained forests and "oak openings" that were fertile and relatively easy to clear. Misconceptions about the quality of farmland in Michigan were not the only impediment to immigration. Until 1825, the only practical way to reach Detroit from New York City was a month's journey up the Hudson River to Albany, across upper New York by coach or wagon to Buffalo, and then by ship along the southern shore of Lake Erie. But two events joined to shorten the trip and to make it possible for immigrants to bring their families, livestock, and farm equipment to Michigan. First, the arrival of steam navigation on Lake Erie shortened travel from Buffalo to Detroit. Whereas writer William Darby took eleven days in 1818 just to sail from Buffalo to Detroit against the prevailing southwest winds,[8] by 1825 the trip took no more than two or three days (if the ship's boiler did not explode). Second, the opening of the Erie Canal in 1825 allowed travelers to avoid the torturous overland trek from Albany to Buffalo that often took three weeks. Traveling on the canal, the same trip could be accomplished in relative comfort in a matter of days.

To farmers, the importance of those developments was not just that they could move their farm operations to Michigan quickly and with relatively little danger. Speed on the return to New York was even more of an inducement to new settlers. Until the establishment of railroad networks a decade or more later, transporting bulk goods by water was tremendously less expensive than transportation by land. For example, it cost as much to transport grain by land from any point more than thirty miles inland as it did to get it the rest of the way to its destination in Europe.[9] In 1825 the Erie Canal changed the economics of farming forever. Suddenly, it was faster and cheaper to ship goods of all kinds to New York City from Detroit than from most towns in New York State. The cost of shipping a ton of wheat from Buffalo to New York City dropped from one hundred dollars to six dollars,[10] and wheat, corn, fish, and fruit began to flow east from Michigan to be sold in New York City at prices that farmers in most of New York state, including those in Chenango County, could not match.

Michigan's other advantage in the 1820s and 1830s was that most of its land was still held by the federal government, which had made it possible for any family with a small amount of cash, usually from the sale of their family farm in New York or New England, to buy a substantial homestead. Although the United States had been selling land in the old Northwest Territory for decades, until 1820 those sales favored speculators over farmers. The minimum parcel size was one-quarter of a section (thus a "quarter-section"), containing 160 acres, at a minimum price of two dollars per acre.[11] Although a buyer had four years to pay the purchase price of $320, the hard economic times that followed the War of 1812 made repayment, even over a period of years, difficult. The situation became so serious that in 1818 Congress had to place a moratorium on foreclosures that was not lifted until 1823.

Finally, on April 24, 1820, just four days after William Simmons distributed John Sr.'s estate, in another part of the District of Columbia, Congress amended the statute governing the sale of public lands. Although the amendment prohibited sales on credit, it also reduced the minimum parcel size to eighty acres and the minimum price per acre to $1.25.[12] A family could buy an eighty-acre farm for one hundred dollars in cash, a viable size for a farm in the fertile lands west and north of Detroit. In Michigan the result was immediate: from 2,860 acres in 1820, sales of public lands in the Detroit district increased to 20,000 acres in 1822 and to 92,000 acres in 1825. Although sales did slow during another recession that lasted from 1826 to 1829, Michigan's federal land offices sold 218,000 acres of public land in 1831, almost all at $1.25 per acre. In 1836 the United States sold 1,475,725 acres of public land in Michigan to new settlers.[13]

DETROIT BEFORE THE BOOM YEARS

Until the late 1820s, Detroit's population was still small and balanced uneasily between the French-speaking, Roman Catholic "habitants" who had lived in the area for a century or more and who led a self-contained life of hunting, trapping, and subsistence farming, and the newcomers whom the habitants called "Bostonians," English-speaking and largely Protestant American businessmen and land speculators who had come to Detroit to make their fortunes.[14] As the numbers of Bostonians increased, the number of American Indians living in Southeast Michigan waned. Few still lived near Detroit, but each summer tribes from the Upper Lakes crowded the city's streets, selling their furs, fish, and sugar and buying supplies as they traveled to Fort Malden, across the river in Ontario, to receive gifts from the British authorities.[15]

Detroit in the mid-1820s was functional instead of pretty. L. D. Watkins, who, like the Simmons family, arrived in Detroit in 1825, remembered that: "At that time there were no railroads nor wagon roads worthy the name, and Detroit could not boast of a paved street, nor even a sidewalk; the streets were not lighted and almost impassable in wet weather; the public buildings were shabby, the hotels were mere hovels; the forest was near by and the woods were almost impenetrable."[16]

For many citizens, the perils of nature began at the city's edge. In the late 1820s wolves still fed on the carcasses of dead animals dumped on Detroit's common, known as the Campus Martius, at the north end of town. The availability of dumped carcasses encouraged some wolves to carry off pigs from nearby homes,[17] and in 1830 wolves could still be heard howling outside town. Children were warned not to leave the settlement after dark.[18] Disease, however, was more of a danger than wolves. In 1838 an author trying to *promote* migration to Michigan listed the "most prevalent" diseases in Michigan: malaria, various forms of autumnal or bilious fever, catarrh, pneumonia, rheumatism, diarrhea, and goitre ("particularly among females").[19] Malaria, known commonly as "fever and ague," was near universal. So was a skin eruption known as the "Michigan rash," a form of erysipelas,[20] which principally affected newcomers.[21]

The climate in Michigan in the first half of the nineteenth century was substantially wetter than at the beginning of the twenty-first.[22] Consequently, mosquitoes swarmed everywhere from the spring thaw to the first hard freeze. The inhabitants did not understand the connection between those insects and malaria, but they did know that mosquitoes were a source of constant misery to them, their families, and their livestock. William Nowlin, who came to Michigan as a boy in 1834, recalled that:

> Myriads of them could be found any where in the woods, that would eagerly light on man or beast and fill themselves till four times their common size, if they could get a chance. The woods were literally alive with them. No one can tell the wearisome sleepless hours they caused us at night. [. . .] Frequently when I awoke I found them as wakeful as ever; they

had been feasting while I slept. I would find bunches and
blotches on me, wherever they had had a chance to light,
which caused a disagreeable, burning and smarting sensation.[23]

Newcomers were also likely to suffer from "derangements of
the digestive organs, owing to the quality of the water."[24] In
Detroit, especially, obtaining clean water was difficult. Robert E.
Roberts recalled that when he arrived in Detroit in 1827, Detroit
had no sewers or wells because of its thick surface layer of clay
soil. Instead, "the inhabitants were supplied with water drawn
from the river in carts and delivered for one shilling per barrel, or
carried in buckets, suspended from wooden yokes on the shoul-
ders, with which most housekeepers were provided."[25] There was
a town pump located at the end of the wharf built by Peter
Berthelet in 1824,[26] but not every supplier of water bothered to
use it. In 1826 the *Detroit Gazette* complained: "It is a well-estab-
lished fact that the water which some of the cartmen are in the
practice of delivering to families is dipped up from within twelve
feet of the shore, and it is generally so filthy as to emit a very
offensive smell after standing one or two hours."[27]

A year later, in 1827, two entrepreneurs, Bethuel Ferrand and
Rufus Wells, did begin to construct a residential water system
using hollowed-out tamarack logs running from the river to a
9,500 gallon reservoir on Randolph Street.[28] That system served
only a small area, was not fully operational until August 1830,
one month before the Simmons hanging, and did not produce
satisfactory pressure until years later.[29] Nevertheless, the Detroit
residents served by those wooden pipes were better off than most
citizens of London, Paris, or Rome at that time.[30]

Indeed, despite its disease, stench, wild animals, lack of modern comforts, and occasional barbarous customs, Detroit in 1827
was not an uncivilized wasteland. The view greeting passengers
on ships arriving at Detroit was reassuring to new arrivals.
Prosperous farms, windmills, and orchards lined the river, while
dozens of century-old pear trees, six to ten feet in girth and sixty
feet high, fronted the many farms to the east of town.[31] Detroit's

skyline was dominated by the towers of St. Anne's Roman Catholic Church and the steeple of the new courthouse. Clustered principally in a small strip of land bordered by the river to the south, Jefferson Avenue to the north, Governor Cass's farm to the west, and the Brush farm to the east, the town's other buildings were small shops or warehouses and plain but cozy cottages, constructed mostly of wood, one or two stories high, with steep roofs and dormer windows.[32]

In 1818 New York visitor William Darby remarked that, despite Detroit's isolation, geographical and emotional, from the rest of the United States, "The resident society of Detroit has all the exterior features of a flourishing and cultivated community, as much so, equivalent to numbers, as any city of the United States."[33] Six years later, when Stephen G. Simmons first invested in Michigan land, the territory had no public schools,[34] but the other principal symbols of American civilization were well established: organized religion and culture, a code of laws, and a newspaper.

Antoine de la Mothe Cadillac established Detroit's first church, a Roman Catholic chapel dedicated to St. Anne, in 1701. In 1825, the twin, tin-coated steeples of St. Anne's Church, begun in 1818, towered over the city. The first organized Protestant congregation in Detroit, with seven members, was not established until 1810, and the first Protestant church in Detroit was not built until 1820. However, by 1827, Detroit's Presbyterian, Methodist, and Episcopal congregations met in their own churches, and a Baptist church was completed in November 1830.[35] By the late 1820s Detroit also had many cultural and professional organizations as well as amateur music and theatrical performances.[36] Clearly, people in the Territory had a sense that they had lived, and were living, in a noteworthy place and time: the first issue of the *North-Western Journal*, published on November 20, 1829, announced the formation of the Michigan Historical Society chaired by Governor Lewis Cass.[37]

Michigan was also fertile ground for lawmaking and lawyers. The Act of Congress that created the Territory of Michigan in

1805 established an executive branch, the Governor, and a judicial branch, a three-judge Territorial Supreme Court, but no separate legislature.[38] Instead, Congress directed the two branches,
known collectively as "the Governor and Judges," to enact all
laws needed to govern the Territory. Their initial effort, first published in 1805, was known as the Woodward Code for brilliant
but eccentric Judge Augustus Brevoort Woodward. In 1816 and
1820 the Governor and Judges published new compilations of
laws known respectively as the Cass Code, for Governor Lewis
Cass, and then the Code of 1820, the last set of laws enacted by
the Governor and Judges.[39] In 1823 Congress transferred the legislative power over the territory from the governor and judges to
a Legislative Council consisting of nine men selected by the
President from eighteen candidates elected by Michigan's voters,
which enacted legislation in conjunction with the Governor.[40]
In January 1827 Congress authorized qualified Michigan voters
to elect the Legislative Council directly.[41]

Over the years, the statutes enacted by the Governor and
Judges and by the Legislative Council added up to a substantial
body of law. An 1827 compilation of Territorial statutes encom-
passed 581 pages, including acts for the organization of the
Territorial government, the militia, and taxation.[42] The legislators also enacted prohibitions on all activity on Sundays except
religious worship[43]; on "immoral practices," including puppet
shows, wire dancers, and jugglers[44]; and on gambling, including
horse racing[45] and billiards.[46] To enforce the ban on betting, the
Council made gambling debts unenforceable[47] and authorized
unlucky gamblers to sue the winners to return their lost money.[48]
In 1830 the Council added a law banning all nine-pin bowling
because the sport led to "idleness and dissipation."[49]

Those statutes were intended to supplement the common law
of England, the foundation of the legal education received by
American lawyers and which they counted on to continue in
effect despite the Revolution. Because the common law evolves
over time, a question that did trouble and divide the American
legal community for decades after the Revolution was which ver-

sion of the common law was to apply in Michigan. Judge Woodward, for example, was of the opinion that Michigan was bound only by the ancient common law of England, unsullied by any English statute passed after September 3, 1189. He explained, in his own grandiloquent fashion: "On that day, being the epoch of the coronation of Richard Coeur de Lion; and the first monarch of the name of Richard on the English throne; the 'Common Law' became complete, and insusceptible of any additions."[50] That battle over the scope of the common law in the United States went on for many years, and Judge Solomon Sibley, who advocated adopting the common law as it existed in 1787, the year the Northwest Ordinance was first enacted, was still arguing the point with his colleagues in 1828.[51]

Although the Woodward Code contained no criminal statutes, the later codes provided for a wide range of crimes. The Code of 1827 enacted by the Legislative Council defined and specified the punishments for more than sixty separate offenses from murder to creating a hazard by felling trees into streams.[52] However, then as now, the presence of a law on the books did not mean that it would be, or could be, enforced. Michigan was still on the frontier, and otherwise upstanding citizens sometimes ignored or circumvented unpopular laws. For example, the first tax laws passed in 1805 were universally ignored; if authorities raised any money by way of those taxes, they never recorded it.[53] The Sabbath law was also disregarded by many citizens. On a Sunday in June 1825, Marshal Adna Merritt called out a posse to help him apprehend several soldiers who refused his order to stop fishing from the public wharf. The soldiers were seized and jailed, but, following a two-day trial, they were acquitted by twelve jurors who clearly considered keeping the Sabbath a private, not public, decision. Alternatively, the jurors may merely have felt that Marshal Merritt was enjoying his work far too much.[54]

In other cases the very existence of prosecutions is some evidence that laws were scoffed at. In 1830 prosecutor B. F. H. Witherell had to bring charges to close down both a bawdy house and a "common gambling house." In the latter case prominent and colorful attorney George A. O'Keeffe, who later defended Stephen at his murder trial, was subpoenaed to testify for the prosecution. He admitted, under oath, that he had frequented the gambling establishment occasionally and had seen some gaming. But, in defense of his own dignity, O'Keeffe insisted that he only went there to partake of its oysters.[55]

The city's first successful newspaper, the *Detroit Gazette*, was published weekly from July 1817 until April 1830.[56] The *Gazette* was a Democratic paper that in 1825 was a fervent supporter of Andrew Jackson and Martin Van Buren. The Federalist/Whig interests in town responded first with the *Michigan Herald* (1825–29) and then, in November 1829, with the *North-Western Journal*.[57] The *Journal*, a weekly, was published by George L. Whitney, a staunch Whig,[58] supporter of the temperance movement,[59] and the organist at St. Paul's Episcopal Church on Woodward Avenue.[60] On April 26, 1830, the *Journal* became Detroit's only newspaper when the offices of the *Gazette* were torched by an angry employee, Ulysses G. Smith.[61] Because the *Journal* remained the only paper in Detroit during the Simmons trial and execution,[62] and because the two other papers in the territory, the *Michigan Sentinel* of Monroe and the *Oakland Chronicle*, published in Pontiac, reprinted the *Journal's* stories and added little reporting of their own, the *Journal* was the principal contemporary source for information about the case.

A TAVERN HOMESTEAD IN THE FOREST

The Simmons family apparently arrived in Detroit in October 1825, just as the last parts of the Erie Canal were being put into service. The family found a town receiving more than three hundred new settlers a week, far more than the hotels and taverns could absorb. The *Detroit Gazette* boasted that the territory would experience a fifty percent gain in population just in that one year. Nor was the traffic growth only on the westward leg. In December 1825 the first wagon load of flour from the Mack mill in Pontiac was loaded on ships for transport to Buffalo and New York City.[63] By 1842 Michigan's exports had expanded to 180,000 barrels of flour, 99,000 bushels of wheat, 19,000 barrels of pork, and 912 tons of potatoes. On October 31, 1825, soon after he and his family arrived in Michigan, Stephen purchased a quarter-acre lot in Detroit from John N. McDonnell, a local politician.[64] This purchase was probably intended to provide the family a place to live while Stephen considered his opportunities. On December 2, 1825, after a month of considering, Stephen paid one George M. Johnson five hundred dollars for eighty acres of forest land located about sixteen miles southwest of Detroit, where the Old Sauk Trail (later called the Chicago Road and now Michigan Avenue) crossed the South Branch of the Rouge River.[65]

The principal economic attraction of this property was a large log cabin. When Johnson bought that property from the government in February 1824, for one hundred dollars,[66] he planned to build a tavern and inn for pioneers traveling west from Detroit to Ypsilanti and beyond.[67] Although initially successful, Johnson was not able to keep the tavern profitable, and he was fortunate to be able to sell the lot and tavern to Stephen for four hundred dollars more than he had paid for it.

Over the years, Stephen added to his inventory of properties in Michigan. In February 1826 he bought 63.1 acres of federal land along the Huron River for the going price of $1.25 per acre.[68] Two years later, on February 15, 1828, he bought another 170 acres of farmland in Springwells Township, on the Rouge River, from a Cleveland businessman named James Bryant,[69] who returned the favor by purchasing fifty-four acres of Stephen's remaining land in Chenango County.[70] However, the eighty acres on the Chicago Road remained the center of family life, what Stephen always called his homestead. By contrast, he referred to his other Michigan properties as "lots," mere investments without any emotional attachment.

Coming to a new place with a pocket full of money, Stephen could have decided to get out of farming altogether in order to concentrate on land speculation, or he would have opted to open a tavern in Detroit or one of the other towns in the territory. Instead, he chose to settle in a remote and uninhabited forest, far from the attractions of civilization, and on a property chiefly notable for a decaying tavern that his predecessor could not make into a success. Why did Stephen make that choice?

He may simply have come to see himself and his family as farmers and the forested acres on the Rouge as potential cornfields and pastures. Or there may have been truth in the *North-Western Journal*'s inference, after Stephen's execution, that Stephen and Levana chose this isolated spot specifically to make sure that Stephen was "separated from such fatal influences" as excessive drinking, thieves, and loose women. But if the *Journal* moralized, in the end "he could not cast off his habits, which seem, like the long-worn chains of the captive, to have become imbedded in his nature."[71] If avoiding temptation was the goal, Stephen's decision to become a tavern keeper seems decidedly odd.

There is a suggestion in the records of another reason for the Simmons family to settle where they did. In August and September 1825, just months before Stephen and his family arrived in Michigan, one Joseph Moss of New Berlin, Chenango County, New York, bought 2,660 acres of government land in Wayne County, including more than 1,200 acres along the Chicago Road and only a short walk from what was soon to be the Simmons homestead. Within the next few months, Moss purchased an additional 1,210 acres in Wayne County, bringing his total holdings to more than 3,800 acres.[72] Stephen must have known "Deacon" Moss, who was the scion of New Berlin's leading family and who, although no older than Stephen, was rich and successful, one of the "chief promoters of New Berlin's prosperity," and the founder of the town's chief industry, a cotton mill.[73] Although there is no evidence that Deacon Moss was involved in the Simmons's decision to move to Michigan or to buy the tavern property, it is very unlikely that it was a coincidence that two men of about the same age, from the same rural village in New York State, decided at the same time to buy parcels of land within a mile of each other in the lonely Michigan forest.[74] Stephen may have worked for Moss, or he may have been trying to copy Moss's investment out of admiration and envy. The true nature of their relationship, or even whether there was one, is a mystery.

Besides running the tavern, Stephen and his family also tried to farm their land and, on occasion, rented out land to tenants.[75] According to the probate inventory taken a few months after his death,[76] the family owned a span (i.e., a pair) of horses, one yearling colt, and a yoke (again, a pair) of steers, three cows, three calves, and two yearling heifers, a wagon, one plough, three axes, one shovel, one hand saw, one ox yoke and a mowing scythe. In those days, before even the most rudimentary farm machinery, that equipment and six children should have been enough to run a good-sized farm or two.

The problem the family faced was making the tavern turn a profit. During the summer of 1824, George Johnson had benefitted from being the only licensed tavern keeper between Dearborn and Ypsilanti[77] and thus the only location on that long stretch of road where a traveler could find a roof for the night or where a neighbor could legally buy a glass of whiskey or rum or a tankard of cider, beer, or ale.[78] But there was more to running a tavern than just selling drinks.

Michigan law required every tavern keeper to have a license from the county court and to reapply each year.[79] The court could not issue a license unless it could certify that the applicant "is of good moral character and of sufficient abilities to keep a tavern and that he has accommodations to entertain travelers, and that a tavern is necessary at the place where the person resides or proposes to keep such a tavern, for the actual accommodation of travelers."[80] The law's specifications for guest comfort were very precise:

> [E]very tavern keeper [shall] at all times be furnished with suitable provisions and accommodations for travelers, and shall keep in his house at least two spare beds for guests, with good

and sufficient sheeting and covering for such beds respectively,
and provide and keep good and sufficient stabling and proven-
der, of hay in the winter, and hay or pasturage in the summer,
and grain for four horses or other cattle more than his own
stock, for the accommodation of travelers.[81]

A tavern keeper could not sell more than "ten shillings" worth
of alcohol (about $1.25) on credit, except to travelers. No tavern
keeper could allow the playing of billiards, or any gambling of
any kind, or any loud disturbances, in or on the grounds of the
tavern, nor could he or she sell liquor at all on Sundays except to
travelers and boarders.[82] Finally, in order to encourage compliance with the requirements of the act, a tavern keeper was subject to fines of up to $200 per occurrence and had to provide to
the court a surety bond in the amount of fifty dollars.[83]

Although those rules do not seem to have discouraged
Johnson, two other factors did: changing travel patterns and
increased competition. The Chicago Road was, by all accounts,
abominable: a swampy, muddy, and rutted trail of tree stumps
running through the wilderness. One pioneer remembered: " . . .
when not frozen it was one continuous mud hole."[84]
Consequently, pioneer families began to bypass the Chicago
Road, and thus Johnson's Tavern, by traveling north from
Dearborn on the Ann Arbor Trail and then to the new
Territorial Road to Plymouth, both built on higher ground.[85]
Johnson also faced competition from the famous inn in Dearborn
owned by Conrad (Coon) Ten Eyck (who claimed to have been
the first person to call Michigan residents Wolverines)[86] as well
as from the Black Horse Tavern, which, because it stood just two
miles to the east along the Chicago Road, was able to snare most
of the settlers heading west from Detroit who were on that part
of the road when night fell.[87] In December 1825, discouraged by
declining business, Johnson sold his tavern on the Chicago Road
to Stephen and opened a new tavern on the Ann Arbor Trail,
which he operated for many years.[88]

There is no existing drawing or picture of the tavern in which

Stephen took up his father's trade with Levana and their children, but it probably was very similar to Thompson's Tavern near Dearborn, a few miles to the east, which was depicted in *The Bark Covered House*,[89] William Nowlin's account of his family's arrival in Michigan in 1834. Thompson's was a rough, single-story, log cabin in a forest clearing along a muddy track. It had a small log barn, surrounded by a rail corral for horses, cattle, and pigs, and a cabin that was distinguishable from a small farm house only by a sign on a post outside the door with the owner's name, as required by the tavern laws.

On October 26, 1826 the Wayne County Court issued Stephen his first Wayne County tavern license, authorizing him to keep a tavern "at his present residence in Range 2, Township 2 on the south branch of the river Rouge on the road leading from Ten Eyck's bridge to Woodruff Grove" near Ypsilanti.[90] Signing the license application with a trembling hand, Stephen promised to "maintain good order and rule and shall not suffer any unlawful games in his said house or any of the dependencies thereof and shall not break any of the laws for the regulation of taverns." Stephen renewed his license in 1827[91] and 1828,[92] and he probably did so in 1829 and 1830 as well, but records from those years have not survived. Two of the licenses that do still exist contain a small irony: in 1827 Stephen's bond was guaranteed by B. F. H. Witherell, who would prosecute him for murder, while in 1828 his guarantor was George A. O'Keeffe, who would defend him in the murder trial.

Despite his solemn undertaking to abide by his legal mandate to keep the tavern clean and well stocked, Stephen and his family apparently did little or nothing to improve the tavern's rough accommodations. Pioneers who did stop at "Johnson's Tavern," as it was still called for years after the Simmons family took over, remembered it as a forbiddingly bleak and spartan establishment. The Norris family stopped for the night at Simmons's "log house" in June 1828. Stephen provided them with little more comfort than they would have had if they had slept on the road. Their supper consisted of fried pork, tea without milk, and "a short-cake

made with fat and water and baked by the fire." Their accommodations were even more primitive: a space partitioned from the
living and dining space "with rough boards and without a door."
There were only two narrow beds for the entire party: all of the
women and girls slept on one bed and all of the males slept on the
other. Understandably, the Norris party did not stay for breakfast;
instead they "got out of their close quarters the best way they
could."[93] Even so, the Norrises were lucky to have been fed at all.
In 1827 Deacon Isaac Mason and a Dr. Pratt found shelter at
Johnson's Tavern, "a log cabin standing hard by the trail, solitary
and alone in the woods, with a rude tavern sign hanging out
before it." On that occasion Stephen offered his guests no food at
all, either for supper or for breakfast.[94]

Strong Drink

According to contemporary accounts, the rough road, bleak
accommodations, and bad fare were not all that made Simmons's
tavern unpopular with settlers and neighbors alike. By now mid-
dle-aged, both Stephen and Levana Simmons were heavy
drinkers capable of violent outbursts when drunk.[95] That they
were often drunk was not surprising because excessive drinking
and chronic intoxication were the usual conditions of life in
early-nineteenth-century America:

> By almost any standard, Americans drank not only near-uni-
> versally but in enormous quantities. Their yearly consump-
> tion at the time of the Revolution has been estimated at the
> equivalent of three-and-a-half gallons of pure, two-hundred-
> proof alcohol for each person. . . . By the late 1820s their
> imbibing had risen to an all-time high of almost four gallons
> per capita. "Beastly intoxication" in public became ever more
> widespread, and many men went from dramming and regular
> "tavern haunting" to spending whole days intoxicated on
> alcoholic binges.[96]

Rural Americans, in particular, regarded water, to drink or to wash with, as a carrier of a variety of diseases. They did not know that they could purify their water by boiling, but they did believe that drinking whiskey instead of water both prevented and cured many ills. Until quinine appeared in Michigan years later, whiskey reigned as the sole remedy available for the cycles of chills and sweating brought on by the "fever and ague" of malaria.[97]

Americans also considered whiskey and hard cider to be "a crucial part of their sociability as well as an essential stimulant to exertion."[98] Michigan's new pioneers, like their French habitant neighbors, considered alcohol to be a necessity of life and serving their guests alcohol in great quantities to be the hallmark of civility.[99] No social or political gathering was held, and no great physical undertaking was attempted, without the consumption of large amounts of alcohol. Throughout the old Northwest Territory

> The use of whiskey was general. As a commodity it was pro-
> duced on innumerable farms, and available at "groceries" at
> from 15 to 25 cents a gallon. From cabin raising and
> logrolling to muster assembly and political barbecue, no
> important work could be accomplished without its use.[100]

Attempts to hold "temperance" barn-raisings or harvesting in Michigan in those years were notorious failures; despite the hosts' best intentions, the work could not be completed without large volumes of alcohol.[101]

Like farmers throughout America, Michigan's pioneers also soon discovered that, once they began to grow more grain than their family and animals could consume, whiskey was an economic boon as well. Unlike raw grain, whiskey made from a surplus crop could be stored for long periods of time and transported to market with little risk of its going bad before it was sold.[102] As one commentator noted fifty years later, "in those days, it was considered as right and legitimate to manufacture corn or rye into whisky as to produce flour or meal from the same grain."[103]

Such excess did finally cause a reaction, and by 1830 attitudes towards drunkenness had began to change. A series of evangelical Protestant revivals aroused religious fervor across the country against all excess and particularly against excessive drinking. The American Temperance Society was founded in 1826,[104] and the frontier was caught up in the movement, albeit gradually. By the time of Stephen's final, and fatal, drunken rage, there were five temperance societies in the Michigan Territory,[105] including the Detroit Society for the Suppression of Intemperance, which was founded in February 1830.[106] But the work of the temperance movement proceeded slowly. In 1830 Wayne County had more than forty licensed taverns, as well as numerous illegal drinking houses, to serve a population of only seven thousand adults and children. Four years later, a committee of the Detroit Common Council reported that the aggregate annual spending on liquor by residents of Detroit was more than $90,000, enough money, the Common Council calculated, to buy 500 sheep, 500 cattle, 500 horses, and still have enough to erect four brick seminaries.[107] Those figures may reflect Americans' growing love of statistics more than an accurate account,[108] but the general message was correct: in the 1830s, despite the efforts of preachers and temperance crusaders, Detroiters continued to consume alcohol on a majestic scale.

Most of Detroit's imbibers could be classified as relatively harmless, or at least harmless to other people, because they drank until they passed out peacefully. Sometimes they fought, and if those fights ended in bloodshed or death, the community tended to consider the result an unfortunate accident. From contemporary accounts, however, it seems that their neighbors put Stephen, and perhaps Levana as well, in a different category—as bullies who were consistently and aggressively violent when they drank. According to contemporary accounts, at fifty years of age Stephen was still an attractive man, tall and rugged, his 250 well-proportioned pounds topped by a strikingly handsome and expressive face.[109] When sober, he was a loving father and husband, but when he drank he became brutally violent. Levana and the younger children, who could not simply avoid his company, apparently lived in terror. Levana, in particular, suffered because of Stephen's drinking. At the time of his murder trial, the *Journal* reported that the Simmons children described Stephen as " . . . a husband sometimes forcing, always encouraging his wife to drink; in his moments of intoxication, beating her with the hand or instruments of wood or iron, and driving her forth at night to seek shelter in the woods, following her and stamping upon her."[110]

After Stephen's execution, the *Journal*, a temperance paper, attributed Stephen's conduct to excessive drinking and to his drinking companions. "Intemperance brutalized and exasperated his naturally violent temper, and his intercourse with shameless females unfitted him for association with a virtuous woman. It was his own confession, that he had been so long accustomed to such society, 'he knew not how to treat a wife.' "[111] The *Journal* concluded that, even isolated from those influences in the forest, his nature could not change completely. "Although separated from such fatal influences, and bound to life by those ties, which are usually most endearing, he could not cast off his habits, which seem, like the long-worn chains of the captive, to have become imbedded in his nature."[112]

On the other side of the marital mattress, Levana was far from the contemporary ideal of a patient, reserved, and dutiful spouse or, for that matter, from the modern ideal of a competent and loving wife and mother. Many later accounts characterized her as the typical innocent and passive victim that was the favorite of most temperance fables. But during the murder trial her children remembered a woman who, when drunk, was just as violent and dangerous as her spouse, "a mother in a drunken carousal with her husband in the presence of their children; or raving like fury, and grasping chairs or boards to beat them, and drive them from the house."[113]

To their contemporaries, Levana's drunken behavior was more disturbing than Stephen's. "Americans traditionally found drunkenness tolerable and forgivable in men but deeply shameful in women."[114] Until the 1840s, and particularly in the West, women drank freely with men, but they were expected to drink cider instead of whiskey and in smaller amounts.[115] Nevertheless, the community did not consider Levana to be any less of a victim, and if Stephen anticipated that a jury's disgust toward her behavior would be translated into sympathy for a killer, he was very wrong.

chapter 4

"A Crime at Which Human Nature Shudders"

The Murder of Levana Simmons

Although alcohol played its part in the death of Levana Simmons, and although accounts written fifty and more years later focused exclusively on intoxication as the cause,[1] contemporary sources blamed jealousy as well. The *North-Western Journal*—paraphrasing the trial testimony—and visiting journalist Calvin Colton—repeating gossip on the street—both reported contemporaneously with the events that Stephen's rage was precipitated by his suspicion that Levana was interested in another man.

Stephen had a lot on his mind in early June 1830, including the disintegration of the marriage of his oldest daughter, Catharine. She had been married for several years to one Fitzpatrick McCarty, known as "Fitz" or "Pat," an illiterate laborer and would-be road contractor.[2] In May 1830 Stephen retained an attorney from Ypsilanti, Elias W. Skinner, to gather evidence against McCarty so that Catharine could get a divorce. On May 11 Skinner went to Ann Arbor, obtained two affidavits, and returned to "the Simmons house," where he drafted "a petition to the Legislative Council for a Divorce of his daughter (Mrs. McCarty)."[3]

Skinner had probably found witnesses who would confirm McCarty's adultery, the sole ground for divorce allowed by Michigan's divorce statute in 1830.[4] Law and practice allowed Catharine McCarty two options for obtaining a divorce under that statute. She could ask for a "chancery" divorce from the territorial Supreme Court by filing a complaint ("exhibiting a bill") alleging adultery and then providing the details of her husband's conduct in open court. That process was public and humiliating, and Catharine, like many others, took the more confidential alternative of petitioning the Legislative Council for a divorce. Although the Council had no statutory authority under federal or territorial law to grant divorces, the Council began doing so in June 1828[5] and did not stop until March 1831.[6] Such "legislative" divorces were far more popular than going to court: the Supreme Court heard only twenty-two proceedings for divorce during the three decades of the territorial period, while the Legislative Council granted seventeen divorces during those three years alone.[7] On July 31, 1830, while Stephen sat in jail waiting to be hanged, the Legislative Council granted Catharine's petition and ordered "that the marriage contract between Catharine M'Carty and Fitz P. M'Carty, be and the same is hereby dissolved."[8]

Stephen had another concern during the first week of June 1830 besides engineering Catharine's divorce. He was notified that he was to appear in Wayne County Circuit Court in Detroit during the week of June 7 to begin a trial in a civil case brought against him. *William H. St. Clair v. Stephen G. Simmons* was about St. Clair's lease right to farm the Simmons homestead, adjacent to the tavern, during the 1828 harvest. Although a jury had already returned a verdict in Stephen's favor in a trial presided over by a justice of the peace, territorial law allowed St. Clair to appeal to the Circuit Court and to have another trial there with a new jury.[9]

Stephen and his son David, who had been directed to appear as a trial witness, left home on Saturday, June 5, or Sunday, June 6, and traveled to Detroit, where they spent the week. It appears from a bill submitted to the executor of Stephen's estate that Stephen and David stayed at the Steamboat Hotel, the most popular lodgings in the territory and the site of a legendary saloon.[10] Stephen probably had a very good time from their arrival until Thursday, when the trial began, especially if he spent his evenings with his attorney for the trial, the flamboyant George

Alexander O'Keeffe, who, like Stephen, enjoyed whiskey and rum far too much for his own good.

Finally, on Thursday, June 10, Judges Henry Chipman and William Woodbridge[11] called the court to order and began the trial of *St. Clair v. Simmons* by selecting a jury. Judge Woodbridge, as was his habit, took detailed notes of the trial testimony.[12] According to those notes, neither Stephen nor St. Clair testified to the terms of their contract. Instead, each relied on other witnesses, including David Simmons, who ended up being called to the stand by both sides to testify. Although the surviving court records and the Woodbridge notes do not make the facts of the case entirely clear, it appears that in 1828 Stephen leased the farm on his tavern property to St. Clair for one year for either fifty or two hundred dollars to be paid for the most part with produce harvested from the farm. It is curious that the lease began in July, when the hard work of planting was over and the growing season nearing its end, and that, as the witnesses agreed, St. Clair surrendered the farm back to Stephen in October or November 1828, after the harvest. It may have been that Stephen and his sons were unable for some reason to harvest the crops that year.

Judge Woodbridge's notes were meant to be an *aide-memoire*, not a full explanation of the claims and the significance of the evidence, but they do reveal that Stephen grew potatoes, turnips, cabbage, corn, and peaches. They also show that Stephen and his family gave up their farm house to St. Clair, who stored their furniture and other goods. Because there is no mention of St. Clair running the tavern, it may be that the Simmons family lived in the tavern itself during this period.

One significant detail in the testimony, for our purposes, concerned the tavern sign. After David Simmons complained that St. Clair had sawed up the sign and used it to cover a barrel, St. Clair called a witness who retorted that "old man Simmons" had told him "that he got in a spree and cut down the sign post himself."

The trial concluded on Friday, June 11. After listening to five witnesses testify, the second jury, like the first, returned a verdict for Stephen in the amount of $15.35.[13] Although "old man

Simmons" cannot have enjoyed having his "spree" described in open court, he seems to have been happy with the jury's verdict. He did not head home after court adjourned Friday afternoon or even early Saturday morning. Instead, it seems that he and David celebrated their victory, probably at the saloon bar of the Steamboat Hotel, and did not set out along the Chicago Road until Saturday afternoon. In any case, when they did return to the tavern late Saturday evening, June 12, Stephen was in a good mood.[14]

On Sunday, June 13, the family was "all happy together," although both Levana and Stephen "drank freely." On Monday morning, June 14, they continued their drinking: both took a dram in the morning and slept the rest of the day "until about an hour before sunset." But all was not well in Stephen's mind as the liquor fueled his imagination to the level of paranoia. Stephen began to wonder if Levana had been unfaithful during his absence with "the stageman who had passed that day." When he woke up on Monday evening, Stephen questioned one of his daughters about the possibility that Levana had had "improper intercourse" with the suspect, a driver for one of the stagecoaches that stopped daily at the tavern on their way to Ypsilanti.

We do not know what his daughter told him except that she did not ease his jealous suspicions. Stephen stormed into the marital bedroom, where he first accused Levana of infidelity and then proceeded to beat her until she cried out: "O, Stephen, don't." Stephen left the room but he soon returned and resumed the beating. Hoping to stop the beating, Levana finally did confess to having committed adultery with the stageman, but that did not stop Stephen's blows. To the contrary, he beat her even harder, an immense man raining blows on his much smaller wife. Stephen left the bedroom again, but he returned and hit Levana until "she was seen to draw up her feet once" in a spasm. As Stephen turned from the battered and bleeding Levana and returned to his drinking, David Simmons and a tavern guest, William Sutherland of Bergen, Genesee County, New York, went into the bedroom to help her. They found her unconscious and decided to take her outside, hoping that the fresh summer air would revive her, but Levana Simmons was dead. When they told Stephen that he had killed his wife, he "manifested great surprise and grief, and urged the bystanders to make various efforts to recover her." Like the bystanders' attempts to help Levana, Stephen's concern came too late.

Calvin Colton, a journalist passing through Detroit on his way to the upper Lakes, was in Detroit on the day Stephen was sentenced. Although he did not see the killing or attend the trial, Colton did see Stephen sentenced, and he was able to pick up the gossip on Detroit's streets that day. In a story written for a New York newspaper and also included in a book about his trip, he confirmed that Detroiters believed that Levana's death was caused by jealousy as well as intoxication: "He had loved his wife excessively, and loved her, strange as it may seem, unto the last. And for that very love he was the more cruel, and the greater monster. He was jealous of her fidelity, without cause. [. . .] And only when intoxicated with strong drink did this terrible passion gain its dominion over him."[15]

ARREST AND INDICTMENT

When they saw what had happened, the other men who were at the tavern that night arrested Stephen and restrained him until he could be delivered to the authorities. The next morning, Tuesday, June 15, Stephen was bound and taken under guard to Detroit, riding in the back of his own farm wagon with Levana's corpse.[16] In town, the wagon driver and guards surrendered Stephen to the custody of the Wayne County Sheriff, Thomas S. Knapp.[17] Levana's body left little doubt as to what Stephen had done. The Detroit correspondent for the *Oakland Chronicle*, published in Pontiac, reported: "The body was examined by physicians the next morning, and bruises were discovered on the face and neck and breast and side. The Coroner's inquest was held the next day and Simmons committed to jail in this City."[18]

Stephen must have been distraught when he arrived at the jail because the sheriff immediately had Dr. Marshal Chapin examine him and prescribe some medicine, possibly laudanum or another sedative.[19] It is uncertain whether that strain was caused by guilt for killing Levana or shame at being known as a killer. Certainly, when Stephen first realized that Levana was dead, and on several subsequent occasions, he expressed sorrow that he had killed her. On the other hand, the *North-Western Journal* reported that, while Stephen was in jail, he demonstrated a "hard and iron insensibility to guilt," a "dogged and resolute fatalism," and an "obstinate disbelief in the retributions of revelation."[20]

Although Chapin was one of the town's most prominent physicians, and also the owner of the territory's first drug store, his medical skills and his potions did not relieve Stephen's emotional torment. According to various sources, Stephen gave in to his despair, whether caused by guilt or shame, and tried to kill himself at least once, and perhaps twice, while he waited for his trial.

On June 18 the *Oakland Chronicle* reported that Stephen tried to commit suicide by slicing his own throat: "[Simmons] is now confined in Detroit jail—during which he made an attempt to cut his throat—cut the windpipe half off. There was a man present during this unfortunate and terrible occurrence and neither interfered or [sic] alarmed others—he is also confined."[21] Although the *North-Western Journal* did not report this incident,[22] it is confirmed by claims made against Stephen's estate by jailer Owen Aldrich and surgeon Randall S. Rice. Among the items in his detailed statement of claim, filed with the Wayne County Probate Court after Stephen's death, Aldrich asked for two dollars for the "expense and extra trouble" he incurred on Wednesday, June 16, the day after Stephen had spent his first night in jail, "in attending on Stephen G. Simmonds [sic] this day, having attempted to take his own life in Jail by cutting his throat."[23] While Stephen bled all over the bed in his cell, Aldrich sent a deputy running to summon Randall S. Rice, another prominent doctor who also served as the Wayne County Probate Court's register or clerk and who, therefore, was often found at the nearby courthouse.

Stephen had botched the job. He missed cutting the carotid artery in his neck, and Dr. Rice was able to stop the bleeding and "dress" the wound. Dr. Rice continued treating Stephen until July 6, the day the trial started, while Dr. Chapin billed Stephen's estate for visits only through June 25. Rice billed Stephen's estate thirty dollars for his services, while Chapin asked for twenty dollars for "attendance & medicine."[24] Jailer Aldrich kept a close eye on Stephen for the next few days, billing the estate five dollars for his "extra trouble" and another four dollars for cleaning Stephen's bed and bedding.

On the same day that Stephen tried to cut his throat, County coroner Benjamin Woodworth completed his inquest, and Levana's death was submitted to the sitting grand jury for Wayne County.[25] The grand jury included foreman Eurotas P. Hastings, president of the Bank of Michigan,[26] prominent merchants Levi Cook and T. S. Wendell, as well as John A. Rucker, a former justice of the peace,[27] all selected by former Sheriff Thomas C. Sheldon just before he was removed from office in a political squabble with the territory's Secretary James Witherell.[28] The grand jurors first heard the testimony of William Sutherland and, after he had given his evidence, required Sutherland to post a hundred-dollar bond to assure his attendance at trial as a witness for the United States.[29] On the next day, Thursday, June 17, the grand jury heard from David, Ellen, and Bathsheba Simmons and had them post bonds as well.[30] The children were probably dressed in mourning clothes made from material purchased from Levi Cook's store (and charged to Stephen's estate) on June 16 and 17: black crape, black silk, bombazine, black silk thread, black braid, black silk handkerchiefs, black gloves, and new shoes for the entire family.[31] It is likely that after they were finished testifying, Levana's children took their mother's body back to the homestead to be buried, although there is no specific record of her burial and any indication of the location of her grave has long since disappeared.[32]

According to the records of the case that Clarence Burton found in the attic of the old Detroit City Hall, the grand jury also heard from two other tavern guests: Benjamin Avery of Waterford in Erie County, Pennsylvania, and Andrew Bell, described by Burton as being from "Castleton in Rutland County,

Vermont,"[33] although census records indicate that Mr. Bell was, in fact, a long-time resident of Michigan and Wayne County.[34] In any case, neither Bell's nor Avery's name appears among the witnesses placed under bond by the Circuit Court, indicating that the prosecution did not care whether they appeared at the trial or not.

Later on Thursday, June 17, the grand jury appeared in court and presented ("exhibited") several indictments,[35] including a "true bill" against Stephen G. Simmons for the murder of "Livana [sic] Simmons, his wife."[36] Stephen was formally presented with a copy of the indictment and a list of potential trial jurors on Friday, June 18.[37] The criminal process against Stephen then adjourned until Monday, June 21. But other court business continued on Friday, June 19, including Stephen's motion, argued by George A. O'Keeffe, for entry of judgment in favor of Stephen and against William St. Clair and also against Joseph Heacock, who had posted the bond for St. Clair's appeal to Circuit Court.[38]

When the court was again in session on Monday, June 21, the District Attorney, B. F. H. Witherell, moved that Stephen be brought into court and arraigned on the indictment. Three days later, Stephen was brought from jail, placed at the Bar, and advised of the charge against him. Stephen pleaded "that he is not Guilty in manner and form as he stands charged in the Indictment."[39] Stephen was then returned to the jail to wait for his trial.

Although he had pleaded not guilty, there was no doubt in Stephen's mind that he had killed Levana. Back in his jail cell, he brooded for a week and then gave way once more to guilt or shame. On June 28, the Clerk of the Supreme Court, John Winder,[40] recorded in his journal that: "Owen Aldrich, jailer, says Simmons asked his daughter to procure poison for him."[41] Stephen was given no opportunity to carry that plan, or any subsequent suicide plan, into effect. After the first suicide attempt, Owen Aldrich took "extra trouble" to watch Stephen himself. After Stephen's request for poison was intercepted, Aldrich hired a man whose sole job was to live at the jail and watch Stephen until the end of the trial (a total of seventeen days) in order to prevent any further suicide attempts. At the same time, Aldrich also took the elementary precaution of hiring a barber to shave Stephen during his tenure in the jail.[42] The cost of both measures was charged to Stephen's estate.

For some reason, none of the three newspapers in Michigan reported Stephen's attempt to obtain poison. In fact, despite the sensational nature of the suicide attempts, the *North-Western Journal* never mentioned either attempt directly. The *Journal* contented itself with a general statement, in its report on the execution, that Stephen had been "anxious to escape the shame of the gallows" and "ready to be his own executioner, to ensure that escape."[43]

"THE FELONY WITH WHICH HE STANDS CHARGED . . ."

Under the laws of the Michigan Territory in effect in 1830, there were two types of felonious homicide: murder and manslaughter. The territory's "Act for the punishment of crimes" provided: "That every person who shall commit murder, or shall aid, abet, counsel, hire, command, cause or procure any person or persons to commit murder, shall, on being thereof convicted, suffer death" to be carried out "by hanging the person convicted by the neck until dead." On the other hand, the law prescribed a far lighter punishment for manslaughter: "a fine not exceeding one thousand dollars, and an imprisonment at hard labor, not exceeding three years, or either of them, at the discretion of the court."[44] Although those provisions seem to be clear and unambiguous, they left unanswered a question very relevant to this case: which homicides amounted to murder and which were manslaughter or justifiable homicide?

Michigan's written laws in force in 1830 did not define either murder or manslaughter. Instead, those definitions were left to the common law. People, or at least judges and lawyers, understood that, in the Anglo-American legal tradition, statutes were intended to be supplemented by the unwritten common law, including common-law definitions of murder, manslaughter, and other crimes. Under the English common law, murder was defined as a homicide in which "a person of sound mind and discretion unlawfully killeth any reasonable creature in being, and under the king's peace, with malice aforethought, either express or implied."[45] In January 1830 Judge William Woodbridge of the Michigan Supreme Court adapted the concept to American conditions in more succinct language: "*Murder* is the 'unlawful killing of a human being with malice aforethought,' " while "*manslaughter* is distinguishable from murder principally in this, that in the former there is no *predetermination* to kill, no *premeditated* malice."[46]

It appeared to observers in 1830, as it does now, that Stephen probably struck Levana deliberately but killed her accidentally, in a drunken rage, and not with any premeditated intent to kill her. Many commentators since then have suggested that, for this reason, Stephen should have been indicted for no more than manslaughter. However, under both the common law and Michigan's statutes in force in 1830, the grand jury was justified in treating Stephen's "accident" as murder. The common law allowed a jury to infer malicious intent both from an act intended to cause death or great bodily harm or from an act committed with the knowledge that it would probably kill or cause great bodily harm, even if the perpetrator was indifferent to the result or actually wished that death or great bodily harm not occur.[47] As Judge Woodbridge explained, the term "malice," as used in this context, included acts committed with "a dangerous recklessness of probable consequences to human life," because such indifference "necessarily implies depravity of heart . . . 'a heart regardless of social duty and fully bent on mischief,' " such as taking a crowbar to discipline a child.[48] Similarly, a section of the criminal code provided that an accidental killing was murder if it occurred as a result of an illegal act "of which the probable consequence shall be bloodshed."[49] The grand jury that indicted Stephen clearly believed that the blows that killed Levana fit those descriptions.

The other obstacle to reducing Stephen's charge to manslaughter was that the common law did not allow a defense of voluntary intoxication to exonerate a defendant from a charge of murder. Michigan now follows the modern rule that a homicide committed while the killer is in a state of voluntary intoxication, if it is so severe that it deprives a person of the ability to form an intent to kill, is charged as second-degree murder, which does not require proof of a premeditated intent to kill.[50] But Michigan did not ever distinguish between first- and second-degree murder until 1838[51] and did not accept intoxication as a defense for any degree of murder until many decades later. Until then, jurors were instructed to ignore the defendant's intoxication and to hold his or her acts, instead, to the standards applied to a sober man—would a person of common understanding reasonably expect his or her acts to endanger the victim's life?[52] Using that definition, the grand jury was well within the law in indicting Stephen for murder.

Michigan and the Death Penalty in 1830

Professor William Wirt Blume, a noted scholar of the laws and courts of the Michigan Territory, calculated that some thirteen offenses were punishable by death in Michigan between 1805 and 1823.[53] That may have been true, technically, between 1805 and 1815 when Michigan had no criminal statute and the common law dictated criminal penalties. Because it never came up, though, we cannot say which, if any, of those crimes other than murder the Governor and Judges would have punished by death before 1815. We do know that Michigan's first "Act for the punishment of crimes," passed in November 1815 and included in the Cass Code of 1816, limited the death penalty to murder; homicides occurring in the commission of a felony; and second convictions for certain specified crimes including manslaughter, sodomy, rape, arson, burglary, robbery, and forgery.[54] The Codes of 1820 and 1827 dropped the death penalty for two-time felons but also added a provision punishing with death any killing of a judge or other officer of the law acting in the line of duty.[55] In 1830 murder, felony murder, and killing an officer of the law were the only crimes still subject to the death penalty under territorial law. In practice, the death penalty was reserved for murderers, and even then was used very rarely.

When Stephen killed Levana, there had been only one execution under the laws of the territory (although two men had been executed in Michigan under federal laws enacted by Congress and prosecuted by the United States Attorney instead of the county prosecutor). By contrast, during the period 1800 to 1840, there were at least seventy-six capital executions in New York State.[56] Although the vast differences in population make any statistical comparison meaningless, hangings were a part of the experience of the people of New York that juries in Michigan sought to avoid by returning verdicts of manslaughter or refusing to convict at all. In the few cases in which the jury returned a murder verdict, the governor granted a pardon, or the defendant thwarted the hangman by escaping into the forest.[57]

The only exception occurred nine years before Stephen went on trial. In 1821 Ke-wa-bish-kim, "of the Menomini Nation," was tried in Detroit for the murder of Charles Ulrick, a trapper, at Green Bay, then part of the Michigan Territory.[59] Ke-wa-bish-kim was defended by B. F. H. Witherell and George A. O'Keeffe[59] who would serve, respectively, as Stephen's prosecutor and his defense counsel. Ke-wa-bish-kim was convicted, as was Ka-tau-kah, a Chippewa, who was tried at the same time under a federal murder statute, for killing an Army physician, Dr. William S. Madison, near Green Bay.[60] Both Ke-wa-bish-kim and Ka-tau-kah were sentenced to death (by Judge James Witherell, the father of B. F. H.[61]), and hanged in Detroit before a crowd of a few hundred people on December 27, 1821.[62]

Since that date, there had been no executions in Michigan, although that did not mean that people in Michigan had stopped killing each other. On the contrary, although homicide was less frequent in Michigan than in many eastern cities, several other homicides went to trial in just the five years before 1830. In a well-publicized case in 1825, the year that Stephen moved to

Michigan, an Oakland County jury acquitted a young man named Imri Fish by reason of insanity after he killed and mutilated his landlady and her daughter.[63] In June 1828 tavern keeper Levi Willard was tried for killing his brother with a butcher knife in a drunken fight during an Independence Day celebration.[64] The jury returned a verdict of manslaughter, and the judges of the Supreme Court sentenced him to just two years in prison, to be served in solitary confinement and at hard labor.[65] On August 14, 1829, John Dickman, a Detroit working man, died from a beating he had received, several weeks earlier, at the hands of his best friend, John McLaren, during a "drunken frolick."[66] On June 15, 1830, just one day after Stephen killed Levana, McLaren was convicted of manslaughter and given the extraordinarily light sentence of merely three months' solitary imprisonment at hard labor, although the judges might have taken into consideration that McLaren had already spent ten months in jail awaiting trial.[67] Both Willard and McLaren served time in the Wayne County jail while Stephen was awaiting trial there, and Stephen was certainly aware of their sentences.

Stephen was surely also aware of another case of homicide in the territory in which Governor Cass pardoned the defendant. On November 14, 1828, a private in the Second United States Infantry, stationed at Fort Gratiot (now the site of Port Huron, Michigan) killed Private John Worthy. Governor Cass later described the incident in the careful, redundant legalese typical of the first half of the nineteenth century:

> . . . the said William Collins with a certain Gun then and there loaded and charged with gun powder and leaden shot did shoot and discharge & the said William Collins with the leaden shot aforesaid by the force of the gun powder aforesaid did give the said John Worthy one mortal wound whereof he died.[68]

Collins was charged with murder, apparently under Michigan's statute. He was tried by a jury in the St. Clair County Circuit Court in July 1829 before Supreme Court Judges Solomon Sibley and William Woodbridge, two of the judges who would preside at Stephen's trial a year later. Despite Collins's clear responsibility for Worthy's death, the jury concluded that he had acted without malice and convicted him of manslaughter instead of murder. Collins was sentenced to eighteen months in prison and payment of the costs of prosecution. Even that sentence was too harsh for Governor Cass, who gave Collins a full executive pardon on September 3, 1829.

The federal government was less forgiving of another soldier stationed in Michigan. In December 1828 Private James Brown was serving with Company G of the Fifth U.S. Infantry Regiment garrisoned at Fort Mackinac on Mackinac Island between Lakes Huron and Michigan. On December 6, Brown shot and killed his squad leader, Corporal Hugh Flinn, in the company mess room. Brown claimed that the shooting was an accident, but he and Flinn had exchanged words the day before, and Brown had a bad reputation because he had gone absent without leave about a year earlier. Charged under federal law with murder committed in a location under the sole and exclusive jurisdiction of the United States, Brown was tried twice before Judge James Duane Doty sitting as a U.S. District Court, once at Mackinac and once at Green Bay, and was convicted by a jury both times. In September 1829 Brown's attorneys, Samuel B. Beach and Joseph W. Torrey, sent Governor Cass a petition asking President Jackson to pardon Brown.[69] Because the case involved a federal crime, Cass had no power to pardon Brown himself, but he did stay Brown's execution until he received Jackson's decision on the petition.[70] Although there was a strong feeling on Mackinac Island that Brown should be pardoned, President Jackson, not surprisingly, had a sterner opinion. Old Hickory communicated his denial of the pardon to Cass, who forwarded the President's letter north on December 8, 1829,[71] although Cass's letter did not reach Mackinac until January 11, 1830. Private Brown was hanged quietly on February 1, 1830, by Sheriff Edward Biddle, somewhere on Mackinac Island; the exact location of the execution is unknown.[72]

Waiting for Trial

After the indictment was announced, Stephen was remanded to the jail[73] to wait for his trial, which began twelve days later, on July 6.[74] The Wayne County Jail was a reasonably clean and comfortable place to wait for a trial. Built in 1819 of white-washed stone, the jail was located at the current site of the down-town branch of the Detroit Public Library at the corner of Gratiot Avenue and Library Street.[75] There was plenty of space in the eighty-eight by forty-four foot, two-story building, partic-ularly as the jail had only ten or twelve other inmates during the summer of 1830.[76] Large barred windows provided light and air while a picket fence served more as a symbol than a deterrent to escape.[77] Territorial law required the sheriff to provide prisoners with food, drink, clean bedding, and linen, free of charge except for those persons jailed to compel payment of debts.[78] A prisoner could also order any "victuals, and other necessary food" that the prisoner was willing to pay for. Although those imprisoned for debt were allowed to buy ale and beer,[79] Stephen and others accused or convicted of a crime were, at least officially, allowed only "small beer" to drink.[80]

Prisoners sentenced to solitary confinement were supposed to be fed only bread and water "unless other food shall be necessary for the preservation of his or her life."[81] If the prisoner was liter-ate, the sheriff was bound to supply him or her with a Bible pro-vided by the local clergy, who had access to the jail to counsel all prisoners, including those in solitary confinement[82] who were otherwise to be separated from the general jail population and allowed no contact with other people.[83] But, like other laws these statutes regulating jails and solitary confinement were only as effective as the people enforcing them.

In April 1830, after inspecting the jail, the Wayne County Grand Jury noted approvingly that "the prisoners therein con-fined, are comfortably provided for, as to accommodations and provisions, and safely and properly secured." The Grand Jury also found that the jail was too comfortable for at least one tenant.

"Levi Willard [was] sentenced to close confinement for manslaughter; instead of which, he has been, and is now indulged in most unjustifiable liberty in that he has been, and is now permitted to be about, and some say, out of the jail buildings; and even has been indulged in keeping in his pockets, some of the keys of the prison."[84] At about the same time, Judge William Woodbridge of the territorial Supreme Court complained to the grand jury about the general disregard for laws in Michigan, including the sheriff's failure to keep "spirituous liquors" from the prisoners in the county jail.[85]

It is unlikely that Stephen, facing a death sentence, was given as much freedom of movement as Willard, even though both of them had, after all, killed a family member while drunk. There is also no evidence that he was allowed any alcohol until July 14, when the jury found him guilty of murder. On that day, he fell off the wagon when the sheriff, understandably, allowed him to buy one and three-quarters gallons of brandy on credit from his friend Levi Cook.[86]

chapter 5

The Bench and Bar of the Michigan Territory

In 1830 the history of attorneys in Detroit and Michigan was still relatively short. There had been no attorneys in the peninsulas during the period of French control. Instead, the military commanders at Detroit and at Michilimackinac in northern Michigan took care of minor crimes and disputes; any serious matter was sent to Montreal or Quebec for trial. The British continued that practice until 1789, when attorney William Dummer Powell was assigned to hold various courts at Sandwich (now Windsor, Ontario), across the river from Detroit. Later, another attorney, William Roe, arrived in Sandwich and began to practice civil law. But Roe also acted as Crown Prosecutor, and criminal defendants coming before Judge Powell did not have trained defense counsel available.[1] The creation of a truly independent bar had to wait until the Americans finally took possession of Detroit and Michigan in July 1796. Even then, there was no real justice system in Detroit for many years because the Northwest Territory and the Indiana Territory, which governed what is now Michigan between 1796 and 1805, held no courts there.

Detroit's first American attorney, Elijah Brush, arrived in the city not far behind Anthony Wayne's troops, but it took almost two years before the second, Solomon Sibley, rode up from Marietta, Ohio, through the Black Swamp, and on to Detroit. With no courts and few land sales, Michigan had little to encourage other lawyers to follow them. On July 30, 1805, when the Supreme Court of the Territory of Michigan opened for business, the only names entered on its roll of attorneys were Brush and Sibley. Despite the creation of the territorial courts, there were still only five attorneys in Michigan (all in Detroit) at the end of

1805. By 1814 only fourteen attorneys had ever been admitted to practice before the supreme court, and several of them no longer practiced in Detroit.[2] During the hard years that followed the War of 1812, the already small number of attorneys decreased further and did not reach fourteen again until 1824.[3] Then the Erie Canal and the lure of cheap public land changed everything, bringing to Michigan the farmers and merchants who could support a law practice. In 1830 fifty attorneys belonged to the bar of the Michigan Supreme Court, almost all of them practicing in or near Detroit.[4]

Thus, Stephen had a good selection of trial attorneys from which to choose his defense team. Although the Sixth Amendment to the United States Constitution dictates that every criminal defendant is entitled to "the Assistance of Counsel for his defence," in 1830 that provision was not understood to require the appointment of counsel to indigent defendants, even those charged with murder. It was not until more than one hundred years later, in *Powell v. Alabama*,[5] that the United States Supreme Court held that the Sixth Amendment entitled defendants in state capital cases to legal assistance. But despite its backwardness in some ways, Michigan was ahead of the country on that issue. A Michigan statute, first enacted in April 1827 by the Legislative Council, required courts to assign to any person indicted of a crime, "if not of the ability to procure counsel, such counsel, not exceeding two, as he or she shall desire; to whom such counsel shall have access at all reasonable hours," all at county expense.[6]

Stephen was, however, a man of property, and he appears to have been wealthy enough to afford two of the most distinguished and able trial attorneys in the territory. One of those attorneys, George A. O'Keeffe, was already representing Stephen in his case against William St. Clair and in other matters. He was joined in the murder case by another trial attorney who was well respected in Detroit, Henry S. Cole. Neither O'Keeffe nor Cole required Stephen to pay cash up front. Instead, violating a cardinal rule of criminal lawyers, they agreed to represent him, a man facing death or substantial jail time, on credit. On June 24, the day Stephen was arraigned, he signed a printed form of a money bond in which he undertook to pay Cole two hundred dollars plus interest by July 1, 1831.[7] As security for payment, Stephen gave Cole a lien on the land containing the tavern and the homestead farm. This lien was in the form of a conditional sale—instead of giving Cole a lien on the property, Stephen transferred the property to Cole outright, but stated that if he paid off the bond by July 1, 1831, the transfer would be void.[8] Cole recorded the mortgage in the county clerk's office on that same day, and he may have felt that the nature of his lien protected him from not being paid. If so, he was wrong.

Although George O'Keeffe had already represented Stephen on other matters, Stephen did not officially retain him in the murder case until July 5, the day before the trial began. On a scrap of paper, now in the files of the Michigan Supreme Court, Stephen wrote out a note promising to pay O'Keeffe $130 plus interest by July 5, 1831.[9] As he had with Cole, Stephen gave O'Keeffe a lien, in the form of a conditional sale, on the tavern/homestead property.[10] Stephen may have pleaded that, like every farmer in the summer before the harvest, he was short on cash and that the lawyers would be paid from the 1830 harvest. Despite receiving such assurances and substantial collateral, however, it is not clear that Cole was ever paid, while O'Keeffe would not see a penny of his fee until 1834, and he would not be paid in full until 1839.

Although both Cole and O'Keeffe had begun practicing law in Michigan in 1820, they had starkly contrasting personalities and styles. "Harry"[11] Cole, a twenty-nine-year-old graduate of Union College in Schenectady, New York, who practiced in Detroit with his college classmate Augustus S. Porter,[12] was a scholarly lawyer, an "elegant gentleman,"[13] and on the fast track politically. Governor Cass had appointed him a probate judge for Wayne County when he was only twenty-five years old, and, at age thirty-two, he would become Attorney General of the Michigan Territory.

George Alexander O'Keeffe, the first prominent Irish member of the Detroit bar, lacked Cole's scholarly temperament but not his intelligence. Of more consequence to Stephen's defense, O'Keeffe was the Detroit bar's best spell-binding orator of the old school, an incomparably dramatic and witty trial lawyer. "[T]all and massive, with large blue eyes, large head, and curly hair," O'Keeffe was "an Irish gentleman in the truest and fullest sense, learned, cultured, brilliant, and witty."[14] Born in 1792 in Cork, Ireland, O'Keeffe claimed to be a graduate of Trinity College, Dublin, a bastion of the Protestant power structure that did not admit Catholics to its degree programs on an even basis with Protestants until 1793. He left Trinity, "in disgust but not in disgrace," after an altercation with other students that may have been related to his Catholic religion.[15] After studying law in England and Ireland, O'Keeffe emigrated to the United States in 1816. In 1820, after studying American law in New York City, he made the unlikely decision to open a practice in Detroit despite its having only twelve hundred residents at the time. The fact that a majority of them were Catholics may have influenced his decision.

O'Keeffe did not limit his wit and energy to the courtroom. Any party or dinner that he attended was likely to dissolve into joyful chaos under his direction. In an 1828 letter O'Keeffe described to John Winder a lively gathering in Mount Clemens where his antics made it "impossible . . . for the Ladies to pre-serve a proper degree of reserve & decorum—I quickly beat down all etiquette—put at bold defiance all ordinary rules of propriety, & the Goddess of Reserve, if there be such a Heathen Divinity had to lament the entire demolition of every thing dedicated to her shrine torn down by the ruthless & devastating [attack] of the Hibernian invader. . . ."[16] Mrs. B. C. Farrand recalled a visit by O'Keeffe to the hotel kept by François McConce, a chief of the Pottawattomies, at Swan Creek in St. Clair County. "Chancellor O'Keefe [sic] was always very well dressed, and one night he is remembered to have become so hilarious as to have danced with his silk stockings fallen down over his slippers much to the amusement of the children of the family."[17] However, there was indeed melancholy behind his antic facade. In the same letter to John Winder, he apologized for his "blue devils," his "somber temperament & egotistical querulousness, with which I so frequently embarrass my young friend." That melancholy, as well as his more congenial traits, are abundantly evident in his only known portrait.

At thirty-seven or eight, O'Keeffe was at the height of his powers of persuasion and invective. Friend Palmer, who was seven years old in 1830, remembered O'Keeffe with great admiration: "with his ample cloak thrown around one shoulder, his right arm free, he would stride up and down, gesticulating and rolling out his adjectives, to the intense wonder and amusement of his audience, myself included."[18] Another contemporary, the Reverend George Taylor, once shared a long and bumpy stagecoach ride with O'Keeffe and remarked on his proficiency "in the vulgar tongue" and for his ability to "pour out a volley of epithets not found in ordinary vocabularies."[19]

O'Keeffe shared Stephen's taste for alcohol, as did most western lawyers in those days. Indiana judge Isaac Nylor remembered that, "When I commenced the practice of law in 1818, I found the besetting sin of early members of the bar to be intemperance and gambling. About nine-tenths of the members of the bar were slaves and victims of those vices."[20] O'Keeffe was definitely part of that majority. When he boasted that he had been admitted to three different bars, William Pettit, a political opponent, remarked sarcastically, "We are carefully left to conjecture, whether the inside, or the outside, of the 'bar' has been so often honored by the presence of this honored Trismegistus, this second Gamaliel."[21]

On one occasion, O'Keeffe's tendency to drink to excess almost brought him, like Stephen, before a court on a charge that he had committed murder, and murder by hanging no less. In 1820, a few months after his arrival in Michigan, O'Keeffe joined other prominent Detroiters in an outing to Pontiac to celebrate the opening of Colonel Stephen Mack's flour mill, the first in Oakland County. The festivities included a good deal of drinking and horseplay. On the way home, a group that included O'Keeffe,

Governor Cass, Colonel Stephen Mack,[22] and Dr. Olmstead Chamberlin[23] continued their "jollification":

> [O]n arriving near Royal Oak, the party stopped at the shanty of a Frenchman, who was also pretty much under the influence of liquor. The party urged him to drink, and on his refusal they put him on trial, found him guilty and sentenced him to be hung. They accordingly tied a rope around his neck, fastened the other ends to the shafts of a cart, got onto the back end and tipped up the cart so that the man was taken off from his feet and actually left hanging for several minutes. On being let down he appeared to be dead, to the great alarm of those who had done execution to him. Dr. Chamberlain [sic], as the attending physician on the occasion, declared that he was dead, but as the body soon came to life he claimed that it was through the great professional skill that the man's life had been saved and persecutors relieved from a serious criminal prosecution. Such were some of the olden times.[24]

Colonel Mack's party was quite famous, or notorious, in its day. According to another source,[25] the "hilarious proceedings" included a mock court presided over by Solomon Sibley who, ten years later, would be one of Stephen's judges. The court tried the party-goers for various offenses and meted out punishment. Fourteen-year-old Charles W. Whipple, a future justice of the Supreme Court of the State of Michigan,[26] convicted of some "misdemeanor," was sentenced to dance in his underwear on the mill floor for half an hour. When Whipple collapsed after fifteen minutes, the jolly crew suspended him out an upper-floor window by his heels until he agreed to finish his sentence. Another source revealed that O'Keeffe himself hid in Colonel Mack's new barn to avoid being judged, but his pursuers set a fire in the barn in order to "burn him out." The fugitive "heard the flames snapping and crackling" and finally gave himself up to his tormentors. He was then sentenced to chew a quantity of resin from a nearby pine tree.[27] According to another report, it was at this gathering, amid the drinking and hijinks, that it was decided that Solomon Sibley would replace William Woodbridge as the territory's delegate to Congress.[28] It would appear that in territorial Michigan it paid to be one of the boys.

The lawyers opposing Cole and O'Keeffe in the Simmons trial were also secure members of the local legal and political establishment. Officially, the prosecution, like the defense, was to be conducted by two attorneys, the territory's Attorney General, William Asa Fletcher,[29] and Wayne County's District Attorney, Benjamin Franklin Hawkins Witherell. Already a relatively mature thirty-four when he arrived in Michigan in 1822, Fletcher wasted no time in advancing his career. He was appointed Attorney General of the territory in 1825, and he would work his way up to justice of the Supreme Court of the State of Michigan in 1836. However, his participation in the Simmons trial was largely symbolic, as he took only a nominal role in presenting the prosecution's case, leaving most of the work to district attorney Witherell.[30]

Known to his friends as B. F. H., and to his enemies as "Big Fat Hog" because of the comfortable 240 pounds that he carried on his six-foot frame, Witherell was thirty-three years old in 1830 and had already served as a judge of the Wayne County Court and as prosecutor for both St. Clair and Wayne Counties. He was handsome, even-tempered, kind, and popular with both the English- and French-speaking communities.[31] He was also one of the few lawyers of the day who did not drink alcohol. B. F. H. came to Detroit in 1819 to join his parents. His father, James Witherell, had served as a judge of the Supreme Court of the Territory of Michigan from 1808 until he resigned in 1828 to become Territorial Secretary.[32] James Witherell, B. F. H. Witherell, and George O'Keeffe had all played parts in the murder trial of Ke-wa-bish-kim. B. F. H. and O'Keeffe were appointed to represent the defendant, while James Witherell was given the duty of pronouncing the death sentence even though he had not presided at the trial.[33]

The Court and the Judges

The dubious honor of presiding over Stephen's murder trial belonged to the three judges of the Supreme Court of the Territory of Michigan but not to the Supreme Court. When they tried Stephen for murder, the Supreme Court judges acted in their other judicial capacity as judges of a territorial circuit court and, in particular, as judges of Wayne County Circuit Court. They had been assigned the additional role of circuit judges in 1825 because, although they had been appointed to the Supreme Court by the President, and given legislative power (as three-fourths of the Governor and Judges) by Congress, the judges of the Supreme Court were also subject to the dictates of a territorial legislature that thought that they needed more work.

When it created the Territory of Michigan in 1805, Congress also created a "superior court" composed of three judges to be "appointed by the President of the United States, by and with the advice and consent of the Senate."[34] On July 24, 1805, at one of their first sessions, the Governor and Judges (consisting at that time of Governor William Hull and Judges Augustus Brevoort Woodward and Frederick Bates) enacted a law that formally established the superior court mandated by Congress as the Supreme Court of the Territory of Michigan.[35] Although the Supreme Court was created by Congress and although the judges of the Supreme Court were appointed by, and could only be removed by, the President, the Governor and Judges undertook, without objection from the federal government, to define the powers to be exercised by the Supreme Court, to establish the duties of the Supreme Court judges, and to create a system of "inferior" courts for the territory.

Initially, the Governor and Judges gave the Supreme Court the power to sit as a trial court over all cases involving the title to real estate; all cases in which more than two hundred dollars was in dispute; all cases of divorce and alimony; and all criminal cases "where the punishment is capital." The Supreme Court was also required to hear all appeals from any inferior courts that might be created by the legislature.

Over the years, the governor and judges exercised their authority to create, and often abolish, various systems of "inferior" courts as well as judges and justices of the peace to run those courts. By the early 1820s those inferior courts conducted the trials of most criminal and civil cases that arose in the territory. Although the Supreme Court continued to act as both an appellate court and as a trial court for a wide range of important civil and criminal cases, including capital crimes, those cases were relatively few, and citizens complained that the Supreme Court was rarely in session. While the judges and justices of the peace assigned to the inferior courts dealt with most of the judicial business in the territory, the Supreme Court held its regular sessions, always in Detroit, for only one month each year,[36] and the Court performed its duty to decide cases involving the United States (principally tax and customs matters) in a few days more.[37] During the rest of the year, the Supreme Court judges carried on private law practices, engaged in land speculation, or pursued some other business.

This leisurely existence began to change in 1823, when Congress authorized the creation of an elected Legislative Council to replace the Governor and Judges as the territory's legislature.[38] For the first time, lawmaking in Michigan was not controlled by the judges of the Supreme Court, and the Council moved to force the judges to provide more service to the public. After some maneuvering, in April 1825 the Council passed a law creating a new inferior trial court, called a circuit court, to be held once a year in Wayne, Macomb, St. Clair, Oakland, and Monroe Counties.[39] To the dismay of the Supreme Court judges, the Council required that at least one of their number preside at each circuit court. In 1828 the Council went further and required that at least two of the Supreme Court judges attend every circuit court session in each county lying east of Lake Michigan.[40] In November 1828 Supreme Court Judge William Woodbridge complained of the strain imposed on the judges by having to attend "*fifteen* Courts annually, instead of one, & to traverse, mostly on horseback, an immense country, over roads not yet half formed &, some of which are exceedingly dangerous."[41]

Besides requiring the judges of the Supreme Court to sit outside of Detroit for the first time, the 1825 statute also increased
the time the Supreme Court judges had to spend holding a circuit court by concentrating more of the judicial work in the circuit courts at the expense of the Supreme Court. In particular,
the Council reduced the Supreme Court to a purely appellate
role by reassigning to the circuit courts all of the trial jurisdiction
of the Supreme Court, including trials of capital cases.[42] Thus
when *The United States of America v. Stephen G. Simmons* came
to be tried in July 1830, five years later, the trial was held in
Wayne County Circuit Court, albeit by the same judges and in
the same courthouse as would have been the case if he had been
tried by the Supreme Court.

Having the Supreme Court judges do double duty may have
been efficient, but it created a disadvantage for Stephen and other
defendants. Because the law required that at least two of the judges
be present at each session of a circuit court, Stephen could be sure
that the judges who would decide any appeal that he might make
to the Supreme Court would be the same judges who had made the
ruling in the circuit court that was the basis of his appeal. Wayne
County District Attorney B. F. H. Witherell expressed the opinion
that, under those circumstances, a decision by a circuit court settled the matter and any appeal was futile.[43]

Although the judges complained bitterly about these new
duties, the caliber of Michigan's judiciary had improved substantially since 1824, and the judges in office in 1830 had the intellectual ability to carry out the Council's mandate. That had not
always been the case: the judges who sat on the Supreme Court
bench from 1805 to 1824 would have floundered or would not
have tried to comply at all. In 1820 William Woodbridge, by
1830 a Supreme Court judge himself, sized up the men he would
one day replace in a letter to a friend: "Our chief Judge [Augustus
Brevoort Woodward] is a wild theorist, fitted principally for the
'extraction of sunbeams from cucumbers.'"[44] Judge John Griffin,
according to Woodbridge, was a gentleman, tasteful and polite,
"but with a mind lamentably inert." Indeed, it was well known in

the community that Griffin believed himself to be incapable of holding court without Judge Woodward at his elbow to tell him what to do.[45] Finally, Woodbridge noted that Judge James Witherell, a veteran of the Revolution whose education was in medicine, not law, was honest and intuitive but that he had a serious failing for a common-law judge: a "deadly hostility to that common law which he is officially called upon to administer,— because of its English descent."

By 1830 Judges Woodward, Griffin, and Witherell had been replaced by Woodbridge, Solomon Sibley, and Henry Chipman, resulting in a marked improvement in the court's reputation in the community for legal scholarship and collegiality. Judges Woodbridge and Sibley had known each other for more than thirty years, ever since both were young attorneys from New England practicing law in Marietta, Ohio. Also practicing law in Marietta at that time was another young, transplanted New Englander, Lewis Cass. As Michigan's governor, Cass would rely on Sibley and Woodbridge to help him dominate territorial government for more than fifteen years.

Born in 1769 in Sutton, Massachusetts, Solomon Sibley was sixty-one years old in 1830. He graduated from Rhode Island College (now Brown University) and was admitted to the Rhode Island Bar at the relatively old age of twenty-eight. Moving west, Sibley practiced law for a short time in Marietta, but he decided that Detroit, which then had only one attorney, Elijah Brush,[46] had more potential. Sibley arrived in Detroit in April 1798 after a seventeen-day ride from Marietta across the Black Swamp. Sibley's intelligence, charm, and romantic good looks soon made him one of the most prominent and influential men of early Detroit, active in business, legal, and political affairs.[47] Before becoming a judge, he served as Wayne County's representative on the Legislative Assembly of the Northwest Territory,[48] as Detroit's first elected mayor,[49] as Michigan's first United States Attorney, and as the territory's delegate to Congress.[50] Sibley was appointed to the Supreme Court bench in 1824 by President James Monroe; he took his oath of office on March 3, 1824, with

James Witherell and John Hunt.[51] By the time of Stephen's trial, Witherell had been replaced by William Woodbridge and Hunt by Henry Chipman.

William Woodbridge, a native of Norwich, Connecticut, was eleven years younger than Sibley and about the same age as Stephen Simmons.[52] Woodbridge was practicing law in Ohio when, in 1813, Lewis Cass was made Governor of the war-devastated Territory of Michigan as a dubious reward for having served on the staff of General William Henry Harrison during the campaign that recaptured Detroit from the British. One of Governor Cass's first official acts was to arrange the appointment of his old comrade Woodbridge to the position of Territorial Secretary, a job that gave Woodbridge wide scope to act as Cass's principal lieutenant in the territory. From 1813 to 1831, when Governor Cass resigned to become Andrew Jackson's Secretary of War, Woodbridge served as territorial Secretary, delegate to Congress (succeeding Sibley), and Supreme Court judge.

Although they worked together very well, the three men were very different in personality. Cass and Woodbridge "were always good friends, but never perhaps very intimate. . . . [T]heir characters and tastes were totally unalike."[53] Whereas Cass was a robust, healthy, energetic man of the world, Woodbridge, always believing himself to be in fragile health, was a quiet homebody who preferred family life and reading over socializing. Forty-nine years old at the time of Stephen's murder trial, Woodbridge has been described as "[d]our, irascible, an inveterate office-holder, a staunch lieutenant,"[54] and as "honest, conservative, and unimaginative."[55] While Solomon Sibley shared personality traits with both men, he was quite capable of behaving like one of the boys and had sufficient energy to keep up with Cass, while he also had the intellectual vigor to match Woodbridge. Sibley also had a gift, not given to Cass or Woodbridge, of being able to avoid controversy and political squabbles. When he saw no benefit in taking a stand, Sibley tended to disappear into the background. As a result, Sibley retained his popularity during local and national disputes that tarnished both Woodbridge and Cass.

From today's perspective, the three seem to have been a strange mix in politics as well as in personality. Sibley and Woodbridge were both National Democrats, the party, later known as the Whigs, that carried on the conservative Federalist tradition,[56] while Cass was, at least nominally, a Republican Democrat and a supporter of Andrew Jackson's populist democracy. Until the 1830s, however, Detroit and Michigan were fairly well isolated from the partisanship of the battles between Federalists and Republicans or Whigs and Democrats. Michigan politics focused almost universally on the local issues on which Cass, Sibley, and Woodbridge could agree.[57]

In contrast to his colleagues on the Supreme Court in 1830, Henry Chipman was a newcomer to Michigan. The son of a Vermont Supreme Court judge and a graduate of Middlebury College, he had practiced law in South Carolina for twenty years[58] before moving to Detroit in 1824.[59] Like Woodbridge, he was a Whig, but with an ardor more common in the east than in 1820s Michigan. In May 1825 he began publishing a newspaper, the *Michigan Herald*, which expressed his political views and was designed to oppose the Jacksonian *Detroit Gazette*, which had been started under the patronage of Governor Cass,[60] but the *Herald* lasted only until May 1829.

In December 1825 Chipman was appointed Chief Justice of the Wayne County Court. This was not a highly sought-after post because the pay was limited to fees collected from criminal defendants, and Chipman resigned a year later. In 1827 his activities on behalf of the Whigs paid off when President John Quincy Adams appointed him to the territorial Supreme Court to replace Judge John Hunt, who had died in office. Judge Chipman was reappointed in 1828, and he soon established a reputation for sound legal reasoning.[61] At the time of the Simmons trial, he was forty-six years old, of medium height, well-proportioned, with blue eyes and thick, curly white hair that he wore long. He was described by a contemporary as having "a countenance full of benevolence and expression."[62] Like B. F. H. Witherell, Chipman abstained from drinking alcohol.[63]

Although the legal skills of the judges of the Michigan Supreme Court in July 1830 were strong, their health was not. Judge Woodbridge was always sickly looking, and he often excused himself from the bench on the ground that he was too ill to preside. The fact that he lived to a ripe old age, and that after being ousted as a judge he served as both U.S. Senator and Governor of the State of Michigan, suggest that his principal illness may have been hypochondria. Whereas Woodbridge made no secret of his fragile health, Judge Sibley tried to hide the fact that he was almost completely deaf.[64] Because his handwriting changed from neat and orderly to illegible at about the same time that his hearing began to fade, his deafness may have been neurological. The third member of the court, Judge Chipman, had a speech impediment,[65] and he was generally silent on the bench except when some comment was necessary. This tended to increase his reputation for quiet, grave thoughtfulness.

As a result of their physical problems, Sibley and Chipman tended to rely on Woodbridge to speak for the court and to keep notes of any arguments or testimony. The Woodbridge Papers at the Clarence Burton Collection of the Detroit Public Library contain extensive notes of the cases he tried. Unfortunately, Judge Woodbridge was not in court to hear the testimony of the witnesses in the Simmons trial, and if either of the other judges made notes, they have not survived.

chapter 6

Trial and Sentence

The trial of *The United States of America v. Stephen G. Simmons* began on Monday, July 6, 1830, during a severe heat wave.[1] At that time, the judges, whether sitting as the Michigan Supreme Court or as Wayne County Circuit Court, conducted trials in the territorial courthouse, also called the Capitol because the Legislative Council, and later the state legislature, sat there as well.[2] Located at the far northern edge of town on what is now Capitol Square at Griswold and State Streets,[3] the courthouse had had a long gestation period. As part of the rebuilding of Detroit after the great fire of 1805, Congress allocated ten thousand acres of land just west of the old town to be sold to finance the construction of a courthouse and a jail.[4] In 1806 the Governor and Judges enacted a law placing the courthouse, "an edifice for the permanent accommodation of the supreme court of Michigan," in the center of the Grand Circus. Grand Circus, which remains one of Detroit's major public squares, first appeared in the drawings for Judge Woodward's master plan for redeveloping Detroit after the fire, but in 1806 its site was in the deep forest, well outside the settlement.[5] The Governor and Judges did nothing about actually building a courthouse for seventeen years except to repeal the courthouse act in 1815.[6] In July 1823 the Governor and Judges finally awarded a contract to two local merchants, Thomas Palmer and David McKinstry, to build a courthouse at the head of Griswold Street. The price of the building was $21,000, to be paid by granting the builders the right to buy, at a reduced price, more than six thousand acres in the ten-thousand-acre tract set aside by Congress in 1805.[7] The courthouse was supposed to be completed by December 1824, but

the practical and financial difficulties of building a large structure
in Detroit delayed completion until May 1828.[8] Even then, the
new Legislative Council had to bail out Palmer and McKinstry,
who were unable to sell many of the lots granted to them.[9]

Despite the delays and difficulties, the result was an elegant
and imposing building that served the community in various
roles for fifty years. When completed, the courthouse was a three-
story, sixty-by-ninety-foot brick building in the Greek Revival
style, distinguished by a portico of six Ionic columns and a pep-
per-box cupola 140 feet high, which offered an unparalleled view
of the city, the river, and the forest.[10] The building housed the
Legislative Council in addition to the courts, and in 1836 it
became the first State Capitol. When the state legislature moved
to Lansing in 1847, the building became a public school. It
housed Detroit's first high school from 1863 to 1878.[11] In 1830
only St. Anne's Catholic Church rivaled the courthouse as the
premier building in the territory.

Long before the trial began, the courtroom was packed with
sweltering spectators, most of whom, at least the men, were
either smoking or chewing (and spitting) tobacco. Although
those activities were tolerated in court, loud noises and sleeping
were not. Courtroom decorum and order were maintained by a
redoubtable constable and crier, "General" Isaac Day, a tall, thin
man with a loud voice who, quite literally, carried a big stick and
was not slow to use it on spectators.[12] Sartorially conservative,
Day "clung to knee breeches, ample coat skirts and waistcoat. He
wore his hair long, brushed straight back from his head and tied
in a queue."[13] Also providing security in court throughout the
trial was Sheriff Knapp, who had the duty of escorting Stephen
between the jail and the court each day. The distance was only a
few hundred yards, so they might have walked, but because of
Detroit's mud-choked streets, Knapp may have chosen to transport his prisoner by cart instead.

On that first day of the trial, all three judges were present and
seated on the bench at 10 A.M., when Day called the court to
order. At the court's command, Sheriff Knapp brought Stephen

into the courtroom and placed him at the Bar.[14] The court's first piece of business, after reading aloud the indictment, was of crucial importance to the defense: selection of a fair and impartial jury, as guaranteed by the Sixth Amendment to the United States Constitution and by the common law. The court's clerk, John Winder, escorted into the courtroom nineteen men who were all that had responded to the twenty-four summonses sent to potential jurors. Winder took the roll and then drew twelve of their names at random and directed those named to take seats in the jury box. The game had begun.

As the jury selection process began, it became apparent that O'Keeffe and Cole were willing to push the county's creaky system for summoning jurors to its breaking point and beyond in order to secure twelve jurors who could be as fair and impartial as was possible under the circumstances. The defense strategy was to challenge every juror called as biased against Stephen and to excuse as many jurors as the court would allow in order to find and seat jurors who were most likely to sympathize with their client, principally modest farmers and tradesmen from the outer townships of the county. And, if in the course of pursuing their strategy, they could create an issue for appeal, so much the better.

From its long experience in Wayne County courts, the defense team knew that most of the men who would be on the county's official jury list would be prominent, respectable Detroiters who would have ties to county government and law enforcement. That was not because there was a deliberate plan to stack a jury against Stephen. Rather, it was a result of a jury system which, despite reform efforts, still favored "character," meaning standing in the community, over broad popular participation in government.

A series of territorial statutes had established the qualifications for who could sit on a jury.[15] According to the statute in effect in 1830, jurors had to be "judicious persons" who had "the qualifications of electors of delegate to Congress"[16]—in other words, "free white male citizens of said territory, above the age of twenty-one years, who shall have resided therein one year preceding an election, and who shall have paid a county or territorial tax."[17] But until the process was reformed in 1828, even most of the men in Wayne County who met those qualifications would never serve on a jury. Between 1805 and 1828, the sheriff of each county had complete power to select who, among those qualified citizens, would be called for jury duty: the clerk asked for so many jurors and the sheriff summoned whomever he pleased. In Wayne County that meant that the same handful of prominent citizens, most of them living in or near Detroit, served on one jury after another.

Naturally, people living in rural areas of Wayne County were suspicious of the ability of prosperous Detroiters to hear their cases fairly. In May 1828 the Legislative Council passed an act meant to remove the sheriff's selection power and to broaden the jury pools geographically.[18] Under that act, each township in a county was required to select, each year, a fixed number of men, in proportion to the township's percentage of the country's eligible jurors, to serve in a body of one hundred trial (or "petit") jurors and one hundred grand jurors. Ten days before each session of the court, the county clerk was to pull the names of twenty-four petit jurors, enough for two full juries of twelve, from a box containing all hundred names, "the sheriff or coroner, as the case may be, having first shook the box, so as to mix the ballots." The clerk was then to order the sheriff to summon the men whose names had been drawn.[19] Because the summons was called a writ of *venire facias*, the jurors summoned in this fashion were called "veniremen."

Unfortunately, this jury system was too complex for the conditions in Michigan, even for those in Wayne County. Sheriffs often ignored the law and continued to fill the jury lists with the same names as before, much to the disgust of Judge Woodbridge.[20] At the same time, poor compliance with the law in the townships resulted in Wayne County having only half the usual complement of jurors on call in 1830, fifty grand jurors and fifty petit jurors,[21] most of whom were, once again, the same familiar group of Detroiters.

The judges let this situation continue because, in virtually all jury trials, the small number of potential petit jurors was not an issue. Usually the twenty-four venire summonses were enough, even if some men did not respond to the summons, to handle a day's trials. If the court was short one or two veniremen to fill a jury, the sheriff simply pulled in off the street men who, because they were not summoned in the regular way, were called "talesmen" instead of veniremen. It soon became obvious, however, that Stephen's trial would put an unprecedented burden on the county's jury-selection system because his defense intended to exploit the large number of potential jurors that a defendant in a capital case was allowed to challenge and excuse.

Parties in a trial were allowed two types of challenges to potential jurors: peremptory challenges and challenges for cause. Both the prosecution and the defense were allowed to challenge an unlimited number of jurors for cause, but it was up to the judges to decide if there was, in fact, cause to excuse a juror. If a juror was excused, he was allowed to go about his business while another candidate was called into the jury box to be examined; if not, the party had to either accept the juror or exercise a peremptory challenge.

A party did not have to give a reason to exercise a peremptory challenge. As Judge Augustus Brevoort Woodward told Ka-tau-kah at his murder trial in 1821, a party was entitled to make a peremptory challenge "without assigning any reason—need only say 'he does not like that man.'"[22] On the other hand, Michigan statutes limited the number of peremptory challenges that each party could exercise. In a noncapital criminal case, the district attorney and the defendant had only two peremptory challenges each.[23] But, because of the gravity of his situation, a defendant who pleaded not guilty to "a crime punishable with death" was allowed to make up to thirty-five peremptory challenges, "and no more."[24] Even thirty-five peremptories might not be enough in this case, so the success of the defense strategy would depend on the court's definition of just what constituted sufficient cause to excuse a juror.

In most common-law jurisdictions, a juror's expression of prejudice against a party has traditionally, and logically, been enough to

excuse a juror for cause, particularly if the juror admits that he cannot give the defendant a fair trial. However, unbelievable as it may
seem, Michigan's statute in effect in 1830 did not include prejudg-
ing the guilt of the defendant as a ground disqualifying a juror for
cause.[25] Instead, the grounds for sustaining a "principal cause of
challenge" included only convicted criminals and persons with a
personal or financial interest or involvement in the case:

> . . . any petit juror who shall have been convicted of any
> crime, which by law renders him disqualified to sit on a jury,
> or who has an interest in the same, or who has been arbitra-
> tor on either side, relating to the same controversy, or who
> has an interest in the same [sic], or who has an action pend-
> ing between him and the party, or who has formerly been a
> juror in the same cause, or who is the party's master, servant,
> counselor, steward, or attorney, or who is subpoenaed as a
> witness in the cause, or who is kin to either party.

The statute specifically stated that a person under "suspicion of
prejudice against, or partiality for either party, or any other cause
that may render him at the time an unsuitable juror" could be
removed only by a peremptory challenge. As the statute was written, then, Stephen's attorneys could excuse only the first thirty-
five veniremen summoned into the box who had already judged
Stephen to be guilty of murder and would have to accept those
who followed even if they admitted having prejudged his guilt.

That result would have defeated to the defense strategy, but
the presiding judges were not inclined to interpret the jury
statute so literally. Although he bemoaned the territorial tendency to disregard the written laws, Judge Woodbridge was quite
willing to ignore this statute because of his fervent belief that the
system of trial by jury could achieve justice only if it were
shielded from the smallest taint of prejudice. Whatever the
statute said, the thought of requiring a party to accept a prejudiced juror disgusted his sense of justice. A year earlier, in a theft
case, *United States v. John Reed*, Judge Woodbridge voted with

Judge Chipman to grant the defendant a new trial because a defense challenge of a juror for cause was denied even though the juror admitted that he had already formed an opinion that the defendant was guilty. In an impassioned written ruling,[26] Woodbridge held that a criminal defendant had both a right to ask jurors whether they had formed an opinion as to guilt and a further right not to be tried by jurors who answered yes:

> From the time of the first establishment of the Saxons in the land of our ancestors, there is good reason to suppose that the right of Jury trial obtained [. . .]. Time, which withers all things, has yet only polished the more, a political con-trivance which does not cease to be a source of exultation—of national pride, of enthusiastic attachment![. . .] If there exist a duty then, more imperative upon this Court than any other, it is, that it should preserve, in all its theoretic purity the right of Jury trial. [. . .] [T]o guard against all extraneous causes of prejudice & bias in jurors,—is emphatically, the duty of this Court [. . .]. In short, it is a mockery of justice to pretend that, *that* is an *impartial* jury, any of whom, had *previously* formed their opinions in this case.[27]

Stephen's lawyers were certainly aware of that opinion,[28] and they probably felt confident that Judges Woodbridge and Chipman, who concurred with the *Reed* opinion, would allow challenges for cause based on a juror's having prejudged Stephen's guilt. That confidence was not misplaced: the number of successful challenges for cause in this case cannot possibly be accounted for by the limited grounds contained in the statute that essentially restricted challenges for cause to criminals and people with a financial interest in the case.[29]

The enormous number of candidates needed to find twelve disinterested jurors in this case, usually reported to have been three hundred, has been interpreted to demonstrate the community's revulsion at Stephen's crime.[30] According to the court's daily journal, the true number of jurors examined and then either excused or seated was only 128.[31] Even if the truth was less than half of the legend, the defense challenges to so many jurors astounded contemporaries and put a severe strain on Wayne County's jury system and on the court.[32] However, the defense realized that this was what they had to do if they were to have any chance of finding, in a county that had fewer than 3,700 "free white males," including minors and foreigners,[33] twelve who might be willing to find Stephen guilty of manslaughter, a verdict of not guilty being plainly impossible.

Cole and O'Keeffe began their search for twelve unprejudiced men with the nineteen veniremen who had obeyed John Winder's summons.[34] The first twelve candidates called up included Harlow Beardsley (a wagon maker), John Roberts (a "soap boiler & tallow chandler"), John Scott (a bookkeeper), Conrad Seek (a tax collector), Stephen Bain (a clerk for the Woodward Avenue produce market), merchants Gilbert Dalson, John Garrison, John Howard, and Samuel Phelps, and three others whose primary occupation is unknown: Aaron Hanley, Elisha Warren, and Robert W. Payne. To a stranger, these veniremen might have appeared to be a fair cross-section of middle-class Wayne County, but Cole and O'Keeffe, who had known most of them and their families for years, would have recognized that they and the seven others summoned that day were members of Detroit's political and civic establishment. We have information about fifteen of them: all were Detroit businessmen, five were past or future city aldermen, another was a future county commissioner, three others were past or future law enforcement officers, and one would lose the election held five months later to succeed Sheriff Knapp.

As the spectators watched with anticipation to see what strategy the defense had adopted, O'Keeffe rose and informed the court that the defendant challenged all twelve members of the panel for cause. The court instructed the clerk to swear in the twelve members of the panel, "on their *voir dire*," to tell the truth. The judges then asked each of the twelve veniremen in turn whether he had prejudged Stephen's guilt or innocence. Their responses were neither surprising nor encouraging: ten of the panel members were excused immediately, presumably because they admitted to a belief that Stephen was guilty.

The court overruled the challenge to jurors Aaron Hanley and Stephen Bain, "whereupon [they] are challenged peremptorily by prisoner & they thereupon retired from the Box." John Winder then called up the remaining seven candidates, including Peter Desnoyers, an attorney and former city constable who was appointed U.S. Marshal a week later; David Thompson, a future constable and U.S. Marshal; and Lewis Davenport, a well-known merchant and ferryboat owner who would, two months later, build Stephen's scaffold. The seven new veniremen took their seats in the jury box, and the procedure was repeated. The defense again challenged all seven candidates for cause, and the court excused four of them, denying the challenges to Desnoyers, Thompson, and Davenport. Although the court's decision as to Desnoyers seems questionable under today's standards because of his law enforcement connections, the court may have felt that Desnoyers would give the defense a fair hearing in this case because he was Harry Cole's brother-in-law.[35] It appears that Cole was not so sure of his brother-in-law's reliability, because the defense made peremptory challenges to all three of the remaining veniremen, and they were excused.

At this point the proceedings had to stop because the court had exhausted its venire and had no more potential jurors on hand. The tally for the first day was nineteen veniremen called but none seated. The court had no choice but to adjourn until Wednesday, July 7, at 10 A.M., after ordering Sheriff Knapp "to summon a Sufficient number of Talesmen to complete the panel in this cause." Clearly, the judges hoped to avoid a repeat of what had been, from their perspective, a fruitless exercise. The sheriff returned Stephen to the jail, and his attorneys probably retired to some establishment where they could have a drink and discuss their next move.

As it happened, the court did not resume Stephen's trial on July 7, possibly because Sheriff Knapp needed more time to round up the anticipated number of talesmen. But the court was not idle: it used the time to sentence several convicted criminal defendants, including three prominent citizens who had been found guilty of assault and battery[36] following a public brawl. United States Indian Agent Henry R. Schoolcraft was fined fifteen dollars, former Sheriff Thomas C. Sheldon was fined twenty dollars, and Robert Beaubien, a member of a prominent French family, was fined ten dollars. In what may or may not have been a separate occurrence, the court fined both Martin and Mary Socier twenty dollars for keeping a bawdy house.

The court then turned to two defendants charged with much more serious crimes. On April 26, 1830, Ulysses G. Smith had burned down the offices of his employer, the *Detroit Gazette*, as well as several other nearby buildings.[37] Smith's bout of arson was aroused by other employees of the *Gazette* who suspected that Smith had stolen publisher Sheldon McKnight's "double-cased silver watch with a steel chain and two gold seals and key" from the *Gazette*'s offices.[38] Smith's fellow employees detained him forcibly and searched his body and luggage, but they found nothing. Outraged, Smith "chose to be the judge and the avenger of the wrong"[39] and set the fire that destroyed the building housing the *Gazette* as well as the homes of John Smith (no relation) and Judge McDonnell, the stores of Major Brooks and Mr. Griswold, and the offices of Dr. Clark and Thomas Palmer.[40] Ulysses Smith was convicted by a jury of arson and, on July 7, the court sentenced him to a fine of $1,000 and ten years imprisonment at hard labor. By contrast, the court sentenced Robert McLaren, convicted of manslaughter for the drunken killing of his best friend, to a mere three months' imprisonment at hard labor and a fine of $250. McLaren's sentence and the two-year sentence given Levi Willard in 1828 for the drunken killing of his own brother[41] may have raised Stephen's hopes for leniency. If so, he probably did not understand the significance, in the minds of the people judging his actions, of the gender and identity of his victim.

Jury selection in *U.S. v. Simmons* did resume on Thursday, July 8. At ten A.M., Stephen was brought back into court, and Judges Woodbridge, Sibley, and Chipman ordered Winder to call another jury panel from the pool of forty-eight potential jurors whom Sheriff Knapp had managed to assemble that morning.[42] Before Winder could do so, however, George O'Keeffe rose and pointed out that the territorial jury statute gave a capital defendant the right to receive the names of all jurors summoned in his case.[43] His client had received no such list for that day. Therefore, he argued, the court must either throw out this pool of jurors or adjourn until he received proper notice of their names. In either case, the court would have to adjourn trial until Friday.

The court was no doubt annoyed by this argument because the problem had been caused by O'Keeffe himself. By rejecting all of the prior jury pool, he had forced the clerk and sheriff to resort to the old method of gathering jurors—going door-to-door or pulling talesmen in off the street because they did not have enough time to summon veniremen according to the statute. Almost certainly, Winder and Knapp had not known, twenty-four hours earlier, who their talesmen would be when the trial resumed on July 8. Faced with the choice of using the informally gathered talesmen despite the defense objection or adjourning trial once more, the court denied O'Keeffe's motion.

The remainder of the proceedings on July 8 repeated many times over the pattern established two days before. As panel after panel was called into the box, the defense challenged every talesman for cause and then challenged peremptorily anyone still in the jury box. On that hot, humid day, Winder called up five panels containing all forty-eight talesmen present. The court excused twenty-eight of them for cause, and the defense exercised fifteen peremptory challenges. The prosecution also used one of its two peremptory challenges to excuse talesman Alfred Hodge, age thirty-five, who lived near Simmons.[44] There was some small progress as both sides agreed to accept four talesmen as jurors to try the case: Guy H. Leonard, Thomas C. Brown, Gaylord Goodell, and Samuel W. Lapham.

The decision to accept Lapham gives another insight into the thinking of the defense attorneys. Lapham had recently been involved in two other criminal cases, one as a victim and one as a defendant. It was for beating Lapham that former Wayne County Sheriff Sheldon was fined twenty dollars for assault and battery on July 7.[45] Lapham had also been indicted in January 1830 on a charge of blasphemy,[46] but he had been acquitted by a jury on June 14, 1830, the day that Stephen killed Levana.[47] Lapham's codefendant in that trial, Abraham Salsbury, had been represented by none other than George A. O'Keeffe,[48] who, no doubt, recognized in Lapham a man with a possible grudge against the government and a partiality for people fighting against authority.

After several hours of jury selection, the pool of talesmen, the judges, and the attorneys were exhausted. When prosecutor Witherell moved for an order adjourning trial, the court gratefully agreed and also ordered Sheriff Knapp to scour the county and gather a large enough pool of talesman to make sure that jury selection would be completed the next time the trial resumed. The court allowed the four jurors who had been seated "to disperse under the charge of the Court," and ordered them "to appear again before the Court upon Monday morning, the 12th July instant at Ten O'Clock." While the jurors left the courthouse, and Stephen was delivered back to the jail by Sheriff Knapp to sit in his cell and wait, the judges and attorneys in the case had more work to finish before their day of rest. On Saturday, July 10, the court conducted three trials in which Witherell prosecuted and O'Keeffe defended. One defendant, Thomas Driscoll, charged with larceny, was released when his jury could not reach a verdict.[49] Two brothers, William and David Hudson, were tried together and found not guilty of larceny.[50] The final defendant, Francis Matevier, was not so fortunate—he was convicted of receiving stolen goods and was sentenced to two months in jail and a fine of $500.[51]

When court reconvened on Monday, July 12, to try to complete jury selection, only two of the three judges were present.[52] Judge Woodbridge sent word that he was too sick to attend court, and Judges Sibley and Chipman continued the trial without him. Woodbridge did not participate in the rest of the trial; whether or not the participants felt his absence, not having his customary notes summarizing the trial testimony is an unfortunate loss to historians. Woodbridge did return to the bench in time to preside at the hearing on Stephen's motion in arrest of judgment on July 21–22, as well as Stephen's sentencing on July 26.[53]

Before any of Monday's pool of talesmen could be questioned, the defense again objected to the fact that it had not received a list of the names of the new talesmen at least twenty-four hours earlier. The court did not explain why it could not have prepared a list of talesmen and delivered it to the defense by Sunday morning. Instead, the court merely overruled the objection and, according to a note in the margin of the official journal of proceedings, directed John Winder "forthwith to furnish" defense counsel with a list of jurors, and the list "was furnished accordingly."

Jury selection proceeded as it had on July 6 and 8, except that the sheriff, after scouring the county, had gathered enough talesmen to finish the job. Panel after panel, a total of sixty-one talesmen were called into the box before the jury was complete. The defense challenged all sixty-one for cause, of which the court sustained thirty-six (including a challenge to George M. Johnson, the former owner of Simmons' Tavern). Fifteen more talesmen were disposed of by peremptory challenges, fourteen by the defense team and the last one available to the prosecution, excusing James Bucklin, another Simmons neighbor and a fellow tavern keeper. Finally, after several hours they were finished, and eight jurors had been seated to complete the panel: John B. Mettez, Eben Beach, Hiram W. Pond, Garry Spencer, Franklin Brewster, Andrew Fisher, Asquire W. Aldrich, and Dean Wyman.

Over three days of trial, the clerk had called 128 men into the jury box, the court had excused eighty for cause and thirty-six on peremptory challenges, including two by the prosecution, in order to seat twelve jurors. This marathon seems to have accomplished part of the defense plan to exhaust the supply of prominent, establishment-minded jurors from Detroit and force the clerk and the sheriff to dip into names of less prosperous and less politically active citizens from the countryside who, the defense hoped, were more likely to be sympathetic to Stephen. In fact, most of the men who actually sat in judgment over Stephen G. Simmons have been forgotten by history. Only two of them ever earned any particular distinction. One, Garry Spencer, a commercial tailor, served in the City Guards, Detroit's militia, reaching the rank of Colonel, and he served as City Treasurer from 1837 to 1840.[54] The other, Asquire Aldrich, had a successful career in real estate and was, therefore, a frequent civil litigant. It appears that Guy H. Leonard was a cooper because the Solomon Sibley papers at the Burton Historical Collection contain an invoice from Leonard to Sibley for the repair of several casks, but not much else is known about him.[55] Eben Beach was probably selected because, like Samuel Lapham, he was willing to stand up to the law, a trait he had demonstrated recently when he was a reluctant witness in the bawdy-house trial of Mr. and Mrs. Socier.[56] Although Beach had been called by the prosecution to testify, he stoutly denied that he had ever seen anything out of the ordinary at the Socier house or that he had been aware of the large number of young men who dropped in there for short visits at all hours.

By the time jury selection was complete, the judges had spent several tiring hours in a sweltering courtroom, and they would not have been criticized if they had adjourned for the day. Indeed, the attorneys on both sides would probably have preferred to rest before conducting opening statements and beginning to examine the witnesses. But the judges obviously felt that too much valuable court time had been spent on this case already. So instead of adjourning, they ordered the prosecution to begin presenting its evidence.

We can only make an educated guess about who testified at trial and, except for Stephen's children, what they said. This court, like most courts at that time, did not have a court reporter to take down the trial testimony verbatim, and, although the court's daily journal recorded the name of every venireman and talesman in the case, it was silent regarding the names of the witnesses, as was the *North-Western Journal*. If Judges Sibley and Chipman made any notes of the proceedings, their whereabouts are unknown. What we do have is Clarence Burton's summary of a record, now lost, that he found among boxes of documents in the attic of Detroit's old City Hall and summarized in his notes.[57] That record, possibly written by John Winder, indicated that the trial witnesses included eyewitnesses Sutherland, Avery, and Bell; David, Ellen, and Bathsheba Simmons; and three men who did not testify before the grand jury in June, Ezra Dunham and Leonard Osgood, both from Seneca County, New York, and Darius Comstock from Lenawee County, Michigan Territory, who had moved to Michigan in 1826 from Niagara County, New York.[58]

Although the *Journal* did not identify them by their first names, the paper did report that the Simmons children testified to a hellish family life:

> The evidence made the hearers acquainted with the conduct
> of the family for some years past. It represented a husband
> sometimes forcing, always encouraging his wife to drink; in
> his moments of intoxication, beating her with the hand or
> instruments of wood or iron, and driving her forth at night to
> seek shelter in the woods, following her and stamping upon
> her. It represented a mother in a drunken carousal with her
> husband in the presence of their children; or raving like fury,
> and grasping chairs or boards to beat them, and drive them
> from the house. Intemperate men and intemperate women,
> can you learn nothing from this?[59]

Visiting journalist Calvin Colton, who did not attend the trial, heard similar accounts of the children's testimony and its effect on the jury: "In telling the story of their mother's dreadful end, they brought their father to the gallows. In the progress of the trial a history of savage violence was disclosed such, we would fain believe, as rarely passes upon the records of crime. What demon of hell can be more fatal to human happiness, and to the souls of men, than ardent spirits?"[60]

The other eyewitnesses no doubt repeated their grand jury testimony, and it is possible that Stephen testified in his own defense.[61] The roles of Dunham, Osgood, and Comstock remain unknown. They may have been present at the tavern on the night of the murder, or they may have been character witnesses, as George Catlin once suggested to Clarence Burton.[62] There is no evidence to support either guess.

The prosecution had not completed its case when the court did, at last, stop for the day. Instead of being sent off for the night on their own, the jurors were sequestered in the custody of jailer Owen Aldrich and Marshal Thomas Knowlton who were "sworn to take charge of the Jury and not allow them to separate." The court then adjourned, "to meet again tomorrow at 9 O'Clock A.M."

As in many contemporary murder trials, the testimony in Stephen's trial did not take nearly as long as the jury selection, but it must have seemed endless to Stephen and his attorneys, an excruciating experience. The next day, July 13,[63] B. F. H. Witherell completed his presentation of the government's case, and the defense began and ended its entire case early enough in the day that the court ordered the prosecution and the defense to present closing arguments before court adjourned that day as well. This was a crucial moment, the last chance for Stephen's defense team to perform a miracle.

Because the facts of the killing were incontrovertible, only George O'Keeffe's ability to convince the jury to ignore the facts and the law could avoid a murder conviction. We do not know what O'Keeffe said, but he probably urged the jury, in his best dramatic manner, with flourishes, lamentations, and tears, to return any verdict but murder. His only viable strategy was to remind the jurors that Stephen had been under the control of strong drink at the time of the crime, that he did not intend, and could not have intended, to kill Levana, that he had lost everything dear to him, and that the jury should exercise mercy and convict him, if it must convict him at all, of manslaughter and not murder.[64]

Unfortunately, no matter how inspired O'Keeffe's efforts may have been, no matter how emotional his appeal to the jurors, there was very little that even he could do to soften the grim facts of the killing. When both sides had competed their closing arguments, the jury "receiv[ed] the Charge of the Court" (the jury instructions) from one of the judges and then "retired to consult of their verdict under charge of Andrew Abbott and Thomas Knowlton the officers sworn to Attend them." When the jury had not reached a verdict by the end of the day, the officers shepherded them to a hotel for the night, and Stephen returned to jail to spend one more night in suspense.

At some time on Wednesday, July 14, word was brought to the jail that the jury had reached a verdict. Soon afterwards, Stephen was "again brought into Court by the Sheriff under the order of Court and placed at the Bar."[65] Word that the jury was returning spread through town, and, by the time Stephen entered, the courtroom was packed with people anticipating both the verdict and the drama of Stephen's reaction. When Judges Sibley and Chipman were ready, John Winder escorted the twelve jurors to the box. There they announced their verdict: "being polled each and every of them say they find the Prisoner Stephen G. Simmons Guilty of the felony with which he stands charged"— murder—for killing Levana Simmons.

If any person in Michigan disagreed with the verdict and truly felt that the verdict should have been manslaughter there is no record of it. Instead, the general feeling in the community seems to have been that the result was tragic but just. The reporter for the *North-Western Journal* hoped that the verdict would be a lesson to others: "We have not room now to say all which occurs to us, in relation to this event, so fearfully appalling, that the heart *stands still* at the contemplation of it. . . . Intemperate men and intemperate women, can you learn nothing from this? . . . We have no comments to make; every reader *will* pause and think; think long and seriously."[66]

After hearing the jury's verdict, Stephen returned to the jail, where he had to wait twelve days before he would be sentenced. He may still have harbored hope for some sentence other than death by hanging, but if he did, he was fooling only himself. While his client waited, George O'Keeffe was kept busy on his behalf. On the day after the jury returned its verdict, Thursday, July 15, O'Keeffe won another victory in a civil case brought against Stephen by one George Foster.[67] On the following Monday, July 19, O'Keeffe obtained a judgment for Stephen, in the amount of $15.35 plus costs, against William St. Clair and his surety, Joseph Hickox, but Stephen would not live to see any of it—the court did not require the surety to pay up until January 1831, long after Stephen was dead.[68]

George O'Keeffe's most important post-trial task on Stephen's behalf was to argue in court a motion "in arrest" of the judgment, which, if successful, would set aside the conviction and death sentence and award Stephen a new trial. All three of the judges of the court attended the hearing when it began on Wednesday, July 21,[69] but Judge Sibley missed the end of the arguments by O'Keeffe and B. F. H. Witherell, on following day, Thursday, July 22, and did not participate in the court's ruling on the motion.[70] According to Judge Woodbridge's notes,[71] O'Keeffe based his argument on the issue he had raised at trial: that the court had erred by failing to provide Stephen and his attorneys the names of the talesmen at least twenty-four hours before the court's sessions on July 8 and 12.

To support his position, O'Keeffe cited several authorities, including an opinion written in 1795 by a Justice of the United States Supreme Court in *United States of America v. The Insurgents of Pennsylvania.*[72] Justice William Paterson, sitting as a circuit court judge in the high treason prosecutions arising from the Whiskey Rebellion, suspended trial and required the prosecutor to provide the defendants the names of potential jurors three days before resuming the case as required by the rules of Pennsylvania courts. The U.S. Supreme Court confirmed many years later that a court's failure to comply with an applicable jury statute did, indeed, mandate overturning a guilty verdict.[73] In Stephen's case, however, Judges Woodbridge and Chipman apparently decided that their own failure to comply with the letter of Michigan's statutory jury procedure jury did not require overturning Stephen's conviction. In their opinion denying the

motion, made public on Saturday, July 24, two days after the
hearing ended, Woodbridge and Chipman reasoned that giving
Stephen's counsel the names of the talesmen at the beginning of
each day was sufficient to satisfy the statute:

> [A] list of the Jury regularly summoned and returned for the
> present term of the Court was duly furnished the Prisoner at
> least twenty-four hours before the Commencement of the
> trial of the cause & that the said Prisoner was also furnished
> with the names of the Talesmen summoned by order of the
> Court previous to the calling of their names.[74]

With that business completed, the court scheduled Monday,
July 26, as the date for the only duty left for the judges to perform: pronouncing sentence. On that day, barely six weeks after
Levana's death and not quite three weeks after trial began,
Sheriff Knapp escorted Stephen back to the courtroom for his
last appearance there. After the titillation and drama of the trial,
the newspapers that had been following the trial with great interest must have anticipated that the sentencing would be bland
and tame. After all, there was no suspense regarding the result
because the law allowed only one possible sentence, death by
hanging. Consequently, the next editions of both the North-
Western Journal and the Michigan Sentinel did no more than report
tersely that Stephen G. Simmons had been sentenced to death,
while the Oakland Chronicle did not mention the hearing or the
sentence at all.[75]

However, another journalist visiting Detroit did find the scene
in court that day worth describing. Calvin Colton happened to
be in Detroit on July 26, on his way to the upper Great Lakes to
study the lives of American Indians. He attended the hearing out
of curiosity and wrote an account that he included in a book
about his trip, Tour of the American Lakes.[76] A graduate of Yale
University and Andover Theological Seminary, as well as a successful Anglican minister, Colton was beginning at the age of
forty-one a second career as a journalist, writing about travel,

religion, and politics. "Prolific rather than profound," he was conservative in politics, a "protagonist of the Anglican Church, the protective tariff, slavery, and the Whig party."[77]

Our other source of information about the hearing is Judge Woodbridge, who pronounced the death sentence. Although the *North-Western Journal* did not provide its own account of the sentencing hearing, two weeks after the hearing it printed Judge Woodbridge's own reconstruction of his sentencing speech.[78] Woodbridge apologized to the newspaper for not being able to provide the speech *verbatim*. Until the last moment, he had not expected to give the customary address to the prisoner because he had been "prevented by sickness from attending Court during a part of the trial." Therefore, his oration had been "extemporaneous," "uttered under the influence and great embarrassment of strong feeling, with which, from its suddenness, I was little able to contend."[79] The best he could do was an approximation, based on his memory, containing "whatever is *appropriately* said on such occasions" and, apparently, omitting some words that he later judged too emotional for the occasion.

As it had been throughout the trial, the courtroom was full as Sheriff Knapp conducted Stephen to the Bar to receive his sentence. Stephen was, understandingly, nervous, but he tried to hide his feelings behind a stoic front. Colton reported that:

> As he entered this now awful chamber of justice he cast his eye around upon the expecting throng, whose presence and gaze could only be a mockery of his condition:—and with the greatest possible effort for self-possession, braced his muscular energies to support his manly frame, while trembling under the tempest of passion, which agitated his soul.

Despite Stephen's obvious anxiety, his physical presence impressed Colton: "[B]earing a face and head not less expressive, than the most perfect *beau ideal* of the Roman . . . Rarely is seen among the sons of men a more commanding human form, or a countenance more fitly set to intelligence and virtue." So long as he stood at the Bar, Stephen was able to maintain his composure, although with difficulty. "But the moment he was seated, all his firmness dissolved into the weakness of a child;—and he wept— he sobbed aloud." Colton did not address the question of guilt or shame—whether Stephen wept for Levana or for himself.

Colton reported that, as the crowd of spectators waited for Judge Woodbridge to speak, "[a] silence reigned through the crowd, and a thrill of sympathy seemed to penetrate every heart." Colton noted that Judge Woodbridge's face was pale from his recent illness and the strain of performing this duty as he broke the silence: "'[Stephen G. Simmons], have you anything to say, why the judgment of the court should not now be pronounced?' The prisoner rose convulsed, and with faltering voice, and in broken accents, replied: 'Nothing, if it please the court, except what I have already communicated'—and resumed his seat."

At this point, we defer to Judge Woodbridge's account of his address to the prisoner,[80] which focused initially on the ways in which the law had protected Stephen's right to due process throughout the case. Woodbridge reminded Stephen that, as a first level of protection, the question of his guilt or innocence had been submitted first to a grand jury:

> Stephen G. Simmons: You have been charged with the crime of wilful and savage murder! a Grand Jury of the county of Wayne, in which was comprised a great deal of moral worth, and respectability of character;—a Grand Jury comprehending men of intelligence, and who doubtless possessed a deep sense of their duty to *you*, as well as in regard to their country and their God, have pronounced you *guilty*. As public accusers, they have brought you forward as fit to be made a sacrifice of, to the violated laws of your country; as one whose unrestrained, violent and vengeful passions render you an enemy to mankind; one whose enlargement, like that of the ferocious beast of the forest, would jeopardise the security of all!

Despite the grand jury's accusations, Stephen had not been presumed guilty as might have been the case in a foreign court: "But the laws of *our* country, have prescribed a different course. They require that we should *presume* you innocent, until your guilt shall have been fully demonstrated; and giving every facility for manifesting your innocence, they have required that we should treat you as one who may be innocent, until the last hope of your being found such, shall have vanished!"

Stephen had received the assistance of "Counsel learned in the law, and skillful in its forms, that your defense might be properly moulded and ably conducted." The court had also labored to find twelve impartial jurors: "But we knew too, and we felt, the full force of our responsibility towards you, towards the country, and to our own consciences; and we felt determined by the blessings of God, to secure to you the *full* protection of *all* your rights. And did we not do so? Was not *that* jury which tried you, emphatically a jury of your own election!"

But now that the jury had found Stephen guilty of murder, the presumption of innocence had expired: "We can no longer throw around you the mantle of charity; we can no longer indulge our personal hope that your innocence might be established [. . .]"

As Judge Woodbridge turned his attention to the crime and its victims, it is apparent that Levana's gender and her position as wife and mother combined in the judge's mind to distinguish this case from the other recent homicides, which had resulted in short sentences or pardons. Stephen had not only taken a life, "a crime at which human nature shudders," he had killed the very person most entitled to his protection:

> And who did you kill! It was one with whom you was [sic] connected by the strongest tie, by which one human being can be connected to another; a tie sanctioned by Heaven! It was the wife of your bosom whom you destroyed! Who was there on earth to whom she could look for protection against the worlds [sic] oppression but you? to whom, but to you, could she apply for solace in affliction?

SIMMON'S TAVERN. Line Drawing by W. Harrison Bayles in his *Old Taverns of New York* (New York: Frank Allaben Genealogical Co., 1915)

THE WAYNE COUNTY JAIL. Drawing by Silas Farmer from his *History of Detroit, Wayne County, and Early Michigan*, 3rd. ed. (Detroit: Silas Farmer & Co., 1890), reprinted by Gale Research Co., Detroit, 1969

THE THOMPSON TAVERN. From Wilson Nowlin's *The Bark Covered House* (Detroit, 1876), reprinted by the Dearborn Historical Commission (Dearborn, 1959) and by University Microfilms, Inc. (Ann Arbor, 1966)

THE COURTHOUSE OR CAPITOL. Drawing by Silas Farmer from his *History* (1890)

GEORGE A. O'KEEFFE. Burton Historical Collection, Detroit Public Library

WILLIAM WOODBRIDGE.
Burton Historical
Collection, Detroit Public
Library

HENRY CHIPMAN. Burton
Historical Collection,
Detroit Public Library

THE MULLETT MAP OF DETROIT. Burton Historical Collection, Detroit Public Library. Although this map shows the developers' optimistic lot lines, in 1830 only the area south of Jefferson Avenue and the portion of the land between Jefferson and Michigan Avenues that is west of Woodward Avenue had been developed. The Territorial Courthouse (shown at the north end of Griswold Street), the County Jail (shown on Fort Gratiot Road to the east of the court house) were built next to farms. St. Anne's Catholic Church is shown south of the jail at the corner of Larned and Bates Streets.

Benjamin Franklin
Hawkins Witherell,
portrait attributed to Alvah
Bradish. Detroit Historical
Society

Solomon Sibley, portrait
by Chester Harding. Detroit
Historical Society

SCENE OF DETROIT'S LAST HANGING IN 1830. Pen and ink drawing, *The Detroit News*, 22 December 1900. Burton Historical Collection, Detroit Public Library

Passing from the victim to the subject of the prisoner before him, Judge Woodbridge addressed Stephen in words that extinguished any hope of a sentence other than death:

> Your days on earth are numbered; a few brief days, and you
> will appear before that God who made you, the Creator of all
> things! Employ this short time, we beg of you, in making your
> peace with that God, whose laws you have so despised.
> Approach him with contrition and remorse; with repentance
> and with prayer. Approach him with a contrite heart and a
> proper spirit through the mediation of the blessed Redeemer,
> and hope may still beam upon you; for upon such terms has
> he not promised you his forgiveness, and that your sins shall
> be washed away, although they be as scarlet!

Woodbridge also noted that whether or not he approved of capital punishment was irrelevant because the law left him with no alternative: "For the rest we are not allowed to act upon our personal wishes." We cannot tell, at this distance, whether he had doubts about the morality or the effectiveness of capital punishment or whether that comment was just a rhetorical device. We can only note that he had made a similar comment to the Wayne County grand jury in January 1830 after summarizing the arguments for and against capital punishment.[81] In either case, he was not a man to take radical action, whatever his personal qualms, and for him the sentence truly was inevitable. Speaking with what Colton described as "that subdued emphasis and touching pathos, which became the responsibility of his office and the nature of the occasion," Judge William Woodbridge sentenced Stephen Gifford Simmons to death:

> Whereupon all and singular the premises being seen and by
> the said Court here fully understood it is considered by the
> Court here and it is accordingly adjudged that the said
> Stephen G. Simmons be taken to the Gaol of the County of
> Wayne from whence he came and from thence on Friday the

twenty-fourth day of September now next ensuing to the place of execution and that between the hours of 10 o'clock in the forenoon and four o'clock in the afternoon of said twenty-fourth day of September *he be hanged by the neck until he be dead.*[82]

And, according to Colton, Judge Woodbridge concluded with the words, "And may God Almighty have mercy on your soul."[83]

chapter 7

Preparing for the Last Drop

The Sheriff Resigns

The task of planning and carrying out the execution was the responsibility of the Wayne County Sheriff Thomas S. Knapp.[1] The date set by the court gave him two months to prepare, but it also gave him time to think about what he was being asked to do. Knapp was an active member of Detroit's Methodist Episcopal Church,[2] and, as September 24 drew nearer, he became more and more uncomfortable with the prospect of executing Stephen. Ultimately, Sheriff Knapp decided that he would not, that he could not, carry out the sentence and hang Stephen G. Simmons. More than fifty years later, memoirist Friend Palmer remembered that "Thomas Knapp was the sheriff at the time, but his heart was too tender to permit him to do a job of that sort. . . ."[3] Rather than act as executioner, Knapp submitted his resignation as Wayne County Sheriff to the new territorial Secretary, John Mason, on September 10, 1830, two weeks before the execution date.[4]

There is no reason to doubt the sincerity of Sheriff Knapp's convictions or that he resigned when he did because he was not willing to be Stephen's executioner.[5] However, there were other forces at work that made his resignation somewhat less of a sacrifice than it appears. In fact, when he decided to resign Knapp had no real hope of continuing as sheriff beyond the end of the year whether he hanged Stephen or not. Why was that? The reason, as in so many other instances, was territorial politics and patronage, which had also been the reason for his appointment as sheriff in the first place.

113

Although the position of county sheriff was not particularly powerful, it was very attractive to men who were looking to increase their income in a completely legal way, and who did not mind losing friends. The sheriff's compensation depended entirely on the multitude of fees that he was allowed by law to charge for supervising the jail, serving legal writs and summonses, attending court, gathering jurors, providing shelter for the poor, conducting the census, and many other duties.[6] The plum, the sheriff's principal source of income, was the fee he received for collecting territorial taxes throughout the county: "five per centum of all monies by them respectively collected and paid into the treasury" for taxes imposed annually on persons practicing certain businesses including all merchants, traders, tavern keepers, auctioneers, and ferry keepers.[7] In Wayne County this collection fee was substantial, and the right to appoint a sheriff was, accordingly, an important piece of political patronage.

Who would get to exercise that patronage had become a source of political maneuvering. From 1815, when the office of sheriff was created,[8] until 1825, the territorial governor had the sole right to appoint sheriffs.[9] In 1825 Congress forced the governor to share the patronage power by requiring him to obtain "the advice and consent of the legislative council" for the appointment of any sheriff.[10] By 1829 there was considerable sentiment in Michigan that sheriffs should be elected by the people directly, like most other county officers.

Thomas C. Sheldon had been appointed Wayne County Sheriff by Governor Cass in September 1826 with the advice and consent of the Legislative Council.[11] On November 5, 1829, the last day of the Council's 1829 session,[12] Governor Cass asked the Council to consent to the reappointment of several incumbent officeholders, including Sheriff Sheldon, whose terms would otherwise expire before the Council would reconvene during the summer of 1830.[13] The Council adjourned, however, without considering any of the reappointments, nominally because a majority felt that it was bad policy to reappoint men whose terms had not yet expired.

The Council had a specific concern about Sheldon. He also held the lucrative federal office of Inspector of Customs for Detroit, an abuse of patronage in a territory where political jobs provided one of the few secure source of income. In fact, Governor Cass had promised the Council informally that he would not appoint men to territorial service who already held a federal position.[14] This was a good opportunity for the Council to remind him of that promise.

Whatever the Council's initial motive, Governor Cass's political opponents seized the opportunity to exercise some patronage of their own when Cass left the territory on a trip to Washington, D.C., just after Christmas of 1829.[15] Federal law provided that when the governor was out of the territory, the territorial secretary, in this case James Witherell, the father of B. F. H. Witherell and a political opponent of Cass, became acting governor with all of the powers of the office including the right to make recess appointments without the Council's consent.[16] Sheriff Sheldon's term expired on December 31, 1829,[17] and less than a week later, on January 5, 1830, Witherell declared a vacancy and appointed his own ally, Thomas Knapp, to replace Sheldon.[18]

This political maneuver would likely have created a controversy no matter who the deposed sheriff had been, but Thomas C. Sheldon was the brother of John Sheldon, editor of the *Detroit Gazette*, and the controversy quickly became a political brawl that ended up costing James Witherell his job. When B. F. H. Witherell defended his father's action on the ground that Thomas Sheldon had failed to file the four-thousand-dollar bond required by law,[19] John Sheldon, in a vitriolic *Gazette* article,[20] protested that his brother had in fact posted the correct bond. John Sheldon also denounced the move to replace his brother was both political and personal: Tom Sheldon was a "decided Jackson man" (which Knapp and James Witherell decidedly were not), and there was still bad blood between Witherell and Sheriff Sheldon from 1828 when Witherell had deliberately delayed authorizing Sheldon to return a runaway slave to his master long enough for the free black men of Detroit to spirit away the slave to Canada and freedom.

Knapp accepted the appointment gratefully, but he must have known that a recess appointment was good only until the end of the Council's next session, some time in the early summer of 1830, unless he was reappointed by Governor Cass and the Legislative Council.[21] Because he was not "a Jackson man," and because of the way the Witherells had sneaked his appointment past both the Governor and the Council, he cannot have held out much hope that this would happen.

When Governor Cass was advised of Knapp's appointment, he was not amused. When he returned to Michigan on April 6, 1830,[22] Cass asked the Council to reinstate Sheldon.[23] Whether or not it had the power to comply, the Council saw its own opportunity to take the sheriff's job out of the realm of patronage. On July 13, 1830, the Council resolved not to confirm any nomination for sheriff unless the nominee was the winner of a popular election.[24] Although Cass was not opposed to electing sheriffs, Congress was not yet ready and would likely refuse to recognize any such election. The solution was an agreement to hold an election in November with the unofficial understanding that the governor would appoint the winner Wayne County Sheriff, and then the Council would confirm his appointment.[25]

The Governor and the Council also agreed that Knapp could hold the position until the new sheriff took office in early 1831,[26] but that neither he nor Sheldon would be a candidate in the election. So, when he resigned on September 10, 1830, Knapp was well aware that he was giving up only a few months of fees, an amount that he believed was not worth staining his conscience and his name with Stephen's blood.

Uncle Ben Takes Charge

After Sheriff Knapp resigned, his duties, including the duty to hang Stephen G. Simmons, devolved upon Wayne County Coroner Benjamin Woodworth as a matter of law.[27] A territorial statute specifically provided that

whenever the office of sheriff shall become vacant in any
county, either by death, resignation, or otherwise, and there
shall be no under-sheriff therein, the coroner of such county
shall perform the same duties, be vested with the same powers, and liable to the same fines, penalties, and other proceedings as are or may be provided by law in the case of sheriffs,
during such vacancy.[28]

Woodworth's legal duty to succeed Knapp has been ignored over
the years in favor of a story that Governor Cass found himself at
a loss for a hangman and that Woodworth volunteered for the
task. In that fable there is a meeting between the two men in
which Woodworth assured Cass that, if chosen, he would not fal-
ter and in which Cass accepted Woodworth's offer of his services
with some relief, appointing him sheriff on the spot.[29]

In fact, Woodworth took over responsibility for the execution
automatically, and Cass did not appoint him sheriff until
December 1,[30] the day before the election for sheriff between John
M. Wilson and Samuel Phelps to decide which would be
appointed sheriff.[31] Although Woodworth may have met with
Cass to discuss the hanging, it is unlikely to have been anything
but a courtesy call. Cass kept himself well insulated from this case,
and the two men were of different political persuasions: Cass supported Jackson while Woodworth was a Whig and "an ardent
[John Quincy] Adams man."[32] Absent the mandate of statute,
Cass would never have selected Woodworth for such a prominent
assignment, but the Governor was probably glad that the choice
was not his to make.

Woodworth approached his new duties with his characteristic
enthusiasm and entrepreneurial imagination. Known to all as
Uncle Ben, he was one of the most energetic businessmen and
ubiquitous public servants in the history of the territory. About
fifty-five years old in 1830, he was broad-shouldered and gray-eyed,
"a great-handed, strong, old-fashioned Yankee."[33] Although he
had a mild and friendly appearance, "when enraged [he became] a
perfect old volcano, whose increasing pallor, and deepening of the

wrinkles of his face, told of the higher barometer of passion within."[34] A carpenter by training, Uncle Ben first arrived in Detroit in 1806 to build a house for Governor Hull.[35] He soon branched out into other activities, both civic and business. In the 1820s he commanded Detroit's volunteer artillery company, and, in later decades, he held many other civic offices, including assessor, alderman, and supervisor.

In 1815 Woodworth was appointed coroner for Wayne County, a position that did not at the time require any medical training. The coroner's job was merely to summon a jury to examine the body of any person "supposed to have come to his death by violence or casualty." The jury questioned any witnesses and any relatives of the deceased and returned a verdict as to whether the deceased died "of felony, mischance or accident, and if of felony, who were the principals and accessories, with what instrument he was wounded, and of all circumstances."[36]

Although Woodworth remained coroner until 1836, he is best remembered as a multitalented businessman and as Detroit's premier hotel keeper: "He keeps a hotel, . . . runs a ferry to Windsor, is captain of an artillery company, carries on a grist mill at Rochester [Michigan] and runs the only line of stages in Michigan between Detroit and Mount Clemens."[37] After the great fire of 1805 that burned Detroit's entire civilian settlement to the ground, Uncle Ben bought four lots for seventy dollars, including one at the corner of Woodbridge and Randolph streets. There he built his first hotel, which, in 1817, was the site of a gala ball for President James Monroe, the first sitting President to visit Detroit. A year later, he built a much larger establishment, called Woodworth's Steamboat Hotel, that quickly became the headquarters of the city's burgeoning transportation industry. Sailors, steamboat men, stagecoach drivers, and their passengers slept in its rooms, drank in its bar, and did business with the stagecoach lines and water transport, including Woodworth's own Detroit River ferry, that had their offices there. The hotel's "long room" was the preferred venue for public meetings and dinners,[38] while the tavern's barn became one of the city's first theaters.[39]

In order to be that successful as a hotel owner, Woodworth had to have a flair for what pleased the public, and he brought that flair to his preparations for the execution. He realized that Stephen's death would bring people to town in unprecedented numbers, more than enough to fill every hotel in the city and to keep every bar, restaurant, and store busy. That was, after all, an incidental benefit of all public executions.

In his history of attempts from 1776 to 1861 to abolish capital punishment in New York State, *Hanging in the Balance*, Philip English Mackey noted that public hangings

> drew vast throngs of spectators to towns which otherwise would not have attracted much attention. The crowd at Troy in 1811 was, in the words of a young onlooker, "beyond everybody's imagination." Between eight and sixteen thousand people attended a hanging in the insignificant town of Mayville, Chatauqua County, in 1835.

An 1827 hanging in Albany "drew a throng estimated at thirty thousand by one source, forty thousand by another." The commercial potential of such crowds was obvious.

> Merchants could look forward to unusual profits as hoards of viewers bought food, drink, or supplies while awaiting the climactic moment. Enterprising homeowners and shopkeepers often sold admission to perches in upper floors and on roofs. Pedlars hawked food and trinkets to the milling crowds. Boys sold broadsides describing in lurid detail the lives and crimes of the person to be hanged and sometimes appended his confession as well.[40]

The execution planned by Uncle Ben included all of those elements except that there is no evidence that there ever were any such broadsides or pamphlets. He also had to anticipate and plan for the barely hidden dark side of some of the people who were likely to be drawn to a public execution. Unless the crowds were kept amused and orderly, the result could be "days of brutal festivity," a camp meeting devoted to drinking, gambling, and fighting.[41]

If Woodworth's plans for the ceremony were conventional, the selection of the execution site was not. The gallows could have been erected in the Campus Martius, the city's largest square, or in front of the courthouse. Either choice would have provided plenty of space for spectators and, because both locations were a few hundred yards from the jail, would also have provided an excuse to hold the traditional procession of the condemned man through the town to the gallows. The prisoner usually rode in a cart next to (or in) his coffin, the noose already around his neck, and was accompanied by a parade of religious, military, and civil officials who were the embodiment of the power of the community. In this case Woodworth decided to hold the execution just outside the jail in the middle of Gratiot Road, the main artery between Detroit and the counties of Macomb and St. Clair to the northeast. Consequently, Stephen would have only a few yards to walk from the jail door to the scaffold, and any attempt to turn that walk into a parade would have been comical instead of dramatic.[42]

The contract for building the scaffold and gallows was awarded to Lewis Davenport, a Detroit merchant, owner of a ferry company that plied between Detroit and Sandwich, Ontario,[43] and, coincidentally, one of the talesmen rejected as a juror at the trial. According to Davenport's final invoice, he was paid forty-five dollars for ten days' labor and for his materials, including 176 feet of timber, 150 feet of studding, 450 feet of planks, and two pounds of nails.[44] This cost was 50 percent more than the $33.88 that the county had paid Thomas Rowland to build the scaffold and dual gallows for Ke-wa-bish-kim and Ka-tau-kah in 1821.[45] There is no record of who designed the scaffold and gallows tree, but it seems likely that Woodworth, a trained carpenter, would have been involved. There is also no record of what the scaffold looked like or how the gallows tree was designed to operate. When the town's most recent scaffold was built in 1821, hanging involved strangling the prisoner, not breaking his neck. The "short drop" universally employed at that time consisted of nothing more sophisticated than pushing the prisoner off of a step or kicking a stool out from under him. The prisoner struggled for several seconds until he lost consciousness, then he convulsed and twitched for minutes until he was dead. In the early 1830s hangmen in Great Britain developed the "long drop" technique using a trap door, which is familiar to us from movie and television dramas. The goal of the long drop was to kill the prisoner instantly by breaking his neck, but the results depended on the skill and experience of the hangman. If the drop was too short, or if the rope was not stretched before use, the prisoner would strangle to death. If, on the other hand, the drop was too long or the hangman was to place the knot in the wrong spot on the prisoner's neck, the result could easily be decapitation.[46] As we shall see, the eyewitness accounts of Stephen's execution are inconclusive as to the length of the drop in his case.

Like any good host, Uncle Ben also planned for the comfort and entertainment of the expected crowd of spectators at the execution. Detroit's only other public execution, the hanging of Ke-wa-bish-kim and Ka-tau-kah, had been a simple and somber event held in a cold, damp Michigan December. Only the presence of some of Detroit's militia, commanded by Uncle Ben Woodworth himself, provided a small dash of color.[47] Uncle Ben apparently decided, however, that the public of 1830 was more demanding and would not be satisfied with merely seeing a man die. His showman's instincts told him that the people who came to see the drama of Stephen's execution would also demand comfort and lighter entertainment as well. To that end, Woodworth ordered wooden grandstands erected on three sides of the scaffolding, uniformed militia to be deployed around the scaffold as a guard of honor, a military band to serenade the crowd while it waited for the main event, and vendors to patrol the grounds hawking food, whiskey, and rum.[48]

"IN VIEW OF MY APPROACHING CHANGE . . ."

While the county went forward with its plans for his death, Stephen sat in his cell in the jail, smoking, drinking brandy, and waiting.[49] From time to time he was visited by his children, or at least some of them, who came into town from the farm. On those occasions, jailer Aldrich provided the children food and a place to sleep in the jail overnight. Like everything else Aldrich did, those accommodations had a price: Aldrich later made a claim against Stephen's estate in the amount of $5.62 for the children's room and board.

After his motion for a new trial was denied, Stephen had the legal right to petition Governor Cass for a pardon, although Cass could not reduce his sentence to a term in prison.[50] However, there is no evidence, either in the *Executive Journal of the Territory of Michigan* or in any correspondence to or from the Governor's office, that Stephen or his attorneys ever asked for a pardon or for clemency. Why they would not at least try is a mystery. Stephen and his attorneys certainly knew that there had been no execution in Detroit for nine years, that the territorial government had never executed a white man, and that even American Indians convicted of murder had been pardoned and that Governor Cass had pardoned Private William Collins less than a year earlier.[51] So why not try for a pardon? Perhaps Stephen was too proud to ask or had become fatalistic. More likely, Cass let O'Keeffe and Cole know privately that he would have to deny any petition for political reasons and that he would prefer not to get involved. The attorneys would be likely to honor such a request rather than make a futile petition that would alienate Cass.

Although there was no last-minute effort to save Stephen's life, Detroit's Protestant clergy did join together, as the day of execution approached, to save his soul. Territorial law allowed clergy free access to jailed prisoners,[52] and several Detroit ministers took it upon themselves to visit Stephen to urge him to prepare himself for the execution itself and for the world to come. At first, according to the *North-Western Journal*, Stephen demonstrated, a "hard and iron insensibility to guilt" in the weeks before he was to be hanged, a "dogged and resolute fatalism" coupled with an "obstinate disbelief in the retributions of revelation."[53] Nevertheless, one of the clergymen, Noah M. Wells, minister of Detroit's First

Presbyterian Church from 1825 to 1833,[54] was not dismayed and met with Stephen daily in his cell to talk.[55] Born in New York in 1781, "Parson" Wells had been called to the ministry relatively late in life after working as a mechanic for years. This early experience gave him a sympathy towards working people and underdogs that, together with the fact that he was about Stephen's age, allowed him, at last, to penetrate Stephen's obdurate shell.

After the execution, the *Journal* reported that Stephen had lost his callous facade forty-eight hours before his death: "We have spoken of the prisoner's state of mind, during his confinement. It was a great relief to the clergymen, who constantly attended him, that in the two days before his death, he manifested a kindlier and better spirit."[56] However, the *Journal* cautioned, the ministers feared that his change of heart might have come too late: "While they were and are grateful for this change, they wish not, we are authorized by them to say, to estimate its value. The efficacy of repentance, at such an hour and under such circumstances, they think God alone can decide."[57]

Having achieved that "kindlier and better spirit," and having put his spiritual affairs in order, more or less, Stephen turned to putting his material affairs in order as well. On September 23, the eve of his execution, he called Henry Cole to his jail cell and dictated instructions for the distribution of his property.[58] Either Cole or a clerk translated those instructions into a last will and testament, which Stephen reviewed, making a few deletions and additions in his own handwriting, and then executed with the same idiosyncratic signature he had used to sign light-dragoon muster rolls in Tennessee so many years before. Stephen then called on four witnesses to sign the will below his own signature: attorney Cole, jailer Owen Aldrich,[59] city constable Adna Merritt,[60] and city sexton Israel Noble, who lived near the jail[61] and whose duties included interring the city's Protestant dead.[62]

As coexecutors of his will, Stephen appointed his older son James and "my friend, Levi Cook." It is not clear whether Stephen really was a "friend" of Cook, a longtime Detroit resident,[63] a respected merchant,[64] the incumbent Territorial Treasurer,[65] and a future Mayor of the City of Detroit.[66] As a grand juror, Cook had voted to indict him for murder, and the defense had used a peremptory challenge to excuse Cook as a petit juror at the trial.[67] If Stephen and Cook were friends, however unlikely, it may have been simply that, as a founder of Detroit's Presbyterian Church,[68] Cook joined Stephen and Parson Wells in their jail cell meetings. Alternatively, they may have had a Masonic connection. In addition to his other distinctions, Levi Cook was a founding member of Detroit's first Masonic lodge.[69] Although there is no known evidence that Stephen was a Mason, his brother John had been one of the charter members of New Berlin's Phoebus Masonic Lodge No. 82,[70] and so Stephen and Cook might have become friends at Masonic gatherings. Whatever the basis for their friendship, in the years to come Levi Cook would demonstrate that he was a good choice to be Stephen's executor, and a good friend indeed. While James Simmons disregarded his duties and soon left Michigan for parts unknown, Cook administered the estate faithfully for more than a decade, even advancing his own funds to pay Stephen's creditors.

Whether or not Stephen's reported religious awakening was completely sincere, the opening paragraph of his will is an appeal to God for forgiveness:

> Be it known that I, Stephen G. Simmons, in view of my
> approaching change, and in possession of my faculties, thanks
> be to God almighty, in whom I place full trust, have made,
> declared & published, and, by these presents do make,
> declare & publish my last will and testament, in manner fol-
> lowing, that is to say—*In primis*—I commit my soul and its
> eternal welfare to the Savior of Sinners.

The will divided Stephen's estate among five of his six children. To his two youngest daughters, Bathsheba and Lavina, he left his 170-acre farm in Springwells on the River Rouge, but he also barred them from selling the farm until the younger of the two reached the age of eighteen, and he directed that "a good person take the place—pay the taxes" and keep his daughters aware of the farm's affairs. To stock the farm, Stephen left Bathsheba and Lavina a cow, three yearlings, and four spring calves as well as "one turned bed-stead each, with a bed and bedding to each, complete."

To his next oldest daughter, Ellen, Stephen bequeathed "my Lot on the river Huron, in the County of Wayne, containing fifty-three acres, and ten hundredths, more or less, to have and to hold the same to my daughter to be disposed of as she may please" as well as a certain cow, "black and white spotted," and the remaining "turned bedstead, with bed and bedding complete." Stephen also directed that Ellen, Bathsheba, and Lavina were to divide whatever "household stuff" was not specifically left to their brothers.

The will left the family's eighty-acre homestead and tavern to Stephen's sons, James and David, along with "my house and lot at Woodruff's Grove," in Washtenaw County, and "all my stock (except such as is above set apart, and granted to my daughters) and also the farming utensils." But Stephen also ordered that

> in the event, that the monies to be collected [from his credi-
> tors] should be inadequate, I direct my said executors to sell
> and dispose of, as they may deem expedient, either at private
> sale or at auction, the homestead, a farm above bequeathed to
> my said sons James & David, and out of the proceeds of sale of
> said farm to pay off the balance of my just debts, dividing
> between my said sons James & David equally, the surplus of
> the proceeds of said farm after payment of the said debts.

Because Stephen's "just debts" included the notes given to Cole and O'Keeffe amounting to $330, plus interest, and because those notes were secured by a mortgage on the homestead property, the bequests to James and David were worth far less that they may appear. Although the homestead property was later appraised, for probate purposes, at eight hundred dollars, a decent profit on the five hundred dollars that Stephen had paid George Johnson for the property five years before, it was clear that little equity would be left if the executors had to sell the homestead to satisfy Stephen's other creditors as well.

If the boys were shortchanged, it may have been because Stephen felt that they could fend for themselves. Stephen's reasons for leaving his oldest daughter, Catharine, the former Mrs. McCarty, essentially nothing—"all her things of which she is now in possession and one yearling"—are not as easy to explain. Why was he so uncharitable toward his first child, the mother of his only grandchildren?[71] Stephen may merely have thought that the 170 acres in New Berlin that Catharine had received from William in 1822 should count as her share,[72] or, less likely, she may have received a substantial settlement from McCarty in the divorce. On the other hand, Stephen may have truly meant to snub her. She had married, probably without Stephen's blessing, a man who was an unskilled laborer, illiterate, Irish, and probably Catholic as well. To a middle-class Protestant father of the time, even if not well off himself, Catharine could not have made a worse choice. If that was the case, it is likely that, despite his supposed religious awakening, Stephen could not forgive Catharine and, instead, deliberately left her dependent on her siblings for support.

chapter 8

The Day of Execution

Day was dawning when they again emerged. A great multitude had already
assembled; the windows were filled with people, smoking and playing cards to
beguile the time; the crowd were pushing, quarreling, and joking. Everything told
of life and animation but one dark cluster of objects in the very center of all—the
black stage, the cross-beam, the rope, and all the hideous apparatus of death.

CHARLES DICKENS, *Oliver Twist*

Although the Wayne County jail was less than half a mile from the
Detroit River, and its location is now in the center of the city's
downtown, in 1830 it was on the edge of the forest. Until later in
that decade, Detroit's businesses and residences clustered in a strip
of land south of Jefferson Avenue that was no more than three hundred yards from the water's edge. For travelers heading northeast
along Gratiot Road to distant Macomb and St. Clair Counties, the
jail marked the end of civilization and the beginning of the wilderness. At that time, the area around the jail had only a few scattered
buildings besides the jail—houses belonging to surveyor John
Farmer and sexton Israel Noble, the new Methodist Church, and
a few shacks[1]—while beyond were only fields and forest.[2] But on
the morning of Friday, September 24, the day set for Stephen's execution, that was the most populated part of the city.

As Benjamin Woodworth had anticipated, the news that a man
would be hanged in Detroit created great public interest throughout southeastern Michigan. Starved for entertainment, entire families, adults and children together, hitched up their wagons,
mounted their horses, or set out on foot to witness the show. An

eyewitness remembered: "People stopped work and came to town with their families in any conceivable vehicle,"[3] some traveling for days to reach Detroit in time. Many years later, both General Lawson Alexander Van Akin[4] and Melvin D. Osband[5] recalled how their neighbors in Nankin Township, who were also neighbors of Stephen and Levana and, some of them, customers of Simmons' Tavern, set out for Detroit to see Stephen hang.

The North-Western Journal estimated that the crowd gathered around the scaffold on Friday morning exceeded two thousand,[6] almost as many people as lived in Detroit then.[7] As Detroit merchants had hoped, the crowds filled Detroit's hotels and taverns, including Woodworth's, and kept the owners of the city's retail stores busy. Those spectators from the countryside who could not afford a hotel room or a tavern meal camped out along Gratiot Road and in the fields near the jail. There they pitched tents or set up bedding beneath their wagons, made fires, cooked supper, and, released from the chores and concerns of home, enjoyed the pleasures of an early autumn evening in Michigan.

On the other hand, many people refused to take part in the event, either because they feared it would degenerate into violence or because they could not stand to watch a person be killed. Although the crowd was enormous in proportion to Detroit's population, it represented only about ten percent of the people living within a day's travel of the scaffold.[8] An unknown number of Detroiters took the opportunity to spend a day in the country, while some people passing through the city agreed with recent arrival Albert Miller, who "had no desire to see the performance" and deliberately left Detroit for his claim near Saginaw before the execution took place.[9]

Those public officials who could avoid attending the execution also found reasons to be elsewhere. Although executions in the east brought out officials en masse to represent and emphasize the civil power, there is no evidence that any county or territorial officials except Uncle Ben Woodworth attended Stephen's execution. Governor Cass conveniently chose the morning of September 24 to set out for Ohio to visit his mother and to console her over the death of his father (in August),[10] while the judges who presided over the trial, and probably the attorneys as well, were off holding court in other counties. There is also no direct evidence that any of the Simmons children were there, although there was a rumor that one of Stephen's sons "brought in a big two-horse wagon load of people to witness the execution."[11]

Despite the absence of those officials, there were more than enough curious citizens to fill Uncle Ben's grandstands, set up on three sides of the scaffold, hours before the time set for the execution. Latecomers stood in rows behind the grandstands, while behind them others watched from horseback or wagons. Even so, the space available was inadequate to give everybody a good view of the proceedings.[12] Some enterprising owners of nearby buildings rented out window space, while many adventurous young people climbed trees or rooftops to see the show. An illustration of the scene, created seventy years later for a *Detroit News* story,[13] gives a general idea of the scene, particularly of the landscape and buildings, but the artist did not include nearly enough spectators, and those that he did depict are altogether too orderly and well dressed.

Despite the large number of people who witnessed the event, and despite its notoriety, I have found only five accounts of Stephen's execution that claim to be based on personal knowledge, four of which were made fifty or more years later: an article in the *North-Western Journal* published a week after the execution; a speech by Edwin Jerome, Sr., to the Michigan Pioneer Society in 1877; an interview given by Robert E. ("R. E.") Roberts to a newspaper reporter in 1885; and two somewhat different accounts by Friend Palmer, one in a newspaper interview from 1900 and the other an excerpt from his book *Early Days in Detroit*, published in 1906.[14] There are also problems with all five accounts regarding the details of what happened that day.

The *Journal's* story would normally be considered the prime source of information simply because it was written on the day, or within a few days, of the events. Unfortunately, however reliable the author might have been, he reported very little about the execution itself and chose, instead, to comment on the moral lessons that it taught. Mr. Jerome's account, although next in time and the source for most of the modern versions of the story, is unreliable for many reasons that I will discuss later. Therefore, I have based my account primarily on the Roberts and Palmer versions, which are very similar but not identical, while at the same time remembering that all three accounts were set down more than fifty years after the event. It is also apparent that both Palmer and Roberts were Detroit boosters who disliked saying anything unfavorable about anybody, dead or alive.

R. E. Roberts, twenty years old in 1830, and Friend Palmer, seven,[15] met in 1827 when they traveled to Detroit on the same steamship.[16] Determined to see the execution, they knew that Palmer and their young cohort, nine-year-old Eben Willcox,[17] would not be able to see over the heads of the adult spectators if they stood in the crowd. So, to get an unobstructed view of the jail and the scaffold, the three stole into the backyard of the home of prosecutor B. F. H. Witherell on the eastern edge of the Campus Martius,[18] and climbed onto the roof of Witherell's woodshed, where they "regaled" themselves with peanuts, supplied by young Willcox, as they waited for the show to begin.[19]

Roberts remembered that "the common was black with people," and that "military was out in gay uniform and good music was present to enliven the occasion." The *Journal* took a more sober view of the proceedings and complained about "the inappropriate music of the military."

Obtaining a military band and a cordon of soldiers to guard the scaffold was difficult in 1830 because Detroit had neither U.S. Army troops nor its own organized militia. The city's last regular army garrison had left in 1826,[20] and the city's only uniformed militia unit had disbanded even earlier and was not replaced until 1831,[21] forcing Woodworth to recruit his troops from the outlying counties. Friend Palmer recalled a company of riflemen from Oakland County who, in their obsolete fringed hunting shirts, plug hats, flintlock rifles and powder horns, sound more like a troop of reenactors than an 1830 military unit, who acted as a body guard and formed a hollow square around the scaffold."[22] An unlikely source provides evidence that the militia of Washtenaw County brought a fife and drum band to Detroit for the occasion. In 1879 seventy-one-year-old Walter Watson petitioned the Michigan Senate seeking back pay (three days at one dollar per day, plus interest at seven percent per annum over forty-nine years) for service as a militiaman at Stephen's execution.[23] According to the Detroit Free Press, Watson's petition alleged that "he was summoned to appear and act as guard on the occasion of the hanging of one Simmons at Detroit," and that, "At that time, Mr. Watson was a resident of Superior, Washtenaw Co., and was obliged to march to Detroit, a journey that occupied two days. Being a musician, he played upon his fife the death march for the procession which led the condemned prisoner to the scaffold."[24] Unfortunately, Watson's petition, with an account of his experience at the hanging, made "with some minuteness," according to the Free Press, has been lost.

The spectators waiting to see Stephen hang included entire families—men, women, and children. The North-Western Journal and Roberts were both disturbed by the presence of so many women and children in the crowd. The Journal expressed its opinion that, although the interest shown by the men was understandable, the women should have been above such sensations:

> It can hardly be wondered at, that so many persons should be
> anxious to behold the execution of one, whose career had
> been so marked with evil, and whose misdeeds, in the hands
> of Rumor, acquired a definite form, and a fearful aggravation.
> But it *was* wonderful, that so many females, some with
> infants in their arms, should mingle in the crowd. It is hard
> to imagine a spectacle, from which a correctly feeling and
> judging woman would sooner intuitively shrink, than from
> that of a fellow being, suspended, in his death-struggle, upon
> the gallows.[25]

Although Roberts and his friends enjoyed this "great gala day" with some relish, he too expressed his opinion that this form of entertainment was not appropriate for the women and children who were "promiscuously assembled" among the men.[26] He also complained that, among all of the spectators, men, women, and children, "very few seemed to appreciate the solemnity of the occasion." Roberts seems not to have appreciated the irony of that remark coming from a man who watched the hanging in the company of two boys, aged seven and nine, all three of whom celebrated the occasion by gorging themselves on peanuts.

One of the children taken to see Stephen hang was Detroit resident Margaret Justine St. Amour who remembered, seventy years later:

> That morning, [Dr. William McCoskry, her family physician] sent for me to go in his carriage to the hanging, together with his wife, his son, and his daughter. I was then twelve years of age and the youngest of the party. He drove us down to the jail at 9 A.M. and left us there in the carriage, while he went around to see his patients. When the horse got restless Mrs. McCoskry drove around, but always kept near the jail. It was quite a sight from first to last, but I don't want to see another of the kind.[27]

Finally, after a long wait, the ceremony began at about four P.M.. From his room in the jail, Stephen must have known about the crowd that had gathered outside over the last day or so of his life. It is likely that he heard their songs, smelled their cooking fires, and knew what they wanted to see. As the time approached, he dressed himself in his best clothes, including a new pair of shoes purchased from Levi Cook's store the day before.[28] We do not know if any of the children spent the last night with their father or if they were with him inside the jail when Uncle Ben and Owen Aldrich came to tell him that it was time to go.

Friend Palmer had a "vivid memory" of Stephen as he strode out of the jail door and towards the scaffold: "I seem to see him now, marching at the head of the county and jail officials, preceded by a band of music consisting of drums and fife." Although pale from his confinement, the former light dragoon did not show the fear that he must have felt. "His bearing was erect and defiant and he kept time to the music." Palmer was impressed by Stephen's "nerve" and "his apparent disregard of death" as he mounted the scaffold's stairway to the platform "with a firm step." Once Stephen stood atop the scaffold, according to Palmer, the end came quickly: "[H]e came to the front, examined the crowd critically, glanced up at the noose dangling over his head and listened quietly to the praying of the officiating minister; then the noose was adjusted around his neck, the white cap drawn down over his face, and he was swung into eternity." Palmer also recalled that some women shrieked and sobbed and that, at the moment of death, "an involuntary 'ah' came from every throat."

Roberts's recollection of events leading up to the drop is consistent with Palmer's: "When Simmons appeared on the high scaffolding that had been erected he seemed calm and self-possessed. My recollection is that he had nothing to say. It seemed strange to me that so powerful and healthy a man was within a minute of his death."

The *Journal* reported that Stephen asked a clergyman, probably Parson Wells, to speak for him: "It was among his last requests, that the clergyman, who attended him on the scaffold, would declare to the people, that intemperance, the habit of his youth and of his manhood, had been his destruction." The *Journal* also noted that Stephen thanked Woodworth: "The sentence of the law was executed on the convict by Mr. Woodworth, the acting Sheriff, whose kind and humane conduct up to the last moment, was gratefully acknowledged by the prisoner, and has been mentioned to us, in strong terms of commendation."

If all three accounts are consistent up to that point, the descriptions by Palmer and Roberts of the method used for the drop itself (the *Journal* was silent on that point) are not. Palmer remembered watching Stephen's death struggle, suggesting that Woodworth used a short drop so that the body remained above the floor of the scaffold, in sight of the spectators, and death was not instantaneous: "Simmons was a large man, full habit, florid face, and when the drop fell it seemed as if his heavy weight must break the rope, the strain was so great. The great body swayed to and fro for a minute or so, the legs contracted two or three times convulsively, and then all was still." Roberts described a somewhat complicated procedure devised by Uncle Ben to open a trap door under Stephen's feet:

> Simmons stood upon the elevated trap. Across the base of the scaffolding were thrown a number of loose planks. To one of these was attached the cord which sprung the trap. The coroner and the deputy sheriff, according to a prearranged program, walked back and forth over the loose planks, guardedly stepping over the one to which was fastened the fatal rope.

This added detail is not inconsistent with Palmer's account, because he might not have noticed this device. However, Roberts's memory of the end of the story is inconsistent in one detail: "While the people had their eyes riveted upon the scene, and were wondering what this movement of the officers meant, the coroner stepped upon the plank *and Simmons shot out of sight* [emphasis added]." After so many years, it is impossible to tell whether Roberts actually meant that Stephen was on a long rope or whether "shot out of sight" is merely a stock phrase like "swung into eternity."

The crowd had seen what it had come to see, and perhaps something more. Men, women, and children dispersed quietly. Although one account written a century later reported that spectators rioted after the execution and tore down the scaffold or the public whipping post, the *Journal's* man on the scene reported no breaches of the peace: "With the exception of a most reprehensible levity in a few persons, the inappropriate music of the military, and the erection of seats for spectators, there was no occasion for regret furnished by the conduct of the immense multitude by which our city was thronged, which came together and dispersed, with unusual quietness and order." Stephen had, in the lexicon of executions, "died game," and most of them probably would have agreed with Roberts's observation that "[t]he execution was a successful one" and with Palmer's admiration of the "taking off of Simmons." Seventy years later, the latter observed: "I have witnessed since then, three executions by hanging at Sandwich [across the Detroit River in Canada], and this taking off of Simmons impressed me more than all the rest on account of the nerve he exhibited on the occasion, and his apparent disregard of death. Besides it was more spectacular."

Other spectators found the whole event disturbing, even revolting. One of them, L. D. Watkins, recalled his disgust at what he had seen: "I witnessed the hanging and being quite young at the time the impression it left on my mind led me to think such punishment both cruel and vindictive. I rejoice today that no gallows nor whipping post except where those victims suffered, has ever been seen in the State. This was enough for Michigan; the death penalty was abolished forever we trust."[29]

A century later, historian George Catlin remarked, in a letter to his colleague Clarence Burton, that Woodworth did not get the reaction he wanted: "Like many an other man who has tried to point a moral and adorn a tale—or a hanging—he overshot his mark and aroused a feeling of sympathy."[30] But there is no evidence that Woodworth felt any personal animosity towards Stephen or that he was trying to stir up the crowd against him. Once Stephen was dead and the spectacle was over, Woodworth had no interest in denying Stephen the crowd's sympathy or in stoking the spectators' enthusiasm for capital punishment. As a property owner and acting sheriff, he certainly preferred the crowd's quiet dispersal to the mayhem and riot that had followed hangings in other towns. It may well be that, all in all, Woodworth achieved exactly what he had planned: a professional execution that was also a commercial boon to the town's businesses.

There is no evidence of how long Stephen's body was allowed to dangle from the gallows before it was cut down. Although authorities elsewhere often left bodies swinging in the breeze for days, that would have been inconsistent with the Wayne County authorities' treatment of Stephen while he was alive. It is more likely that they lowered his great bulk into a cart soon after he was declared dead. We do know, because of a claim against Stephen's estate, that a local cabinetmaker named William Durell charged Stephen's estate a total of thirty-six dollars "for making [a] coffin and taking the Boddy of the deceased to his farm for burial."[31]

Presumably, the children buried Stephen there, on the homestead, perhaps next to Levana or perhaps not; there is no evidence of where either of them was buried. There was also apparently a rumor that can be interpreted to mean that Stephen's corpse was disposed of in a less than decorous and respectful manner. A. D. P. Van Buren remembered a story current when he was young:

> There was another tavern kept in these woods [other than Bucklin's or Ten Eyck's], I do not remember by whom. It was on the rise of ground, west side of the bridge that crossed the Rouge. The house was on the east side of the road, and a well on the opposite side. It was said that a man had been murdered here and thrown into this well, which was then filled with stone. Search was afterwards made for the body but none was found.[32]

That story or rumor may have had nothing to do with the Simmons case, but it might be a garbled account of how the Simmons children avenged their mother's death by dropping Stephen's corpse down a well.

Did the Condemned Man Sing?

In the most enduring image of Stephen's execution, he stands repentant on the scaffold before a hushed throng, delivers an impassioned sermon on the evils of intemperance, and then breaks into a solo hymn in which his deep baritone asks God's forgiveness. That dramatic scene was the cornerstone of George Catlin's 1923 account of the Simmons case[33] (quoted *in toto* in the introductory chapter of this book), and it has had a place of honor in virtually every account since then. Stephen may well have known the hymn, because it had been a staple of Protestant hymnals since the 1780s.[34] But I doubt that Catlin's account is accurate; in particular, I do not think that Stephen performed a hymn solo.

What are my reasons for doubting Catlin's version? First, the eyewitness accounts by Friend Palmer, R. E. Roberts, and the *North-Western Journal* did not mention any such thing. To the contrary, Palmer and Roberts agreed that Stephen said little or nothing while on the scaffold, while the *Journal* did not report Stephen saying anything, but instead noted that Stephen asked a minister to speak for him. It is very unlikely that all three of those sources, all staunch supporters of conventional Protestant religion and the temperance movement, and with an eye for drama, would have failed to include such a tremendously powerful moment in their accounts of the moments before Stephen's death. Second, Catlin's version owes too much to the conventions and cliches commonly used in tales of the scaffold and in the popular press, and it sounds too much like one of the pamphlets sold at other hangings that purported to report the prisoner's last acts before they happened. Third, Catlin's account of the crime and trial are filled with details that are demonstrably incorrect. Finally, Catlin misinterpreted his own source, which, in any case, is of doubtful reliability.

I am not suggesting that Catlin made the story up or deliberately distorted the facts. From many of Catlin's details, it is clear that he relied heavily, and in good faith, on a speech given at the 1877 annual meeting of the Michigan Pioneer Society that was published in the society's chronicles a few years later. The speech was written and presented by one of Michigan's earliest surveyors, Edwin Jerome, Sr., who was then seventy-two years old. His subject was one of his favorites, the history of the Jerome family.[35] Towards the speech's climax, Mr. Jerome talked about events, both memorable and mundane, that had occurred in Michigan when he was young—including Stephen's crime, trial, and execution. Mr. Jerome's description of the execution itself is brief:

On the platform, Simmons sang the hymn in proportion to
his size, his voice rising smoothly to a very high key, far
above all others, descending with a gentle harmonious
melody, and as the last closing cadence sank to rest, one loud,
simultaneous, sympathetic sound gushed forth from twelve
hundred surrounding voices. Like Simmons or the yearly pil-
grims seeking a holy place for penance, it has ever been my
privilege to atone by once a year singing that hymn at the
topmost key my voice can reach.

> Show pity, Lord, O, Lord forgive,
> Let a repenting rebel live;
> Are not thy mercies large and free?
> May not a sinner trust in Thee?
> My crimes are great, but can't surpass
> The power and glory of Thy grace.
> Great God, Thy nature hath no bound,
> So let Thy pardoning love be found. Etc.

There are two obvious differences between the Jerome and
Catlin accounts. One is interesting but not crucial: Jerome
emphasized that Stephen sang "in a very high key" while Catlin
described a "strong baritone voice." However, the other discrep-
ancy is indeed key: Jerome described Stephen's voice rising "far
above all others" suggesting that he sang the hymn with the spectators and not, as Catlin asserted, alone. It was, in fact, customary for the minister presiding at a hanging to lead the crowd in
singing hymns and for the condemned man to join in.[36]

That interpretation is supported by Friend Palmer. Although
Palmer said nothing about singing in his principal account of the
execution in *Early Days in Detroit*, in two other places he mentioned singing. In *Early Days* Palmer wrote: "Simmons, on the
scaffold, *joined in the hymn sung on the occasion:*

> Show pity, Lord; O, Lord, forgive,
> Let a repenting sinner live—

in a loud voice that I could distinctly hear from where I was on the roof of Lawyer Witherell's woodshed [emphasis added]."[37] In his 1900 interview, Palmer said that Stephen sang with the minister.[38] I conclude from this evidence that, if Stephen did sing on the scaffold, it was with the congregation, not solo.

Whether he did sing at all, though, is still open to question. In 1830 Jerome was twenty-five years old and living in Detroit, and he certainly could have been present at the hanging, but he never actually claimed in his speech that he was there. Moreover, Jerome gave his account forty-seven years after the event and at a time when he was in extreme physical torment, which might have put an added strain on his memory and caused him, instead, to embroider on the conventional cliches. Four years earlier, in 1873, Jerome's spine had been severely injured when he was run over by a horse and carriage. For the rest of his life, he was confined to an invalid chair, and, although he fought against his disability with "an indomitable will, united with wonderful vitality," he had been "gradually and hopelessly failing for some little time" before his death in June 1880.[39] Under such difficult circumstances, it would not be surprising if Jerome took some literary license to improve his story and fill in gaps in his memory. Indeed, he seems to have added many dramatic touches to other parts of the Simmons story, many of which are contradicted by contemporary records and by other documentary evidence.

The structure of Jerome's account is a common temperance theme: an educated, refined husband, rendered a monster by drink, destroys his innocent, loving wife in a moment of irrational violence. Stephen and Levana do not fit this mold, and other details are wrong. For example, Jerome referred to the day of the murder as "the fatal Sabbath," when in fact it took place on a Monday; he described Stephen forcing Levana to drink when she needed no such encouragement; and he asserted that Stephen killed Levana with one blow to the abdomen, although the coroner reported that Stephen had hit Levana many times before she died. For many reasons, therefore, the Jerome version is suspect, and I prefer not to rely on it.

WHY DID STEPHEN GIFFORD SIMMONS HANG?

Stephen was far from being the only white killer in Michigan between 1805, when the Michigan Territory was created, and 1846, when Michigan became the first state to abolish capital punishment for first-degree murder. Twelve murder cases were begun in the Michigan Supreme Court between 1805 and 1836, and Michigan prosecuted many other murder cases from 1836 to 1846, while an unknown number of homicides were prosecuted as manslaughter or not prosecuted at all. Why then was he the only convicted murderer hanged who was not an American Indian? (Repugnant as the distinction is to us, it is obvious that, to European Americans living in the early nineteenth century, the moral and emotional questions raised by executing American Indians were different from those raised by executions of European Americans.) A review of the information available on other cases suggests several superficial reasons as well as one satisfactory explanation.

The superficial reasons relate to causation: Stephen was hanged because he did not escape into the wilderness, failed to kill himself in jail, was convicted of murder, and did not receive a pardon.[40] Contemporary accounts indicate that the most common way in which Michigan killers avoided execution was to flee before being arrested or to escape from jail. A number of others committed suicide, including Kish-kau-ko, a chief of the American Indians along the Saginaw River who was convicted in 1826 of murdering a member of his tribe but who killed himself in jail before he could be executed. His son, known to Detroiters as Big Beaver, was sentenced to hang for the same murder, but he escaped from jail and was never recaptured.[41] Other murderers were pardoned by Michigan governors, including two American Indians convicted of a murder in Green Bay and Private William Collins at Fort Gratiot.

There seems to be, however, a deeper reason why Stephen was executed that is related to the question of why the jury did not disregard the letter of the law and convict him of manslaughter instead of murder. Prior to Stephen's trial, Michigan jurors had proved themselves unwilling to return a murder verdict against a defendant who killed while insane, like Imri Fish, or drunk, like Levi Willard and Robert McLaren. Jury leniency towards drunken brawlers continued after Stephen's death. In January 1836 Sheldon McKnight, the former publisher of the *Detroit Gazette*, was indicted on a charge of murder when he killed a man in a bar fight, but the jury acquitted him.[42]

Why was Stephen's case different? Some have argued that he had a reputation as a bully and that the community was glad to get rid of him,[43] but there is no evidence to support either part of that theory. The true reason why he was convicted of murder, and why Governor Cass did not pardon him, may well be because he killed a woman, and not only a woman but his wife. Consider Judge Woodbridge's words in pronouncing the death sentence: Stephen had killed "one with whom you was [sic] connected by the strongest tie, by which one human being can be connected to another; a tie sanctioned by Heaven! It was the wife of your bosom whom you destroyed! Who was there on earth to whom she could look for protection against the world's oppression but you? to whom, but to you, could she apply for solace in affliction?"[44]

In her book *Inheriting the Revolution, the First Generation of Americans*, Joyce Appleby traced the lives of hundreds of men and women of Stephen's generation. One of her findings was that as couples and families left the towns and cities of the east and moved west, the bond between spouses became stronger and more sentimental. They left behind the extended families of parents, grandparents, brothers, sisters, and cousins, as well as the generations-long friends and neighbors on whom much of pre-Revolutionary society was based. Out on the frontier, spouses often had only each other to depend upon for physical and emotional support. The result was that "husbands and wives grew closer together in communities of strangers."[45] This emotional bond between spouses was also intensified by the spiritual image of women popularized by the preachers of the great religious revivals that swept the country during this time. Therefore, it is not surprising that the men of Wayne County were sufficiently outraged, on a conscious level, by this "crime at which human nature shudders" to send Stephen to the gallows.

Levana's gender may also have motivated the judges and the jury on an unconscious level. The three classic justifications for pun-ishing criminals—deterrence, retribution, and reformation—do not provide a reasoned distinction between Stephen's case and those of Willard or McLaren. But if there are unconscious reasons why people decide how to punish, then guilt, one of the strongest of human emotions, may explain the difference. I do not mean the guilt of the defendant but, rather, the feelings of guilt that people in the community experience whenever a person is killed.

A generalized but unconscious sense of guilt is a common attribute of people in a developed society. When a person is killed, community members' unconscious guilt becomes specific: they did not stop the killing (even if they had no opportunity to do so); they did not die instead of the victim; and they harbor vio-lent emotions themselves. Sometimes this guilt is strong enough to cause people to confess to crimes they did not commit. More commonly, it is expressed in the punishment meted out to the actual killer. The need to punish to exorcize this unconscious guilt is intensified if the victim is in a class of people viewed by soci-ety as particularly worthy of love and protection.

As Professor Appleby has demonstrated, in the first decades of the nineteenth century, women, especially wives and mothers, were such a class. Because women arouse strong unconscious and conscious emotions in men in any case, the violent death of a wife and mother may have created an intolerable level of guilt in the judge and jurors that could be assuaged only by killing the mur-derer himself.[46]

chapter 9

The Abolition of Capital Punishment

The Very Worst Use You Can Put a Man To

Public opposition in Europe and America to capital punishment on moral grounds began, according to tradition, in Italy where Cesare Beccaria published *On Crimes and Punishments* in 1764. In fact, as Professor Stuart Banner has pointed out, Beccaria drew on a tradition many decades old. For example, in the 1640s leading Quakers in England were suggesting abolition, and in the Colony of Pennsylvania capital punishment was used only to punish murder until 1718. Beccaria did, however, provide and popularize a systematic argument in favor of abolition that spread quickly. Although the first American edition was not published until 1777, John Adams quoted Beccaria in 1770 when he defended the British soldiers accused in the Boston Massacre.[1]

The publication of American editions of *On Crimes and Punishments* coincided with the birth of movements to reform prisons and to abolish capital punishment in both Philadelphia and New York City. In the heady post-Revolutionary period, Americans were proud that their criminal punishments were milder than those in Europe. Because of the large number of executions in Great Britain for crimes less than murder, capital punishment, in particular, was regarded by many people in America as a punishment only suitable for use by tyrants (although, ironically, abolition occurred first in European states ruled by empresses and dukes).[2]

In 1794, prodded by reformers like Dr. Benjamin Rush and William Bradford, Pennsylvania took a first step toward abolition by dividing murder into first degree (premeditated murder) and second degree (all other murder) and ending hanging for all crimes except first-degree murder. In New York Governor George Clinton led a campaign to adopt Pennsylvania's reforms which, although unsuccessful, did result in the passage in 1796 of a law limiting capital punishment for use only in cases of treason and murder. However, there would be little further progress in the United States toward abolition for decades although the writings of, among others, Samuel Whelpley, Edward Livingston, and John L. O'Sullivan did keep the cause before the public throughout the first half of the nineteenth century.[3]

In the former Northwest Territory, abolition had a few very strong advocates, but most public interest in the issue seems to have been driven by specific cases rather than by sustained commitment to the cause. For example, there is no evidence of general opposition to the death penalty in Michigan at the time of Stephen's execution. But nine months earlier, in January 1830, as Private James Brown waited in Fort Mackinac to hang for shooting Corporal Hugh Flinn, the Reverend William Ferry collected signatures of residents on Mackinac Island for a petition that was sent to President Jackson urging a pardon.[4] Three years later, on 18 July 1833, the federal government convicted a Chippewa Indian, Wau-ben-e-mickee, also known as White Thunder, of the murder of Jean Baptiste Brunet in the Indian country along Lake Superior.[5] Once again, residents of Mackinac Island sent a petition, this time to George B. Porter, the federal officer in charge of the Michigan Superintendency of Indian Affairs, seeking a pardon.[6] Neither petition was granted, the federal government hanged both men, and neither public appeal seems to have had any broader impact or to have been a part of any campaign to oppose capital punishment generally.

That does not mean, though, that the arguments for and against abolition were not known, or of interest, to people in Michigan. Only a few months after Stephen's execution, the *Oakland Chronicle* published a lengthy article on an attempt, ultimately unsuccessful, by delegates to the French Chamber of Deputies, including the venerable General Lafayette, to obtain "the *total* and *immediate* abolition of capital punishment."[7] In January 1831 Governor Cass, in his annual message to the Legislative Council,[8] noted that: "A recent event in the administration of the criminal justice of the Territory, has directed public attention to that part of our penal code which prescribes the punishment of death." He deplored the fact that Michigan law did not distinguish between premeditated killings and those that are "the result of sudden and violent passion." The latter, Cass argued, although "unjustifiable," are "far more excusable" and should be subject to a lesser punishment than death. He predicted that: "The period is probably not too far distant, when it will be universally acknowledged, that all the just objects of human laws may be fully answered, without the infliction of capital punishment." He recommended that, until then, Michigan governors should be given the power to commute death sentences to a term of imprisonment instead of being forced to choose between allowing an execution to proceed and pardoning the defendant entirely.

Two years later, in 1833, Detroit's *Democratic Free Press*, citing local interest in the recent execution in New Jersey of Joel Clough for the notorious murder of Mrs. Mary Hamilton, printed excerpts from Edward Livingston's proposed criminal code for the State of Louisiana which included a section abolishing capital punishment. The *Free Press* expressed the opinion that:

> Capital punishment has nothing to plead for its longer reten-
> tion in our criminal jurisprudence, save antiquity, and the
> barbarous features by which it is distinguished—the former a
> weak excuse in modern legislation, and the latter a strong
> argument against it. [. . .] We are glad to see that the public
> mind has commenced a serious examination into this relic of
> barbarism, and we cannot doubt as to the conclusion of its
> enlightened and liberal spirit.[9]

The first practical step taken in Michigan to abolish that relic had, in fact, occurred more than two years earlier. On March 4, 1831, less than six months after Stephen was hanged, the

Legislative Council passed an act that abolished the territory's only other form of corporal punishment, whipping.[10] For decades, the territorial government maintained a whipping post in the public marketplace in Detroit where "idle and disorderly persons" might receive up to ten lashes. Although the statute defined "idle and disorderly" very broadly ("any vagrant, lewd, idle or disorderly persons, stubborn servants, common drunkards, common night-walkers, pilferers, or any persons wanton and lascivious in speech, conduct or behavior, common railers or brawlers, such as neglect their calling and employments, misspend what they earn, and do not provide for themselves or their families")[11] whipping, like hanging, had been used very infrequently in Michigan. Nevertheless, removing the whipping post was a step, symbolic and psychological, towards removing the gallows as well.

Michigan's first direct attack on the death penalty occurred at the convention that met in Detroit, in May and June 1835, to draft the first constitution for what would soon become the State of Michigan.[12] One of the Democratic delegates to the convention from Oakland County was Elijah F. Cook, a tailor who became a lawyer and the owner of the only distillery in Farmington.[13] On May 14, in the same courthouse where Stephen G. Simmons had been tried and sentenced to death, Cook moved "that a committee of seven members be appointed to take into consideration the propriety of so framing the contemplated Constitution, as to abandon the practice of capital punishments."[14] The committee, chaired by Cook, reported that the view of its members was that: "Capital punishment ought not to be inflicted; the true design of all punishment being to reform, not to exterminate mankind."[15] Consequently, the committee recommended that the state's constitution should include a provision "that the legislature of this state shall pass laws prohibiting capital punishment."[16]

However, after what the *Democratic Free Press* called "a brief and cursory, but handsomely conducted debate,"[17] the delegates defeated the proposal, thirty-eight to thirty-five.[18] Although prevailing religious and moral opinions played their part in defeating the committee's motion, there were also two strong practical reasons why the convention rejected it. In order to demonstrate that the territory was ready for statehood, convention leaders wanted a constitution passed with a strong consensus. Therefore, the leadership needed to avoid controversial provisions, especially those that were "more properly within the sphere of legislative authority."[19] Also, as other delegates pointed out, Michigan lacked a prison capable of housing prisoners for any extended period of time, much less for life.[20]

Despite their setback at the Constitutional Convention, within two years abolitionists in the new state legislature proved that, with the application of some deft maneuvering, partial reform of capital punishment was well within their reach. The reformers' tool was the legislature's decision to enact as state statutes all of the existing territorial laws. The effect of statehood on the validity of the territorial statutes was not clear, and, in any case, the most recent collection of statutes, published in 1833, was both incomplete and disorganized. In March 1836 the state legislature asked William Asa Fletcher, chief justice of the new Michigan Supreme Court (and one of the prosecuting attorneys at Stephen's murder trial) to collect, digest, and arrange the statutes into a comprehensive code of laws that could be reenacted by the legislature.[21]

Fletcher's mandate authorized him to collect a complete set of the territorial statutes, to weed out those that were obsolete, and, for the first time, to organize the statutes by subject matter, but he could not himself suggest new laws or amendments to existing statutes. However, after Fletcher submitted his proposed code to the state legislature, members of the House of Representatives and of the Senate were entitled to propose new laws and amendments without going through the normal committee process. Many legislators played this game, but the abolitionists were particularly adept.

On the initiative of Elijah F. Cook, who was a Senator in 1838 and 1839, a subcommittee was formed in the Michigan Senate to

consider whether Michigan should abolish capital punishment.
When, despite Cook's efforts, the committee issued an unfavorable
report,[22] the reformers decided to set their sights on more attain-
able goals. The code that emerged from the legislative process,
known as the *Revised Statutes of 1838*, included several important
reforms in the application and administration of the death penalty.
Following the example of Pennsylvania, which had already been
adopted by many other states, the *Revised Code* divided murder into
first and second degrees and limited the death sentence to persons
convicted of first-degree murder, defined in the code as either "murder perpetrated by poison, lying in wait, or any other kind of wilful, deliberate and premeditated killing" or murder committed in
the course of "arson, rape, robbery, or burglary."[23] Another new provision stayed the execution of any convict "who has become
insane," unless and until the governor issued an order lifting the
stay, as well as the execution of any pregnant woman until the governor determined that she was "no longer quick with child."[24]
Finally, the new code followed New York, Pennsylvania, and New
Jersey in abolishing all public executions. County sheriffs were
directed to conduct all executions "within the walls of the prison
of the county in which the conviction was had, or within the
enclosed yard of such prison."[25]

Some abolitionists, then and now, have criticized those partial
reforms, when passed in various states, as counterproductive.
These critics argued that reforms short of abolition made capital
punishment more palatable to the public and, thus, caused the
abolition movement to lose momentum and fail.[26] Indeed, no further capital punishment reforms were proposed in either the
Michigan House or Senate until 1843, five years later. On the
other hand, the issue lacked urgency in a state with no executions
and no serious interest in actually executing anybody.

Neither the legislators' speeches nor newspaper reports of the
debates indicate why abolition was added to the legislative agenda
in Michigan in 1843. There was more support for abolition in the
legislature than there had been in previous years, and this may

reflect a feeling in the general population of the state that the stain of tyranny had returned to the institution of capital punishment by executions carried out in nearby Canada over the previous several years. In contrast to Michigan, executions were not uncommon in Canada at that time, including several that took place in Sandwich, across the river from Detroit.[27] Until as late as 1835, authorities there not only hanged criminals, they also exhibited their bodies in gibbets, iron cages suspended from a pole, until they rotted away.[28]

One Sandwich execution was particularly tragic and troubling to people in Michigan. In 1837 a man named Fitzpatrick was convicted of molesting a young girl.[29] Petitions by prominent residents of Sandwich for clemency were rejected by the Lieutenant Governor of Upper Canada, and the condemned man declined to take advantage of a jailer who, perhaps deliberately, rendered himself unarmed and drunk. Still proclaiming his innocence, Fitzpatrick was hanged on October 9, 1837, in front of a "bustling" crowd of Canadians and Americans, many of whom had been part of the crowd of three thousand who had attended Sandwich's previous execution just one week before. Three years later, in 1840, a man named Maurice Sellers confessed, on his deathbed, that he, and not Fitzpatrick, had molested the girl. Because Detroit had a large Irish-American community, an erroneous execution in Canada by British authorities sparked strong emotions across the river.

Even more disturbing were the executions by the British government of Canada of twenty-seven participants in the citizen uprisings in Canada in 1837 and 1838, known in Canada as the Mackenzie Rebellion and in the United States as the Patriot Wars. At least five of the men hanged were Americans, and dozens of other Americans were among the hundreds of men "transported" to Tasmania.[30] One event in those uprisings occurred especially close to home for the people of Michigan. During a poorly planned assault across the Detroit River from Detroit to Sandwich, Ontario, by American and Canadian "patriots," four captured raiders were summarily shot on the orders of a British officer who had just learned that other raiders had killed one of his friends.[31] In 1843 memories of the execution of so many men, who in their eyes were trying to assert their rights against an entrenched aristocracy, were fresh enough to cause people in Michigan to link the gallows with British "tyranny" once more.

When Elijah Cook left the Senate after two terms, the abolition campaign moved to the House of Representatives where Flavius J. Littlejohn and Charles P. Bush led a major effort in 1843. Flavius Littlejohn was born in 1804 in Herkimer County, New York. He moved to Allegan County on Michigan's frontier in 1836 to improve his health. Although trained as a lawyer, he spent most of his time working outdoors as a surveyor, engineer, and geologist.[32] One of Littlejohn's principal opponents in the House on capital punishment was Samuel F. Anderson who represented Cass and Van Buren Counties. In many ways, Littlejohn and Anderson were alike. Both were born during the first decade of the nineteenth century to families with New England roots, both grew up in western New York State, both were lawyers, both emigrated to the frontier counties of Michigan just as the territory became a state in 1836, both were Democrats in 1843, and both subsequently joined the anti-slavery Free Soil Party.[33] They agreed on most other issues, but in the debates over capital punishment they were bitter opponents.

Most of the other members of Michigan's legislature in 1843 were similar in background to Littlejohn and Anderson. They had been born between 1800 and 1810 and raised in rural New York State, had emigrated to Michigan after 1830 to seek their fortune, and were Democrats. And, as was the case with Littlejohn and Anderson, those similarities hid deep divisions on the issue of capital punishment. That phenomenon was apparent to observers at the time. One newspaper, *The Michigan Western Statesman*, published in Marshall, Michigan, remarked that the campaign to abolish capital punishment "finds its friends, as well as its foes, among all political parties, and we may add all religious creeds.

Whigs and Democrats and Abolitionists, Presbyterians, Episcopalians and Methodists, and indeed, those of all sects have been found arrayed on both sides."[34]

For their 1843 campaign, the abolitionists replaced their subtle legislative maneuvering that had resulted in the reforms of 1838 with a well-publicized frontal assault on capital punishment. The debate began in the House of Representatives on Saturday, January 28, 1843, when Flavius Littlejohn rose to speak in support of his own bill to change the penalty for first-degree murder from death by hanging to life in prison. The public interest in the subject had grown to the point that the publisher of the *Democratic Free Press,* in several issues, used precious space usually reserved for national news and advertising to print all of the speeches for and against the bill.[35] According to a summary of the debates in the *Free Press,* several representatives made "powerful and eloquent appeals in favor of the bill" that day including Littlejohn; Bush, representing Livingston and Ingham Counties; George O'Keeffe from Wayne County; Fidus Livermore, a lawyer from Jackson County; Simeon M. Johnson, a lawyer from Grand Rapids representing Kent County; and William Gage, the first settler in Holly, Michigan, representing Oakland County. On the side favoring retention, five representatives "were clear and forcible in their remarks in opposition": Democrats Anderson, Purdy, and Fielder F. Snow, a merchant and miller from Lenawee County; and Whigs Stephen Vickery, a surveyor from Kalamazoo, and W. Norman McLeod, a defrocked Presbyterian minister from Mackinac County who was second only to O'Keeffe in wit, charm, florid oratory, and liquor consumption.

The *Free Press* summarized the principal arguments made by the speakers:

> On the one hand, it was contended that the principles inculcated by our present laws, of blood for blood, materially engendered in the mind of man, feelings of vengeance against his fellow man for real or supposed wrongs, and that mild and humane laws would exercise a material moral influence upon

society in the prevention of crime; while on the other hand, it
was urged that the protection and welfare of society
demanded the fullest vengeance on the heads of those who
"shed innocent blood."

Although Littlejohn began his opening speech with concilia-
tory words (capital punishment "is a question on which gentlemen
might well differ"), it soon became clear that each of the orators
believed that no true gentleman could hold a view inconsistent
with his own. Quotations from the Bible, charges of barbarity, and
disparaging personal references flew across the chamber where
Stephen Simmons had been sentenced to death almost thirteen
years before. But, there was nothing new in the arguments propounded by the abolitionists or by the retentionists.

This lack of novel arguments on both sides was not limited to
Michigan. In his history of the national movement to end capital punishment, *The Death Penalty: An American History*, Stuart
Banner remarked that by the 1840s the debate had ossified everywhere in America:

> The capital punishment debate in the North revolved around
> three issues familiar since the 1780s and 1790s. Was the
> death penalty necessary to deter crime, or would prison be a
> more effective deterrent? Was the death penalty a legitimate
> act of retribution, or did government—for reasons rooted in
> the nature of crime, the characteristics of criminals, or the
> limited power of the state—lack the authority to punish
> crime with death? Was the death penalty a useful means of
> encouraging repentance, of reforming the criminal's soul, or
> would prison do the job better? All three were contested
> issues throughout the North in the first half of the nine-
> teenth century. The debate quickly crystallized into stock
> arguments for and against abolishing the death penalty, argu-
> ments that drew standard responses. When the debate
> reached its peak, from the 1830s through the 1850s, there
> were no new moves available to participants on either side.[36]

What is even more remarkable is that, with one exception, there have been "no new moves available" from 1843 until today. Except for the discriminatory application of capital punishment, every argument propounded on either side of the debate today, and every response, was part of the debate in the Michigan House of Representatives in 1843.

Central to the arguments of the abolitionists was their belief in human progress, not only in its possibility but also in its manifestation in the society in which they were living. Littlejohn applauded "the enlightened views of the present generation," and Simeon Johnson expressed his pride "in the advanced state of science and of civilization, in the progress of liberty and our near approach to the perfection of civil government." Fidus Livermore denounced capital punishment as "a disgrace to the age in which we live," while Charles Bush declared his generation's independence from the thinking of their forefathers:

> But I am gratified with the thought that at this age of the
> world, under our government, knowledge goes hand in hand
> with improvement, and laws are framed not so much to keep
> up customs of olden times as the spirit and principles of consti-
> tutional liberty. We have declared ourselves free from the gov-
> ernment of the old world—we have adopted new and more
> correct principles in the exercise of which, we aim at happiness
> instead of power. Our government instead of being sustained
> by cruelty or terror, must be kept up by intelligence and virtue.

Also key to the abolitionist position was a belief in the possibility of reformation. Dr. William Mottram, from St. Joseph County, put this argument succinctly: "He desired only to say that as all men, however bad, are susceptible of amendments so he thought that the very worst use you can put a man to, is to hang him."

Retentionists viewed those arguments as presumptuous and insulting to earlier generations and to institutions sanctioned by centuries of experience. Although Robert Purdy professed his life-long loyalty to "the liberal political principles of Jefferson," he based his argument on the traditions of "all nations, in all ages of the world." He noted that: "The sense of mankind has universally been that the man who would deliberately and maliciously take the life of his fellow man, is not fit to live on the face of the earth. . . ." Stephen Vickery deplored the fact that: "This is an age of speculation. A spirit of innovation marks the period." He concluded with a plaintive rhetorical question that summarizes the retentionist views: "Is there no end to the experiments made by political quacks upon the body politic?"

Speakers on both sides repeated the arguments of Beccaria, Benjamin Rush, William Bradford and their eighteenth century opponents. They debated the deterrent effect of mild and harsh criminal penalties, the relative importance of punishment and reformation as goals of the judicial system, the possibility of mistaken convictions, and whether a sentence of death was more humane than life in prison. They argued the reluctance of juries to convict if the punishment is death and the possibility that a prisoner serving a life sentence might escape and kill again. On a philosophical plane, they made opposing arguments as to the limits of society's right of self defense and whether abolishing the death penalty for murder exalted or degraded the value of human life.

The Bible could not be kept out of the debates, although Littlejohn expressed "regret, that, on a subject so purely civil in its character, that sacred volume should have been drawn into the controversy, and made the subject of invidious remark." Here, again, the arguments on both sides were adopted from their eighteenth century predecessors. Does the Sixth Commandment, "Thou shall not kill," prohibit or mandate hanging murderers? Was God's admonition to Noah, "He who sheddeth man's blood, by man shall his blood be shed," a command or, by use of "the correlative auxiliary verb," a cautionary prophecy? Did God intend the lessons of the Old Testament to apply only to the ancient "Jewish nation," and not to the presumably more civilized Americans, or did the laws of Moses apply to all people?

The debate on capital punishment continued until it was time for the House to adjourn for the day.[37] After more maneuvering when the House reconvened on Monday, on Tuesday, January 31, 1843, the House voted in favor of Littlejohn's bill, thirty-five to fifteen.[38] The result was historic, the first time that a legislative house of any state had voted to abolish capital punishment. But their victory in the House could not be repeated in the Senate. On February 3, 1843, the Senate judiciary committee reported adversely on the bill, and, on February 17, a vote by the entire Senate killed it, eleven to seven.[39] The House tried to press the issue, but in the end the representatives decided to "recede from their amendment" and allow capital punishment to remain on the books a while longer.[40]

By 1844 the membership of the House of Representatives had changed substantially, shifting the balance of power in the House toward retention. The House and Senate were sufficiently motivated to form a joint Select Committee on the Abolishment of Capital Punishment, and the committee's majority recommended abolition. But, despite petitions from abolitionist citizen groups in Lenawee and Washtenaw Counties, and despite an eloquent committee report, the House defeated an abolition bill soundly, thirty-four to ten.[41] However, another legislative development in 1844 gave the reformers an opportunity that opened the way to achieving their final goal two years later.

The 1844 legislature investigated the condition of the written laws of the state and concluded that during the preceding six years the *Revised Statutes of 1838*:

> had been amended and modified by successive legislatures, until scarcely a single chapter remained as originally passed, and the numerous general statutes enacted in addition to, or amendatory of the revised statutes, had undergone so many mutations as to produce that state of confusion and uncertainty in the laws, which is always a most fruitful source of vexatious and ruinous litigation.[42]

In March 1844, to alleviate that confusion, the legislature directed the governor to appoint "a man learned in the law" as a commissioner to revise and consolidate the general laws of the state.[43] The governor appointed Senator Sanford M. Green of Oakland County to this difficult task, and in January 1846, after almost two years of effort, Green finally submitted his report to the legislature in the form of a bill.

Unlike the legislative act that authorized the 1836 revision, which barred Judge Fletcher from amending or adding to the existing statutes, the 1844 act specifically authorized the commissioner to make "such modifications, amendments, and additions" as he cared to propose.[44] Among the changes contained in Sanford Green's 1846 bill was a provision, based on an 1837 Maine statute, that barred any execution until at least one year had passed from the date of conviction, and, even then, allowed the execution to take place only when Michigan's governor issued a warrant that specifically authorized the county sheriff to proceed with the execution. Senator Green expected that, as had been the case in Maine, no governor would be willing to issue such a warrant once the passion of the moment had died down.

This proposal passed easily in the Senate where abolition's champion, Flavius Littlejohn, presided as both president *pro tem* and chair of the Senate's committee on the revision of the statutes. But Littlejohn and his allies in both the Senate and the House were not satisfied. On April 25, the abolitionists in the Senate proposed an amendment to the Green report that would end capital punishment in Michigan altogether by replacing death as the punishment for first degree murder with solitary confinement in the state prison for life.[45] Two days later, the Senate approved the amendment by a vote of nine to three—six Democrats and three Whigs in favor, two Democrats and one Whig opposed.[46]

The fight now moved to a conference committee. Despite the efforts of the brilliant Austin Blair from Jackson County (who would serve as governor during the Civil War), the House of Representatives rejected an identical amendment, twenty-five to seventeen.[47] On April 29, the House voted not to concur in the

Senate amendment, but the margin was tiny this time, just seventeen to sixteen.[48] When the Senate voted, twelve to four, to refuse to back down,[49] the House agreed, in a face-saving compromise, to abolish capital punishment for first degree murder in return for the Senate's agreement to add the words "at hard labor" to the Senate bill's mandatory sentence for first degree murder—"solitary confinement for life." In fact, as the legislators were well aware, the state lacked adequate prison facilities to enforce either solitary confinement or hard labor.

The abolitionists had prevailed, and when Governor Alpheus Felch signed the statute approving the revised code on 18 May 1846, Michigan became not only the first state, but also the first government in the English-speaking world, to abolish capital punishment for first degree murder. The historic section of the code, which went into effect on March 1, 1847,[50] provided:

> All murder that shall be perpetrated by means of poison or lying in wait, or any other kind of wilful [sic], deliberate and premeditated killing, or which shall be committed in the perpetration or attempt to perpetrate any arson, rape, robbery, or burglary, shall be deemed murder of the first degree, and shall be punished by solitary confinement at hard labor in the State Prison for life; and all other kinds of murder shall be deemed murder of the second degree, and shall be punished by confinement in the penitentiary for life, or any term of years, at the discretion of the court trying the same.[51]

The Reaction

Less than a year later, various groups in Michigan began to clamor for a restoration of the death penalty. In February 1847 a citizen group led by Representative Edmunds submitted a petition to the legislature seeking a return of the death penalty.[52] In January 1848 a public rally was held in Detroit in favor of capital punishment, at

which George Duffield, a Presbyterian minister and well-known
proponent of capital punishment, preached a sermon in which he
established, to his own satisfaction at least, that the Bible not only
allowed capital punishment, it mandated executions of murderers.[53] In 1848 and again in 1849 Wayne County grand juries submitted their own petitions to the legislature, arguing that murder
had become common, whereas, prior to abolition, it had been
"practically almost unknown to our criminal jurisprudence."[54] The
petitioners failed to point out that homicide was just as common
before abolition as after, the difference being juries' reluctance to
convict on a capital crime.

Those protests and others during the nineteenth century were
ineffective because Michigan's experience with the new law was,
in fact, reasonably positive. An 1869 study by H. H. Bingham,
Agent of the Michigan State Prison,[55] found that between 1847
and 1869 only fifty-eight people, including six women, had been
convicted of murder in the first degree. Significantly, six of those
defendants were later retried and acquitted of murder, an error rate
in excess of 10 percent, while four others earned a pardon. Bingham
also reported that the rate of convictions for first-degree murder
decreased substantially between 1848 and 1869, whether measured
as a percentage of the state's population (from one in 99,000 inhabitants to one in 550,000) or of the population of the state's prison
system (from 12.1 percent to 0.8 percent).

Serious campaigns to reinstitute the death penalty have, nevertheless, been mounted from time to time. One house or another of
the legislature considered bills on that subject forty times between
1847 and 1963, but none was ever made law.[56] The margin was only
seven votes (forty-three to thirty-six) at the Constitutional
Convention of 1867[57] and only two votes in the House of
Representatives in 1921. In 1929 both houses actually passed a bill
that would have returned capital punishment to Michigan, but
Governor Fred W. Green, from Ionia, vetoed the bill. His confidence that a majority of voters in the state did not support capital
punishment was confirmed in 1931, when a state-wide referendum
to reinstate capital punishment was defeated by a substantial mar-

gin of 352,594 votes to 269,538; fully eighty percent of voters in the Upper Peninsula voted against capital punishment.[58] In 1952 the House approved a bill to electrocute any "incarcerated felon" who committed first-degree murder while in prison, but the measure died in committee in the Senate.[59]

When delegates met in 1961 to begin drafting a new constitution, one of them, a young Republican lawyer from Lansing named Eugene Wanger, decided to try to provide Michigan's anti-death penalty tradition the protection of constitutional status.[60] His Delegate Proposal was taken up by a bipartisan group that included Frank G. Millard, a former Michigan Attorney General, General Counsel of the Army, and Brigadier General; Delegate and Republican National Committee member Ella Koeze; and Convention Vice-President and Democratic leader Tom Downs. The result was a near-unanimous vote to include in the final version of the Constitution of 1963 a new Article 4, section 46, which reads: "No law shall be enacted providing for the penalty of death."[61] Those eleven words guarantee that capital punishment cannot be reinstated in Michigan by the legislature alone but only by one of the methods provided to amend the constitution, all of which require, *inter alia*, a majority vote by the electorate.[62]

The Reasons for Abolition in Michigan

In *Rites of Execution*, a study of the ritual aspects of capital punishment in post-Revolutionary America, Louis P. Masur commented that: "If there is any reason why Michigan first abolished capital punishment, we will never know it."[63] It is certain that Stephen's death was not the sole catalyst: no legislative speech cited Stephen's case as a reason for abolition. That is not surprising; very few of the legislators who voted for or against abolition had lived in Michigan in 1830.[64] If they had heard of Stephen's case, it was as just one sad gallows tale among many in the country—indeed, only one legislator referred to any specific case.

Instead of a reaction to any particular instance or instances of capital punishment, the reason why Michigan took the initiative in achieving abolition was probably a more general collision of history and psychology. In *The Death Penalty: An American History* Stuart Banner concluded, I think correctly, that a person's stand on the death penalty is influenced more strongly by personality than by other personal or societal factors.[65] Edward W. Bennett reached the same conclusion in his search for patterns in voting during 1843 and 1846 in the Michigan legislature.[66] Generally speaking, as was evident in the speeches in the Michigan House of Representatives in 1843, abolitionists tended to be optimistic and people-oriented while retentionists tended to be skeptical of change, traditionalists, and rule-oriented.

Age or personal experience may make a person more or less optimistic, but self-selecting factors such as occupation, religious affiliation, and political party tend to be evidence of personality rather than independent factors. Michigan was settled later than other states, and its population exploded with young families looking for opportunity just at the time, the 1830s and 1840s, that agitation to abolish capital punishment reached its peak. People in Michigan at that time tended to be younger and more adventurous, more optimistic, than the people they left behind in New York State. The distribution of wealth was more even than in older states, and there was greater opportunity, in a smaller population, for individuals to affect changes. Of course there were skeptical, pessimistic people in Michigan as well, and the differences in personality between people in Michigan and elsewhere may not have been great. But the margin of victory or defeat was so small in both states that a modest difference one way or the other was decisive. The spirit that animated those reformers, based on respect for human dignity, optimism for the possibility of improvement, and a willingness to oppose the forces of precedent and authority, was common in Michigan during the rest of the nineteenth century, possibly even more common than in other "progressive" states. In retrospect, that spirit can be seen in its infancy in those ritual aspects of executions that Woodworth and other officials chose to omit from Stephen's execution.

Historically, public executions owed much of their continuing legitimacy to the use of ritual. "Each execution, with its formal reading of the judgment and sentence, the prayers of the ministers and the last statement of the condemned, was a highly charged piece of public theater, whose intention was to confirm the power of the law and the solidarity of society against the offender."[67] As Professor Masur noted, "As a civil ceremony, the execution exhibited the authority of the state. It sought to bolster order and encourage conformity to a republican code of social values. As a religious ceremony, ministers used hanging day to remind the crowd of its own mortality and to demonstrate that God alone could redeem the sinful. . . . Execution day served as both a warning and a celebration."[68]

An execution in 1832 in Stephen's former home, New Berlin, New York, contained all of the traditional elements identified by Masur: the curious throng; the white-robed prisoner riding to the scaffold "willingly" with his coffin; military guards; a series of "eloquent and highly appropriate prayer[s]" from the clergy assembled on the scaffold; an improbably eloquent speech by the twenty-seven-year-old prisoner in which he acknowledged violating both "the laws of my country and the laws of my maker," blamed his crime on his use of "ardent spirits," and warned the crowd to embrace temperance; then two sermons given "with great earnestness," followed by another prayer lasting twenty minutes. Finally, a full two hours after the prisoner left the jail, he " 'paid the penalty' with scarcely a struggle" and was left to hang for thirty-five minutes before his body was cut down.[69]

At Stephen's execution the authorities omitted most of the more humiliating and demeaning rituals. The event was over minutes after Stephen walked out of the jail, and Stephen was not placed on display either before or after his death. The role of religion and of the clergy was kept distinctly separate from that of the civil authority—there was no procession to a church for a long sermon before moving on to the scaffold. Stephen walked to the scaffold in his own clothes and without a noose draped around his neck, his arms pinioned behind him, or his coffin at his side. There was no sermon explaining to the prisoner and the crowd the legal and moral necessity of capital punishment. There was no muster of the civil leaders of the community in order to emphasize to the crowd the scope of their power. To the contrary, it seems that all of the government officials who could do so avoided the ceremony, and none of them later expressed deriving any satisfaction, or to have seen any great moral benefit coming, from the event. The fact that they did not attempt the exercise again during the sixteen years that would pass before capital pun- ishment was abolished is, in itself, telling.

chapter 10

Afterword

Except for Levana and Stephen G. Simmons, the people involved in this story went on with their lives. All three judges enjoyed long and prosperous careers. Solomon Sibley remained on the bench until Michigan became a state in 1836. He was active in business, banking, and civic affairs. He died in 1846 at the age of 77.[1] William Woodbridge and Henry Chipman returned to the private practice of law in 1832 when their four-year terms were not renewed due to "political reasons"—they were Whigs and, thus, anathema to President Andrew Jackson.[2] Chipman continued his law practice for many years and died in 1867 at the age of eighty-three.[3] Woodbridge focused his efforts on politics and the Whig Party. He served as a U.S. Senator in 1838 and 1839 and, in 1840, he became the last Whig to be elected governor of the State of Michigan. He left that position in February 1841 to serve again as U.S. Senator until 1847.[4] He died in Detroit in October 1861 at the age of 81.[5]

For George A. O'Keeffe, the Simmons case ended on a doubly sour note: his client was hanged, and he was not paid for his efforts. O'Keeffe's problems began, of course, when he agreed to represent Stephen, a man facing a death sentence, on credit. Henry Cole made the same mistake, but in February 1831 he convinced O'Keeffe to buy Stephen's $200 bond for $175 cash.[6] When the two debts became due in July 1831, O'Keeffe tried without success to get the money from Stephen's executors. According to the papers he later filed in the Supreme Court, the coexecutors made up several excuses to delay payment, saying that the estate had an equity of redemption or that the debt had been paid in full.[7]

In June 1834, after being rebuffed several times, O'Keeffe hired former Judge Woodbridge to foreclose on the mortgages securing the two debts. According to the rules, O'Keeffe had to name as defendants all of the Simmons children, coexecutor Levi Cook, and Ezra Derby, a businessman from Ypsilanti, by way of Massachusetts, who bought the tavern/homestead property in November 1832.[8] One of the defendants paid O'Keeffe one hundred dollars in December 1834, but the balance remained outstanding.[9]

Although none of the defendants ever appeared to oppose O'Keeffe's suit, he was not able to obtain a judgment until two years later, on June 27, 1836, when the Supreme Court, sitting as a court of chancery, entered a judgment in his favor in the amount of $362.06, plus taxed costs. Even then, with a judgment of foreclosure in hand, O'Keeffe was not able to obtain full payment until June 1839, almost nine years after the trial, when he recorded a discharge of both mortgages.[10] Ezra Derby apparently paid the debt because he continued to be the owner and to develop the property into what is now the City of Wayne.

George O'Keeffe continued in the practice of law until he retired in the late 1840s for health reasons related to his drinking. He served as Wayne County's first elected probate judge, from 1837 to 1840, and in 1843 he was a member of Michigan's House of Representatives. After his term in the legislature, O'Keeffe turned his attention to the cause of Irish independence and the rights of the people of Ireland. When he died on June 16, 1853, at his home in Detroit, his fellow attorneys eulogized O'Keeffe as "a warm friend, a courteous lawyer, and an honorable and kind-hearted gentleman."[11]

Levi Cook, Stephen's coexecutor, served as territorial treasurer from January 1830 to February 1836. He was elected Mayor of the City of Detroit three times, in 1832 ("unanimously," with 148 votes[12]), 1835, and 1836. In the 1840s Levi Cook served as president and director of the Bank of St. Clair.[13] He died in 1866. As coexecutor of Stephen's estate, he, like O'Keeffe, endured the delays and frustrations of the court system. Shortly after

Stephen's will was admitted to probate in January 1831, his son James, the other coexecutor of the estate, left Michigan without having done anything to help Cook.[14] The estate remained open until December 1841, during which time Cook advanced funds to the estate to pay creditors and administration expenses. Except for a small payment by James Simmons in 1831 and a larger one by Ezra Derby in 1833, he was not reimbursed until the estate was closed.[15]

Henry S. Cole, Stephen's other defense attorney, was appointed Attorney General of Michigan Territory in 1833, but he died in 1836 at the age of thirty-five.[16] His daughter married Eben Willcox, the boy who supplied the peanuts as he watched the hanging from B. F. H. Witherell's woodshed with Friend Palmer and R. E. Roberts. A lawyer and lifelong Detroiter, Willcox was also a founder of Detroit's street railway system.[17] He died in 1891 at the age of seventy.[18]

Benjamin Woodworth's tenure as acting sheriff was short. On December 2, 1830, John M. Wilson was elected to the post, defeating Samuel Phelps 403 to 81.[19] In March 1831 the Legislative Council directed the Wayne County Board of Supervisors to pay Woodworth a hundred dollars to reimburse him for "all services and disbursements made by him and deputies in officiating as sheriff at the execution."[20] Although he lived to the age of ninety-one, his later life was blighted by the loss of his popular and energetic son Samuel, who died in 1844 when the boiler of his steam ferry, the *General Vance*, exploded on the dock at Windsor.[21] Benjamin Woodworth died in 1874 at St. Clair, Michigan.

In 1833 Noah M. Wells, who ministered to Stephen in jail, resigned his post in Detroit because of heart trouble and moved west to Illinois.[22] There he preached, engaged in business, and served as an Army chaplain before returning to Detroit to work in the Bethel Mission. He died in Erie, Michigan, in 1879 at the age of ninety-eight.[23]

Many people in this story were affected by the outbreaks of Asiatic cholera that ravaged Detroit in 1832 and 1834. The 1832 epidemic, introduced by soldiers heading west to suppress an uprising of American Indians under Black Hawk, seeking to recover tribal lands, killed ninety-six people, including Judge Sibley's mother, Governor Cass's eldest daughter, and Father Gabriel Richard.[24] In two months the 1834 epidemic killed more than ten percent of Detroit's population of 3500, including Governor George B. Porter, former Sheriff Thomas Knapp, court clerk John Winder's wife, and Mary Ann Sprague Witherell, the first wife of B. F. H. Witherell, who married twice more and lived a long life full of accomplishment and honors.[25] Witherell served in the legislature, as a judge of the Wayne County Probate, Recorder's, and Circuit Courts, as a justice of the Michigan Supreme Court, and as a regent of the University of Michigan. An amateur historian, he wrote newspaper articles about the history of Detroit and the Michigan Territory under the pen name "Hamtramck" and held the position of president of the State Historical Commission. He died in Detroit in 1867 just before his seventieth birthday.[26] His father, James Witherell, Revolutionary War veteran, doctor, congressman, judge, and territorial Secretary, died in Detroit on January 6, 1838, at the age of seventy-eight.[27]

Friend Palmer lived in Detroit for most of his life. During the Mexican War, he worked for the U.S. Quartermaster; after that he engaged in the stationery and blank-book business in Detroit for about ten years. In 1851, at age twenty-eight, he married Harriet Witherell, a daughter of Judge B. F. H. Witherell and Mary Sprague Witherell.[28] At the beginning of the Civil War, Friend Palmer was appointed Michigan's Assistant Quartermaster General and, later, Quartermaster General, earning the nickname "the General," which he bore proudly for the rest of his life. After resigning from that position in 1871, he bought and sold real estate with his cousin Thomas Palmer, who later became a United States Senator and who donated Palmer Park to the city. Like B. F. H. Witherell and his friend R. E. Roberts, Friend Palmer also became a chronicler of the city's past, writing gossipy newspaper stories about the people who lived in Detroit in his younger days. He died at the age of eighty-three on October 9, 1906, just as a compilation of his articles, *Early Days in Detroit,* went to press.[29]

Robert E. Roberts spent his life in public service in Detroit. From 1844 to 1850, he served as city clerk, and from 1850 to 1872 he was secretary of the Detroit Water Board.[30] Roberts also held positions on the Board of Education, various fire companies, and the Detroit Young Men's Temperance Society.[31] He published two volumes of historical memoirs, *Sketches of the City of Detroit,* and *Sketches of the City of the Straits.* Roberts died in 1888, at age seventy-nine.

Journalist Calvin Colton served four years in London as correspondent for the *New York Observer* and then became the editor of the *True Whig,* a newspaper published in Washington, D.C. In 1844 he moved to Ashland, Kentucky, to become the official biographer and editor of his idol, Henry Clay. Colton spent his last years as professor of public economy at Trinity College in Hartford, Connecticut. He died in 1857, in Savannah, Georgia, at the age of sixty-seven.[32]

The Simmons children dropped out of the public records of Michigan a few years after the execution. According to an affidavit filed in George O'Keeffe's foreclosure action, by February 1835 none of the Simmons children lived in the territory and they were "beyond the reach of the process of this Court."[33] In November 1832 David and James Simmons sold the tavern property to Ezra Derby,[34] and in January 1834 Ellen Simmons "of Ypsilanti" sold Stephen's lot on the Huron River to one Isaac Bush.[35] The three other Simmons daughters all married in Washtenaw County in the early 1830s. Catherine Simmons was remarried in July 1833 to James Forman, Bathsheba married Silas A. Tuless in November 1832, and Lavina married William Butler in December 1833.[36] In June 1832 the Wayne County Probate Court appointed one Aaron Thomas to act as guardian for Bathsheba and Lavina Simmons for purposes of managing the farm in Springwells that Stephen had left them.[37] Although both married shortly thereafter, that guardianship apparently continued for several years. In 1841 Lavina's husband, William Butler, had to petition the court to obtain custody of that farm and to require Mr. Thomas to file a final account.[38]

Simmons' Tavern passed into the hands of Ezra Derby and became the core around which developed what is now the City of Wayne. The Simmons case, still very much a part of Wayne's historical identity, is memorialized by a Michigan Historical Commission marker where the tavern once sat, now the site of a bank building on Michigan Avenue.

appendix a

To a very large degree, this book is indebted to the record keepers of early America and to the people who made the effort to
preserve those records when many governments saw them as
merely a nuisance taking up storage space. Without them, filling
in the blanks of the lives and deaths of Stephen and Levana
Simmons, two entirely unknown and undistinguished people
except for the circumstances of their deaths, would have been
impossible. If their contemporaries in Michigan knew anything
about their lives before they moved to Michigan, that knowledge
was not passed on. The authors of prior accounts of the story say
nothing specific about their birthplaces, parents or siblings, lives
before coming to Michigan, or why they came. When I began my
research for this work, I did not really think that I could do any
better, and I regret that for Levana Simmons I could not.
However, bit by bit, I was able to unearth records in Michigan,
New York, Tennessee, Ohio, and Washington, D.C., which
allowed me to fill in some of the blanks in Stephen's life. In particular, I owe a great debt to the collectors of Michigan records
of the early nineteenth century, including George Catlin, Agnes
and Clarence Burton, Professor William Wirt Blume, and many
others, who managed to save, and make available to the public,
so many original materials.

Stephen's trail began with the records of land transfers in
Wayne County. When he purchased the Johnson tavern in 1825,
Stephen identified himself in the deed as "Stephen G. Simmons
from Chenango County, New York."[1] In the Burton Historical

Collection at the Detroit Public Library, I found two nineteenth-century histories of that county that reported that a Stephen G. Simmons and his brother John, natives of New York City, settled lots owned by their wealthy father in the town of New Berlin, Chenango County.[2] The real estate records of Chenango County in the office of the county clerk in Norwich, New York, revealed that the estate of one John Simmons of New York City[3] transferred lots to his son, Stephen G. Simmons, in 1815 and 1820.[4] One of those deeds referred to John Simmons's "last will and testament dated the third day of August A.D. 1794 registered in the office of the Surrogate of the County of New York."[5] That will had the same date as the will of a John Simmons referred to in the genealogical column of a 1927 edition of the *Boston Transcript*: "Page 312 of New York Wills, 1786–1796, has the will of one John Simmons, innkeeper, dated August 3, 1794, which mentions wife Catherine and children William, John, David, Stephen, Gifford, and Catherine."[6]

This Simmons family, then, had a father John as well as sons Stephen, John, and William. Moreover, Michigan records, including a lawsuit filed in Michigan against Stephen G. Simmons's heirs and Stephen's own will, filed in the records of Wayne County, Michigan, reveal that he had named two of his children Catharine and David,[7] names that also appeared in the *Boston Transcript* column. Review of the actual "New York Wills" entry[8] cited in the *Boston Transcript* contained the name of another son of John Simmons, James, which was the name that Stephen G. Simmons of Michigan gave to his other son.

Two other Chenango deeds and a Michigan court clerk's note complete the circle and connect the Stephen G. Simmons of New York City and Chenango County to the man hanged in Michigan. In September 1828, "Stephen G. Simmons of County of Wayne and Territory of Michigan Territory [sic], and Levana his wife" sold part of the land Stephen inherited from his father, John[9]; and, in October 1828, "Stephen G. Simmons and Levana his wife of the Territory of Michigan" sold more of the lots inherited from John Simmons.[10] This both tied the Chenango

County/John Simmons connection to the Stephen G. Simmons of Wayne County and confirmed Clarence Burton's discovery that the name of the victim of the murder was Livana [sic] Simmons.[11]

Discovering Stephen's military career began with an Internet reference to a Lieutenant Stephen G. Simmons in a light dragoon troop in Tennessee in 1800–01. At the National Archives in Washington, D.C., with the assistance of that institution's remarkably helpful staff, I found several muster rolls and payrolls of a light dragoon company or troop that did, indeed, include one Lieutenant Stephen G. Simmons. Luckily, Lieutenant Simmons was left in charge of the troop for a month and had to sign the roll. That signature was the same idiosyncratic scrawl that was in the journal of tavern license applications for Wayne County in 1826 and on Stephen's will.

Stephen's baptism on February 3, 1780, recorded in the archives of Christ Church in Philadelphia, established his age and indicated that his family had fled New York during the British occupation. I could only estimate the ages of the rest of the Simmons family, using principally the original, handwritten returns from the 1820 and 1830 U.S. censuses that are preserved on microfilm in various collections, including the Library of Michigan in Lansing and the Library of the New York Historical Association in Cooperstown. I also used references to the children's ages in documents in the Wayne County Probate Court's file for Stephen's estate, preserved on microfilm in the Michigan State Archives in Lansing. For example, besides Levana and her daughter Catherine, the Simmons household in 1830 contained one female between ten and fifteen and two between fifteen and twenty, all of whom had been ten years old or younger in 1820. The oldest of these three was almost certainly Ellen. In his will Stephen left her some land to sell or hold as she pleased. Bathsheba and Lavina were barred from selling the farm left to them until the younger reached the age of eighteen. Therefore, it appears that in 1830 Ellen was between eighteen and twenty years old. In June 1832, when Wayne County Probate Court appointed a guardian for Bathsheba and Lavina to operate the farm Stephen left them, the letters of appointment stated that both wards were then over fourteen years old. If that notation and the 1830 census records are accurate, one of them was between twelve and fifteen and the other was fifteen or sixteen when their father killed their mother.

The ages of Stephen and Levana's sons are easier to approximate because there were only two of them. In 1820 one was less than ten years old and the other was between ten and fifteen. The elder son must have been James, whom Stephen named as a coexecutor of the will that Stephen executed on the day before he was hanged. Under Michigan law, no person who was less than twenty-one years old could serve as executor of a will.[12] Therefore, James must have been between twenty-one and twenty-five in 1830. His brother David was between ten and twenty years old in 1830, but probably at least eighteen because Stephen bequeathed land to David outright.[13] Neither David nor James was included in their father's household for the 1830 census, but it does appear that David was at the tavern at the time of the murder. One of the sons was reported to have witnessed the killing's aftermath and to have tried to resuscitate Levana, and David, but not James, testified against Stephen before the grand jury and at the murder trial.[14]

The databases at http://www.ancestry.com helped immensely in filling out the Simmons family tree. The will of Mary Dalley, who died in Philadelphia in 1811, provided evidence of the maiden name of Stephen's mother and led to the record of her first marriage.[15] Those databases also provided information about Stephen's siblings and his nieces and nephews, but not his own children. Thanks are due to William F. Archerd, who maintains the database that includes the Simmons family.

appendix b

Jury Selection

United States v. Stephen G. Simmons
The names of the veniremen and talesmen who were examined on July 6, 8, and 12, 1830, are listed in *Journal A* of the Wayne County Circuit Court. A microfilmed copy of that journal is in the collection of the Bentley Historical Library on the North Campus of the University of Michigan, Ann Arbor. Because the journal is, of course, handwritten, there may be discrepancies in spelling of some names. I have also noted information about an individual's occupation or public offices that I have been able to discover.

July 6, 1830
　　19 veniremen
　　14 excused for cause
　　5 defense peremptories (*)
　　0 prosecution peremptories
　　0 seated

First Panel:

Harlow Beardsley	Wagon maker
John Roberts	Dry goods merchant; "soap boiler & tallow chandler"; alderman, 1832
John Scott	Bookkeeper; alderman; city marshal, 1833
Aaron Hawley*	

Samuel Phelps   Candidate for Wayne County Sheriff,
                         December 1830

Stephen Bain   Merchant
Elisha Warren
Robert W. Payne
John Garrison   Alderman
Conrad Seek   Constable, 1804; militia officer; tax
                         collector

John Howard   Constable, 1826
Gilbert Dalson   Merchant

Second Panel:
Peter Desnoyer*   Attorney; Constable; Alderman,
                         1827–30

David Thompson*   Constable, 1831; City Marshal, 1836;
Alexis Farran
James Williams   Grocer, County Commissioner
                         (1826–27)

James Hanmer   Tavern keeper; alderman; coroner;
                         militia officer

Lewis Davenport*   Merchant and ferry owner
George Hunt

July 8, 1830

48 talesmen
28 excused for cause
15 defense peremptories (*)
1 prosecution peremptory (#)
4 seated (+)

Third Panel:
Abner C. Canniff   Tax collector
Israel Noble*   City sexton
George Moran*
Guy H. Leonard+

William Durell	Furniture and cabinetmaker; built Stephen's casket and drove the corpse back to his farm for burial
Horace Wilson*	
John Martin*	Laborer
Charles Moran	"Gentleman"
George LaForge	
Thomas C. Brown+	
Victor Moross	
Charles Bigalow*	

Fourth Panel:
    Peter Van Avery
    Louis Moran*
    Louis Goulette
    Joseph Allair
    Bazil Criquee*
    Antoine Campau
    Robert Ladouceur
    George Lyon*
    Daniel Thompson
    John Rosseter

Fifth Panel:

Levi G. Scherenck	
Jesse Hicks	
John Andrews*	Boot and shoemaker
Richard Godfroy	
Samuel W. Lapham+	
Louis Rouleau*	
Gaylord Goodell+	
James Butterfield	
Joel Thomas	Tavern keeper
Warren Fenton*	

Sixth Panel:
    John Brown
    George W. Martin   Hardware merchant
    Alfred Hodge #
    Elias Woodruff
    John A. Sager
    Titus Dort
    John Dix*
    Christian Kelley

Seventh Panel:
    Coleman Funston*
    Eustache Chapeton   Mason and bricklayer
    John Grant
    John Steinback*
    William Spears
    Jacob Dix*
    Eleazer Ray   Grocer
    Louis Beaufait

July 12, 1830
    61 talesmen
    38 excused for cause
    14 defense peremptories (*)
    1 prosecution peremptory (#)
    8 seated (+)

Eighth Panel:
    Ira Andrews
    Levi Cook   Merchant; Mayor of Detroit (1832);
                         coexecutor of Stephen's will and estate

    Jonathon Wright*
    Charles Jackson*
    Amos Chaffee*   Blacksmith
    Alva Ewers Cooper;   volunteer fireman; "city magnate"

Jonathon B. Mettez+
John J. Garrison*   Grocer; volunteer fireman

Ninth Panel:
  Edward Brigham*
  Eben Beach+   Clerk, Detroit produce market
  George Dunks (sp?)
  Lemuel Goodell   Restauranteur; ship's steward
  David French*   Merchant; Detroit city treasurer
  John Smythe
  Paul D. Anderson

Tenth Panel:
  Hiram W. Pond+
  Ruel Robinson
  Francis Van Antwerp*
  John B. Lapiere
  Charles N. Delisle
  James O. Lewis   Engraver

Eleventh Panel:
  Knowles Hall   Carriage maker
  Alexander Grant
  Garry Spencer+   Tailor; militia officer
  Thomas B. Gagnier
  Peter N. Girardin

Twelfth Panel:
  Franklin Brewster+
  Matthew Moon*   Grocer
  John Bronson
  James Campbell*   Judge

Thirteenth Panel:
  Jonathon Kearsley   Militia Major and Mayor of Detroit
  Horace Jerome*   Judge

Andrew Fisher+

Fourteenth Panel:
    John Waring
    Andrew Moon

Fifteenth Panel:
    Phillip Warren
    Ephraim Farnsworth

Sixteenth Panel:
    Otis G. Eels
    Griffith Roberts

Seventeenth Panel:
    George Bowen
    Jeremiah Moon*

Eighteenth Panel:
    George Young*
    Daniel D. Orn

Nineteenth Panel:
    Samuel Smith
    Joseph Visger   Well-known citizen; served with Cass
                                  in campaign of 1813

Twentieth Panel:
    Asquire Aldrich+   Land speculator
    Daniel Goodell

Jurors Called Individually:
    Louis Campau   Wealthy businessman
    James Bucklin #   Tavern owner; politician
    Hezekiah Gridley
    Robert Abbott   Territory auditor general

Eraites Hussey
Dexter Coulter
George M. Johnson   Tavern keeper; former owner of
                                    Simmons Tavern
Benajah Holbrook*   Militia major in Black Hawk War
John Cahoon
Joseph Kingsley
Nathaniel Eldridge
William Smith
Daniel L. Cady
Dean Wyman+

Total:

  128 veniremen and talesmen
  80 excused for cause
  34 defense peremptories (*)
  2 prosecution peremptories (#)
  12 seated (+)

notes

In citing works in the notes, short titles have generally been used. Works frequently cited have been identified by the following short titles or abbreviations:

Abstract	Abstract of the Last Will and Testament of John Simmons.
Chen. Rec.	Deeds recorded in the deed books kept by the Clerk of Chenango County, New York, at the Clerk's Office, Norwich, New York.
Early Days	Friend Palmer, *Early Days in Detroit.*
Jour. A	*Journal A*, Wayne County Circuit Court, Bentley Historical Library.
LTM	*Laws of the Territory of Michigan.*
Mich. Bios.	*Michigan Biographies.*
MPHC	*Michigan Pioneer and Historical Collection.*
Mus. Roll	Muster Rolls of Troop of Light Dragoons Van Rensselaer.
NWJ	*North-Western Journal.*
Pap. in Box.	Clarence M. Burton, "Papers in Boxes in Attic of City Hall."
Stats.	*Statutes at Large of the United States of America.*
Story	George M. Catlin, *The Story of Detroit.*
TSCM	*Transactions of the Supreme Court of Michigan*
Wayne Prob.	Wayne County Probate Court, Files and Papers.

CHAPTER 1

1. The only other person executed by the Territory or State of Michigan
    was an American Indian named Ke-wa-bish-kim in 1821 (see discussion,
    Chapter 5). At least four people have been executed within the current
    boundaries of the State of Michigan by the United States for violations
    of federal law. Three of them were convicted of murder on lands con-
    trolled by the federal government. In addition to Ka-tau-kah, who was
    hanged with Ke-wa-bish-kim, two men were hanged on Mackinac
    Island: Private James Brown in February 1830 (see discussion, Chapter
    4) and Wau-ben-e-mickee of the Chippewa in September 1833 (see dis-
    cussion, Chapter 9). In July 1938, Anthony Chebatoris was hanged at
    the federal penitentiary at Milan, Michigan, for killing a bystander dur-
    ing a bank robbery. *Detroit Free Press*, sec. 1, p. 3 (July 8, 1938); Lincoln,
    1785–87; Post, 44–50.
2. For a tally and brief description of executions in Michigan under French,
    British, and American rule, see Burbey, 442–457; Lincoln, 1765.
3. The accounts of which I am aware are, in chronological order with year
    of publication: *NWJ*, June 23 to September 29, 1830; *(Pontiac, Mich.)
    Oakland Chronicle*, June 18 to October 1, 1830; *(Monroe) Michigan
    Sentinel*, July 10 to October 2, 1830; Colton, 48–52 (1833); Jerome Sr.,
    17–18 (1880); "Great Gala Hanging" (1885); Farmer, 181 (1884);
    "Hanged in 1830" (1900); *Early Days*, 705–6 (1906); Ross, 154–55
    (1907); *Story*, 289–93 (1923); Fuller, 264 (1924); Hawley (1924);
    Quaife, "Capital Punishment," 47–48 (1929); Deravigne (1929);
    Burbey, 450–52 (1938); Hoch (1938); Catlin, "Early Settlement,"
    331–33 (1942); Stark, 259–62 (1943); "Big Steve" (1960); Woodford,
    Yesterdays, 177–79 (1969); *Memories of a Community*, 4–6 (1969);
    Gilpin, 99 (1970); Barfknecht, 44–46 (1983); Lincoln, 1773–75 (1987);
    Massie, 46–48 (1988); Dunbar, 208 (1995); Jones, 40 (1996); Wanger,
    766 (1996).
4. *Story*, 289–93.

CHAPTER 2

1. The nation's prior organic law, the Articles of Confederation, did not
    include a national executive branch.
2. Villard, 107; Thomas Smith, 121 (Simmons' Tavern at northwest corner
    of Wall and Nassau Streets); Wilson, 287–92 (in April 1776 lists of per-
    sons selling alcohol and paying excise taxes included "John Simmons,
    tavern keeper" on "Wall Street near City Hall").
3. Thomas Smith, 219–34 (a description of the day's ceremonies).

4. Contemporary records spell the given name of Stephen's mother as both Catharine and Catherine. For consistency, I use the former spelling for Stephen's mother's name and for the names of her daughter and the various granddaughters who were named for her, except when making a direct quotation that uses a different spelling.

5. Tucker, 351.

6. "Earliest Trinity Church Marriages," *N.Y. Gen. & Bio. Record* 19 (1888): 147, 149. The mechanics of tracing Michigan's Stephen G. Simmons to New York's Stephen Gifford Simmons are explained in Appendix A. It seems that Stephen's middle name was important to his father, John Simmons—in his will, John referred three times to his son "Stephen Gifford" but does not mention a middle name for any other child. It is likely that Stephen was named for Stephen Gifford, the doorkeeper of New York's City/Federal Hall. Stephen does not seem to have had any affection for his middle name as he did not use it as an adult, although he did always use his middle initial.

7. The Dally/Salter marriage is recorded at *id.*, 149. The Dally connection can be deduced from the will of Mary Dalley [sic], *Abstracts of Philadelphia Wills*, 3: 439.

8. Scott, *Rivington*, 103 (in February 1775 a newspaper notice stated that "the overseers of the public pumps and wells of the city are to meet at the tavern of John Simmons, near City Hall"); Bayles, 341–42 (in August 1790 the Regents of the State University of New York met at Simmons' Tavern).

9. Bayles, 340.

10. *Id.*, 340.

11. Thomas Smith, 121; Villard, 107.

12. Villard, 107.

13. (*Cooperstown, N.Y.*) *Otsego Herald*, August 28, 1795; Scott, *New York Magazine*, 266.

14. Because there is no direct evidence of William's birth date, it is possible that William was actually the son of William Salter. If not, John must have been a very understanding eighteenth-century husband indeed to agree to name his first son after his wife's first husband.

15. Abstract, 312. Although the first mention of the children is printed in the Abstract as "Stephen, Gifford, and Catharine," it is clear from the rest of the will that there was no son named Gifford and that the comma between "Stephen" and "Gifford" in that one instance was a typographical error.

16. *Wayne Prob.*, Case 440, Will of Stephen G. Simmons.

17. "New Jersey Marriage Licenses, 1727–34, with Additions to 1751," *Genealogical Magazine of New Jersey* 21, 1 (January 1946): 64, 65 (on January 6, 1746, Bathsheba Bozorth, spinster, married Thomas Simmons

of Northampton, Burlington County, NJ; John Simmons stood witness to the marriage).

18. Abstract, 312 (William and James); *Wayne Prob.*, Case 440, Will of Stephen G. Simmons.

19. Abstract, 312.

20. Mather, 1017. Colonel Clinton was the brother of General (later Governor) George Clinton. Although it is not certain that this militia-man was Stephen's father and not his brother, John Jr. was born in October 1761, so he would have been only fourteen years old in April 1776. There were, certainly, more than a few fourteen-year-olds in the American army during the Revolution, but the Patriot Index of the Daughters of the American Revolution does list both John Sr. and John Jr. as veterans of the war, and amateur militia bands like the one raised by Col. Clinton were more likely, particularly early in the war, to be made up of men who were too old rather than boys who were too young.

21. *General Index*, Nos. 5302 (John Jr.) and 5304 (William); White, 3: 3136 (John Jr.). The identity of the John Simmons cited in White is confirmed by his date and place of birth as well as by the comment that he lived in Chenango County, New York, for twenty years.

22. Ellis, 170–73.

23. Bayles, 308.

24. For discussions of the animosities between New York's Patriots and Loyalists during the period of British occupation, see Barck; Abbott.

25. Fenn, 109. Although British and German troops were largely immune to smallpox, people born in North America, whether of Native, European, or African descent, were not.

26. Bayles, 307.

27. *Public Papers of George Clinton*, 8: 295.

28. *Id.*

29. *Baptismal Record 1769–1794*, 953, Archives of Christ Church, Philadelphia, PA.

30. Fenn, 82–86.

31. Heitman, 1: 887.

32. Villard, 107.

33. Fleming, 98–99.

34. *Id.*, 187–88; *Dictionary of American Biography*, s.v. Tayler, John; Wilber, 63.

35. *Chen. Rec.*, February 27, 1793. For some reason, this deed was not recorded in Chenango County until October 4, 1839, although it was witnessed by Robert Gates, Chief Justice of the State of New York, in 1793.

36. Alan Taylor, 328.

37. Fleming, 98–99.

38. John Simmons, Jr., appears in the United States Census returns for Town

16 1800 and 1810. Town 16 was named New Berlin in 1813, renamed Lancaster in 1821, and returned to the name New Berlin in 1822. In an 1812 deed of fifty acres to local merchant Levi Blakeslee, John Jr. described himself as a farmer. It appears that at least two more generations of his descendants also farmed the Unadilla country. John W. Simmons appears as a head-of-household in the United States Census for 1810, and John J. Simmons appears in the United States Census for 1820. In both cases the census information indicates that the head-of-household was a relatively young man.

39. (*Cooperstown, NY*) *Otsego Herald,* August 14, 21, and 28, 1795 and September 4, 1795.

40. *Chen. Rec.,* April 2, 1793.

41. A deed recorded in Chenango County in 1797 stated that William was a resident of Philadelphia. In deeds recorded between 1800 and 1820, he was "William Simmons of the City of Washington in the District of Columbia."

42. *General Index,* No. 5406; *Digested Summary,* 3: 322.

43. *Chen. Rec.,* November 30, 1822 (gift of 170 acres from William Simmons "of Coshocton County, Ohio," to "Catherine D. Simmons, daughter of Stephen G. Simmons"); *Coshocton County, Ohio, Records,* Will Book 2b, p. 81, December 10, 1825 (probate of estate of William Simmons).

44. Abstract, 313 (John's will was "proved"—i.e., accepted for probate—on August 20, 1795); *Marriage and Death Notices,* 128.

45. The older Catharine Simmons died between 1811 and 1815. In 1811, she signed a deed with son William as surviving coexecutors of her husband's estate. In 1815 William signed deeds as sole surviving coexecutor.

46. Abstract, 312.

47. *Chen. Rec.,* June 17, 1806.

48. *E.g.,* Colton, 1:49.

49. Abstract, 312–13.

50. Heitman 1: 887; U.S. Sen. Exec. J. (July 10, 1797). For a roster of cavalry officers as of April 1797, see Hamersly, 47.

51. *NWJ,* September 29, 1830.

52. "An Act to Ascertain and fix the Military Establishment of the United States," *Stat.* 1:483 (1845), enacted May 30, 1796; Heitman, 562–63.

53. Clary, 71.

54. Weigley, 107–09.

55. "An Act to Ascertain and fix the Military Establishment of the United States," sec. 10, *Stat.* 1: 483 (May 30, 1796).

56. Risch, 117–20.

57. Weigley, 107.

58. Fleming, 27–28, 71–72.

59. *Philadelphia Aurora*, December 16, 1798.
60. "An Act to Ascertain and Fix the Military Establishment of the United States," sec. 1, *Stat.* 1:483 (May 30, 1796).
61. Heitman, 1:892.
62. Stephen and Tharp had not yet arrived when the troop's muster roll was prepared at the end of November. Mus. Roll, November 30, 1797.
63. Corlew, 96, 108–11.
64. Mus. Roll, January 31, 1798. Stephen's signature on that document is identical in style to the signature on his 1826 tavern license (although the latter shows signs of a definite tremor possibly caused by age or alcohol).
65. Mus. Roll, August 31, 1798 to August 31, 1799.
66. *NWJ*, September 29, 1830.
67. Corlew, 112. For a discussion of the frontier ethos of violence, see Burgess-Jackson, 46–49.
68. Corlew, 112. Duels, although illegal in Tennessee, were also common. Moreover, all of this punching, gouging, shooting, and stabbing was not limited to the dregs of society. Members of the bar were just as likely to indulge in violence. Two of the premier brawlers of the day were lawyers: future President Andrew Jackson and future Senator Thomas Hart Benton. Corlew, 115–16.
69. From August 1799 to September 1800, the troop muster rolls reported that Stephen was "absent with leave." Mus. Roll, August 31, 1799 to September 30, 1800.
70. Heitman 1: 887.
71. "An Act authorizing the President of the United States to raise a Provisional Army," *Stat.* 1:558 (May 28, 1798).
72. "An Act to augment the Army of the United States, and for other purposes," *Id.* 1:604 (16 July 1798).
73. "An Act giving eventual authority to the President of the United States to augment the Army," *Id.* 1:725 (March 2, 1799); "An Act for better organizing the Troops of the United States; and for other purposes," *Id.* 1:749 (March 3, 1799).
74. Heitman, 1:983. Captain Van Rensselaer certainly was a passionate Federalist. A decade later, in 1807, when he was a leader of the Federalists in Albany and a militia general, he instigated a notorious and brutally violent street brawl between Federalists and Republicans. See Alan Taylor, 367–68.
75. McCullough, 533. See Resolution of Congress, *Stat.* 2:86 (December 24, 1799), ordering the parade and other proceedings.
76. Stephen claimed to have lost a horse due to "the fatiguing and harassing service in which he was employed," H. R. Jour., 6th Cong. 640 (February

25, 1800), but Congress denied his petition for compensation. *Digested Summary*, 3: 321.

77. Clary, 82; "An Act to suspend, in part, an act intituled [sic] 'An Act to augment the Army of the United States, and for other purposes,' " *Stat.* 2:7 (February 20, 1800) (authority to stop enlistments); "An Act supplementary to the Act to suspend part of an act intituled [sic] 'An Act to augment the Army of the United states, and for other purposes,' " *Id.* 2:85 (May 14, 1800) (authority to stop appointing officers and to discharge officers and men of the provisional army).

78. Mus. Roll, October 31, 1800 (Stephen carried "in arrest").

79. Heitman, 1:887; U.S. Sen. Exec. J. 381 (December 22, 1800).

80. *Id.*, 1:951.

81. Snyder Roberts, 183: "The muster rolls and payrolls for the militia and regular troops stationed at Fort South West Point from 1792 until 1807 have not been found except for one company, as follows: "Payroll of Capt. JAMES BALL'S Company of Light Dragoons under command of Lt. WILLIAM THARP, January 1801: . . . Stephen G. SIMMONS, Lt.. . . ."

82. Heitman, 1: 187 (Ball), 951 (Tharp), 983 (Van Rensselaer). Both Ball and Van Rensselaer returned to the army to command cavalry units during the War of 1812. *Id.* Ball faced a mutiny by officers not used to his regular army methods, but he was exonerated. *A refutation of charges exhibited by sundry officers of the late United States' regiment of light dragoons, against Brevet Lt. Col. James V. Ball of the same regiment* (Winchester, VA: John Heiskell, [1815?]).

83. "An Act for fixing the military peace establishment of the United States," sec. 9, *Stat.* 2:132 (March 5, 1792).

84. Pap. in Box., 180. The failure of earlier accounts (including that of Detroit's *North-Western Journal* in 1830) to mention Levana's name may seem strange, and it certainly is susceptible to interpretations that are not favorable to nineteenth-century attitudes about women in general and female victims in particular. On the other hand, literary convention may have had some role as well. In 1878 Maria Norris presented a biographical account of her mother (Norris, 504–21) to the annual meeting of the Michigan Pioneer and Historical Society. In her sketch Norris described her mother's entire life, lovingly and with great admiration, at a published length of more than eighteen pages, without ever once referring to her mother except as "Mrs. Norris."

85. *NWJ*, July 20, 1830.

86. Russell, 162.

87. *Population Schedule, Fourth Census of the United States*, Chenango County, NY, Town of New Berlin, p. 371.

88. *TSCM*, 6: 1443.
89. See Appendix A.
90. *Abstracts of Philadelphia Wills*, Book K346, file 84.
91. *Chen. Rec.*, May 17, 1815.
92. For a description of the credit system for buying land in western New York, see Alan Taylor.
93. *Id*. Although Chenango County is at a slightly higher altitude than Otsego County, its neighbor to the east, life in New Berlin in 1815 was probably very much like life in an Otsego village ten years earlier, as described by Alan Taylor in *William Cooper's Town*.
94. Hyde, 40.
95. *Id.*, 41.
96. White, 3: 3136.
97. *Chen. Rec.*, May 2, 1812, May 1, 1813, July 1, 1813, May 6, 1815.
98. That sale is referred to in a deed from Stephen and Levana Simmons to Stephen Goodrich, *Chen. Rec.*, August 6, 1818.
99. *Id.*, February 6, 1819.
100. *Population Schedule, Fourth Census of the United States*, Chenango County, NY, Town of New Berlin.
101. *Chen. Rec.*, April 20, 1820.
102. Lippincott, 263; Martin, 304.
103. *Id.*, November 8, 1821. The couple sold twenty-two acres in the Town of Lancaster (Lot 2 of Township 16) to local residents John and Rever Dillie for $200, or $9.10 per acre. Given the era's relaxed approach to spelling, the buyers may have been named Dally and related to Stephen through his mother. *Id.*, February 7, 1822. Stephen and Levana deeded thirty-two acres in Lot 69, Township 16, also part of Lancaster, to Stephen Wood of that town for $320, or ten dollars per acre. The delay in recording these deeds may indicate that the buyers gave promissory notes that took a few years to be paid.
104. *Id.*, August 17, 1825 (two deeds). Those parcels sold for $3.60 and $8.60 per acre.
105. Quaife, *Michigan*, 149–51.
106. *Chen. Rec.*, October 1, 1828.

CHAPTER 3

1. *Early Land Transfers* 4: 208 (Stephen G. Simmons granted a U.S. patent for 56.10 acres in Section 21 of Van Buren Township, which was then called Huron Township).
2. Quaife, *Michigan*, 149. The number of people in the territory was

undoubtedly higher because such censuses did not count American Indians.

3. *Population Schedules, Fourth Census of the United States*, Chenango County, NY, Town of New Berlin.

4. Roberts, *Sketches*, 10; *Idem.*, "Recollections," 567.

5. Burgess-Jackson, 49.

6. *Detroit Gazette*, September 1, 1820.

7. Quaife, *Michigan*, 153.

8. Darby, 172.

9. Burns, 57.

10. *Id.*

11. "An Act to amend the act entitled 'An Act providing for the sale of the lands of the United States, in the territory northwest of the Ohio, and above the mouth of the Kentucky river," *Stat.* 2: 73 (May 10, 1800).

12. "An Act to make further provisions for the sale of the public lands," *Stat.* 3: 566 (April 24, 1820).

13. For land sales data, see MacCabe, 86.

14. In 1827 households in the City of Detroit with French surnames were outnumbered by those with English surnames by only 161 to 191, while French surnames were the great majority in Hamtramck and east of the City. However, to the west of Detroit, English names predominated. For example, in Bucklin township, where the Simmons tavern was located, only five percent of households had French surnames. Russell, 150–60.

15. *NWJ*, July 14, 1830; Roberts, *Sketches*, 11.

16. Watkins, 63.

17. Roberts, "Recollections," 569.

18. Leake, 127.

19. Blois, 126–27.

20. Dunbar, 205.

21. Van Buren, "The Fever and Ague," 300; Hoyt, 426.

22. Keen, 101.

23. Nowlin, 33. Although malaria and mosquitoes both plagued Michigan's settlers, they did not understand the connection between the two. Indeed, it is apparent that neither did Mr. Nowlin in 1876, Mr. Van Buren in 1882, or Dr. Hoyt in 1889.

24. Blois, 126.

25. Roberts, "Recollections," 570.

26. "An Act authorizing Peter Berthelet, to erect a Wharf on the river Detroit," *LTM* 2: 214–15 (August 5, 1824); Gilpin, 135.

27. *Detroit Gazette*, October 10, 1826, quoted in Fannie Anderson, 130–32.

28. Farmer, 63–64.

29. *Id.*

30. Friedrich, 136 (in 1860, only one Parisian home in five had piped water).

31. Roberts, *Sketches*, 11; "Annual Report," 356.

32. Roberts, *Sketches*, 10.

33. Darby, 190.

34. Farmer, 735–36. In February 1809 the Governor and Judges passed an act creating a school system, but no schools were ever opened under that law, although private schools opened and closed from time to time. In April 1827 another law was passed authorizing townships to establish a grammar school. It is unclear when Detroit's grammar school actually first held classes. It may have been as late as 1832.

35. *Id.*, 527–637 (history of Detroit's religious congregations and buildings).

36. *Id.*, 357–58 (theaters); 597–642 (churches); 695 (bookstore); 711 (societies).

37. *NWJ*, November 20, 1830.

38. "An Act to divide the Indiana Territory into two separate governments," sec. 2, *Stat.* 2: 309 (January 11, 1805).

39. This description is a simplification of the fractious, sometimes chaotic, progress of legislation in the Michigan territory's early days. For a more detailed account, see Blume, "Legislation on the American Frontier," 341–72.

40. "An Act to amend the ordinance and acts of Congress for the government of the territory of Michigan, and for other purposes," *Stat.* 3: 769 (March 3, 1823).

41. "An Act to allow the citizens of the territory of Michigan to elect the members of their legislative council, and for other purposes," *Stat.* 4: 200 (January 29, 1827).

42. *Laws of the Territory of Michigan* (Detroit: Sheldon McKnight, 1827).

43. "An Act to enforce the observance of the Sabbath," *LTM* 2: 303–4 (March 12, 1827).

44. "An Act for the Prevention of Immoral Practices," sec. 5, *LTM* 2:606–7 (April 13, 1827) (barring "any puppet show, wire dancing, or tumbling, juggling, or sleight of hand" performed for profit).

45. "An Act to prevent Horse Racing," *LTM* 1: 417 (October 12, 1819).

46. "An Act to prevent Gaming," sec. 6, *LTM* 1: 412, 415 (October 12, 1819).

47. *Id.*, sec. 1, at 412.

48. *Id.*, sec. 2, at 413.

49. "An Act relative to Nine-pin alleys," *LTM* 3: 821 (July 21, 1830) ("the playing at Nine-Pins [so called], is productive of great waste of time, and leads to habits of idleness and dissipation, and is attended with great noise and disturbance"). Passage of Act noted in *NWJ*, September 1, 1830.

50. Blume, "Territorial Courts, Part II" at 489, quoting from *James Grant v. Thomas, Earl of Selkirk, TSCM* 3: 431, 436.

51. Blume, *id.*, at 490, quoting from *Josette Lariviere v. Joseph Campau, TSCM* 5: 305, 309–13.

52. "An Act for the Punishment of Crimes," *LTM* 2: 542–57 (April 12, 1827).

53. Gilpin, 26–27.

54. Farmer, 201.

55. Woodbridge Papers, U.S. Cases Folder, *U.S. v. Mary Socier, dit Brown* (bawdy house); *U.S. v. Alexander McArthur* (gambling den).

56. Farmer, 671–72.

57. The anonymous author of a biographical sketch of John Roberts, the brother of Robert E. Roberts, reported that: "In the presidential campaign of 1828, when General Jackson was elected over Mr. [John Quincy] Adams, there were only three democrats in Detroit. They increased, however, very fast when it became known that Jackson was, or was to be, the president. It was easy to see how the cat was jumping. There were then two newspapers published in Detroit, one the Gazette, published by Sheldon & Reed, and the other the Michigan Herald, published by the late Judge Chipman. These had both been Adams papers, but it was said that they had run a sharp race to see which would get over first when it was known that Jackson was elected. The Gazette succeeded and became a democratic paper, while the other, as a matter of policy, remained an opposition journal." "Biographical Sketch of John Roberts," 224.

58. MacCabe, 33.

59. Whitney's devotion to the cause of temperance is apparent from the amount of space devoted to it in his newspaper.

60. MacCabe, 95 (George Whitney listed as church's organist).

61. Farmer, 672; *Early Days*, 332–33.

62. Farmer, 686.

63. Dain, 16–17.

64. *Early Land Transfers* 4: 208.

65. *Id.* At about this time, Stephen must have received word of the death of his brother William Simmons at the age of about sixty-five years. William had moved to Coshocton County, Ohio, in 1821 with his son, Charles W. Simmons, to run the federal land office there. The Court of Common Pleas of Coshocton County appointed Charles the administrator of the estate of his father, "late of the county aforesaid," on December 10, 1825. Coshocton County, Ohio, Records, Will Book 2b, page 81.

66. Johnson received his patent in October of that year. Peck, *Landsmen of Wayne County*, 147; *Memories of a Community*, 4.

67. Orange Risdon's 1825 map showing the tavern's location and a map showing the first landowners in Wayne are reproduced on the interior of the front cover of *Memories of a Community*. The building now on the tavern site, formerly a branch of the National Bank of Detroit and more recently an antique store, has a Michigan Historical Commission marker commemorating the history of "Johnson's Tavern," including the Simmons murder case.

68. *Early Land Transfers* 4: 208.

69. *Id.*

70. *Chen. Rec.*, September 17, 1828.

71. *NWJ*, September 29, 1830.

72. Peck, *Landsmen of Wayne County*, 85, 86, 112, 156, 157, 259.

73. See James Smith, 1: 385; Hyde.

74. Peck, *Landsmen of Wayne County*, 85, 86, 112, 156, 157, 259; James Smith, 1: 385 (Moss's business interests); http://www.Ancestry.com (Moss family information).

75. Such a tenancy contract was the basis for the lawsuit between Stephen and William H. St. Clair discussed in Chapter 4. See *Jour. A*, June 11, 1830.

76. *Wayne Prob.*, Case 440, inventory of assets of estate.

77. *Memories of a Community*, 5.

78. "An Act to regulate Taverns," sec. 1, *LTM* 2: 417 (April 12, 1827). Other merchants could only sell alcohol in bulk (e.g., a quart or more of liquor, a gallon or more of beer) and could not allow consumption on their premises. *Id.*, sec. 4. However, there is some doubt as to the extent to which this law was enforced. In January 1830 Judge Woodbridge of the Michigan Supreme Court complained bitterly about the large number of unlicensed merchants in the county selling alcohol illegally. *NWJ*, January 27, 1830.

79. The Governor and Judges first regulated taverns in the original Woodward Code of 1805. "An Act concerning ferries, tavern-keepers, and retailers of merchandise," sec. 7–10, *LTM* 1:42–43 (August 29, 1805). They increased the regulatory controls on taverns twelve years later. "An Act to regulate Taverns," *LTM* 1: 407–12 (September 10, 1819). The elected Legislative Council reenacted that law in 1827. "An Act to regulate Taverns," *LTM* 2: 417–19 (April 12, 1827).

80. "An Act to regulate Taverns," sec. 2, *LTM* 2: 417 (April 12, 1827).

81. *Id.*, sec. 3.

82. *Id.*, sec. 7.

83. *Id.*, sec. 8, 9.

84. Dewey, 528.

85. *Memories of a Community*, 5.

86. Julia Moore, 1:106–7 ("Ten Eyck tavern a wild and rough place"); Dewey, 528 ("Ten Eyck Tavern 8 miles from Simmons' tavern").

87. Van Buren, "Pioneer Annals," 244.

88. *Early Land Transfers* 4: 208.

89. Nowlin, illustration facing p. 40.

90. *Journal of Ferry and Tavern Licenses*, October 25, 1826.

91. *Id.*, January 2, 1827.

92. *Id.*, February 10, 1828.

93. Norris, 510–11.

94. Van Buren, "Deacon Isaac Mason," 397.

95. Although they differ on many other details, the chroniclers of this incident, beginning with the contemporary newspaper accounts, are unanimous in citing Stephen's alcoholic excesses. See, *e.g.*, *NWJ*, September 29, 1830.

96. Larkin, 286.

97. Crawford, 590 (The author recalled "one Chittenden, with his whiskey factory at full blast, making medicine to kill the ague and cure mississauga bites [. . .].") ; Blois, 127 ("[T]he diseases most prevalent in Michigan, are such as have their origin in *malaria*, or marsh exhalations."). For other folk remedies, see Van Buren, "The Fever and Ague," 301–2; Hoyt, 426–29.

98. Larkin, 284 (alcohol was considered "an essential stimulant to exertion").

99. *Id.*, 284–85.

100. Buley, 1: 370.

101. *History of Oakland County*, 168–69, recounts two such failures in Farmington Township in the 1830s. In both of those instances, the more sober citizenry reluctantly conceded that a barn could not be raised without the "strong reinforcement" of liquor.

102. Colborn, 60–61.

103. *History of Oakland County*, 233.

104. Larkin, 295.

105. *NWJ*, February 24, 1830.

106. "Detroit Young Men's Temperance Society," 457. Founded in February 1835, the society did not require absolute abstention. Instead, members resolved to avoid "immoderate use of wine" and to use "ardent spirits" only "when required as a medicine." *Id.*, 458.

107. *Detroit Journal and Michigan Advertiser*, April 22, 1834.

108. See, *e.g.*, Cohen, 150–74.

109. Colton, 1:49.

110. *NWJ*, July 21, 1830 (note incorrect date in internal masthead).

111. *Id.*, September 29, 1830.

112. *Id.*
113. *Id.*, July 21, 1830.
114. Larkin, 287.
115. *Id.*, 286.

CHAPTER 4

1. *E.g.*, Jerome Sr., 17–18; *Story*, 290. During the middle decades of the nineteenth century, Michigan's temperance movement watched what had seemed to be a victory slip from its grasp. In 1855 the legislature prohibited the manufacture or sale of intoxicating liquors, but enforcement proved to be impossible. Two years after the law was passed, Detroit still had 420 operating saloons, fifty-six hotel and tavern bars, twenty-three breweries, and six distilleries, and in 1875 the prohibition law was repealed. Dunbar, 352–53. Smarting from that defeat, temperance advocates tended to emphasize the anti-alcohol aspects of any story, historical or current, to the exclusion of other, distracting factors.

2. Although Chenango County did not keep marriage or birth records in the 1820s, it may be that the McCartys were married in 1822, when Catharine received a gift of land from her uncle William. *Chen. Rec.* November 30, 1822. The probate court file on Stephen's estate contains a contract dated November 11, 1829, in which a James Maybee agreed to subcontract some road-building work for "Pat McHarry." *Wayne Prob.*, Case 440. That "McHarry," who must have been Mr. McCarty, signed the contract with a mark instead of a signature. McCarty did not pay Maybee, who, apparently, tried to collect from Stephen's estate instead.

3. *Wayne Prob.*, Case 440, (Claim of Elias W. Skinner).

4. "An Act concerning divorces," sec. 1, 4, *LTM* 2: 363–64 (April 12, 1827). In 1832 the Council added impotency as a ground for divorce. "An Act concerning divorce," sec. 1, *LTM* 3: 931 (June 28, 1832). Under both laws, a divorce *a mensa e thoro*, a kind of legal separation, was available on the sole on ground of extreme cruelty. The 1832 act added wilful desertion as a permissible basis for divorce *a mensa e thoro*.

5. "An Act for the relief of Mary C. Yancey," *LTM* 2: 665 (June 3, 1828). The Council granted Mary C. Yancey a divorce from Smith H. Yancey because he had abandoned her "for several years past."

6. The last recorded legislative divorces were awarded to Clarissa Remington and Martha Garlic. "An Act for the relief of Clarissa Remington," *LTM* 3: 907 (March 4, 1831); "An Act for the relief of Martha Garlic," *Id.*

7. *TSCM* 5: xlii, 134–35.

8. "An act for the relief of Catharine M'Carty," *LTM* 3: 840 (July 31, 1830).

9. "An Act in addition to the several acts concerning the Supreme, Circuit and County Courts of the Territory of Michigan, defining their jurisdiction and powers, and directing the pleadings therein in certain cases," sec. 11, *LTM* 2:7 59, 761 (November 5, 1829).

10. Benjamin Woodworth, county coroner and proprietor of the Steamboat Hotel, made a claim against Stephen's estate in the amount of $11.21 "on account." *Wayne Prob.*, Case 440 (Claim of Benjamin Woodworth).

11. *St. Clair v. Simmons,* Wayne County Docket, 1830 Term, Woodbridge Papers ("since Thursday June 10 on trial"); *Jour. A,* June 11, 1830 (Woodbridge and Chipman presiding).

12. *St. Clair v. Simmons,* notes, Legal-Misc. Folder, Woodbridge Papers.

13. *Id.*

14. Unless otherwise stated, details about the murder are from the account in *NWJ,* July 21, 1830, which claimed to be based on the trial testimony.

15. Colton, 1: 52.

16. *Memories of a Community,* 6.

17. By law, the sheriff was in charge of all "gaols and prisons" in the county. "An Act concerning sheriffs," sec. 7, *LTM* 2: 376, 378 (April 12, 1827).

18. *(Pontiac, Mich.) Oakland Chronicle,* July 30, 1830.

19. *Wayne Prob.*, Case 440, claim of Marshal Chapin, M.D.

20. *NWJ,* September 29, 1830.

21. *(Pontiac, Mich.) Oakland Chronicle,* June 18, 1830.

22. The third newspaper in the territory, the *(Monroe) Michigan Sentinel,* copied the *Chronicle*'s story in its issue dated July 10, 1830.

23. *Wayne Prob.*, Case 440 (Claim of Owen Aldrich).

24. *Id.* (Claim of Randall S. Rice, M.D.); (Claim of Marshal Chapin, M.D.).

25. *NWJ,* June 23, 1830.

26. Pap. in Box., 180.

27. *NWJ,* January 27, 1830 (Wendell, Cook, and Rucker listed as members of a committee of the grand jury that sent a note to Chief Judge Woodbridge asking for a written copy of his instructions to the grand jurors).

28. The makeup of this grand jury was the subject of controversy. Under an 1827 statute, the grand jury was supposed to have been selected annually from men nominated by township officials.

29. *Jour. A,* June 16, 1830. Sutherland's bond was posted by Jesse Osborn. *Id.,* June 21, 1830.

30. *Id.,* June 17, 1830.

31. *Wayne Prob.*, Case 440 (Claim of Levi Cook for store purchases by the deceased).

32. There is no evidence as to the disposition of Levana's body. However, Stephen's corpse was returned home for burial, and it is reasonable to assume that the same was done for Levana.
33. Pap. in Box., 180.
34. Russell, 118 (1820 U.S. Census), 160 (1827 Territorial Census).
35. *Jour.* A, June 17, 1830.
36. Pap. in Box., 180.
37. *Id.*, 31; *Jour.* A, June 18, 1830.
38. *Jour.* A, June 19, 1830.
39. *Id.*, June 24, 1830.
40. Farmer, 186.
41. Pap. in Box., 180–81.
42. *Wayne Prob.*, Case 440 (Claim of Owen Aldrich).
43. *NWJ*, September 29, 1830.
44. "An Act for the Punishment of Crimes," *LTM* 2: 542–57 (April 12, 1827). Section 1 covered murder, sec. 2 manslaughter, and sec. 65 hanging.
45. *People v. Garbutt*, 17 Mich. 8 (1868) (opinion by Chief Justice Cooley).
46. *NWJ*, January 27, 1830. Woodbridge presumably made his comments in anticipation that the grand jury would be asked to indict Robert McLaren for killing his best friend in a drunken brawl. Although the judge did not name McLaren in his comments, McLaren's was the only other case of homicide tried in Wayne County in 1830. *Id.*, June 23, 1830.
47. *Id.*, January 27, 1830.
48. Holmes, 51–53.
49. *Id.*
50. "An Act for the Punishment of Crimes," sec. 58, *LTM* 2: 542, 547 (April 12, 1827).
51. *People v. Vasquez*, 184 Mich. App. 443 (1990).
52. The first criminal code enacted after Michigan became a state in 1836 did divide murder into first and second degrees. *Revised Statutes of the State of Michigan*, Part Fourth, Title I, ch. 3, sec. 1 (Detroit, 1838): 621. First degree murder, which included any homicide "perpetrated by means of poison or lying in wait, or any other kind of wilful, deliberate and premeditated killing, or which shall be committed in the perpetration or attempt to perpetrate any arson, rape, robbery, or burglary" carried a mandatory death penalty. The punishment "for all other murder" was imprisonment "for life, or any term of years." *Id.*, sec. 1. The punishment for manslaughter was imprisonment for not more than twenty years, a fine not to exceed $1000, or both. *Id.*, sec. 6.
53. Holmes, 55.
54. Blume, "Criminal Procedure," 294.

55. "An Act for the punishment of crimes," sec. 1, 57, and 61, *LTM* 1: 109 (November 4, 1815).

56. "An Act for the punishment of Crimes," sec. 1, 58, *LTM* 1: 561, 584–85 (May 17, 1820); "An act for the punishment of crimes," sec. 1, 58, *LTM* 2: 542, 556 (April 12, 1827).

57. Mackey, 111–12.

58. See Burgess-Jackson, 46–74, for a study of violent crimes in Michigan up to 1829.

59. *Detroit Gazette*, December 28, 1821.

60. *TSCM* 2: 485.

61. *Detroit Gazette*, December 28, 1821.

62. *TSCM* 2: 244.

63. *Detroit Gazette*, December 28, 1821.

64. *Id.*, July 4, 1826.

65. *Id.*, July 10, 1827.

66. Pap. in Box. 29, 30; *Detroit Gazette*, July 10, 1827 and January 17, 1828.

67. *Detroit Gazette*, August 27, 1829.

68. Pap. in Box., 30; *NWJ*, June 23, 1830.

69. *Exec. Jour.*, 1: 481–82, September 4, 1829.

70. Samuel Beach to Lewis Cass, September 24, 1829, William Lawler Papers, Burton Historical Collection, Detroit Public Library, Detroit, MI.

71. *Exec. Jour.*, 1: 486, October 24, 1829 (stay); Lewis Cass to Edward Biddle, December 8, 1829, William Lawler Papers, Burton Historical Collection, Detroit Public Library, Detroit, MI (transmittal of petition denial).

72. Muster Rolls, Company G, 5th Infantry Regt., December 31, 1829–February 28, 1830, National Archives. For a detailed and well-documented account of the Brown case, see Widder.

73. *Jour. A*, June 24, 1830.

74. *Jour. A*, July 6, 1830.

75. *Id.*, June 24, 1830; Roberts, "Recollections," 569.

76. Wayne County Grand Jury, "Report on Prisoners in County Jail," June 1830, Woodbridge Papers (Jail held ten inmates, including Levi Willard, who had been convicted of manslaughter).

77. Farmer, 215.

78. "An Act concerning Sheriffs," sec. 12, 16, *LTM* 2: 376, 379–80 (April 12, 1827).

79. *Id.*, sec. 16.

80. "An Act for Providing and Regulating Prisons," sec. 6, *LTM* 2: 384, 386 (April 12, 1827).

81. *Id.*, sec. 7.

82. *Id.*, sec. 10.

83. *Id.*, sec. 7.
84. *NWJ*, April 17, 1830.
85. *Id.*, January 27, 1830.
86. *Wayne Prob.*, Case 440 (Claim of Levi Cook for goods purchased by the deceased on credit).

CHAPTER 5

1. Riddell, 49, 57–58, 62.
2. *TSCM* 1: 41–43.
3. *Id.*, 3: 15, citing *Detroit Gazette*, January 2, 1824.
4. *TSCM* 5: 24, citing *NWJ*, September 15, 1830.
5. 287 U.S. 45 (1932).
6. "An Act regulating general proceedings in criminal cases," sec. 22, *LTM* 2: 459, 463 (April 12, 1827). For a discussion of this statute, see Blume, "Criminal Procedure," 242–43.
7. Cash bond, Stephen G. Simmons to Henry S. Cole, June 24, 1830, Case File 1443, Box 20, Supreme Court of Michigan Collection.
8. *Id.*, Mortgage (recorded in Mortgage Book 1, pages 85–86, Wayne County Records).
9. *Id.*, Note, Stephen G. Simmons to George A. O'Keeffe, July 5, 1830.
10. *Id.*, Mortgage, idem. (recorded in Mortgage Book 1, pages 80–81, Wayne County Records). The clerk, physician Randal S. Rice, apparently kept longer hours than is customary today—a notation on the mortgage states that it was recorded at 7 P.M.
11. *Early Days*, 218.
12. *TSCM* 5: 29.
13. *Early Days*, 316.
14. *Id.*, 482.
15. *Mich. Bios.*, s. v. O'Keeffe, George A.
16. George A. O'Keeffe to John Winder, April 6, 1828, John Winder Papers.
17. Farrand, 433.
18. *Early Days*, 482.
19. George Taylor, 15.
20. Buley 1: 370–71.
21. *Detroit Gazette*, March 12, 1834.
22. Colonel Stephen Mack (b. 1763, d. 1826), a prominent Oakland County pioneer, businessman, and founder of the City of Pontiac, Michigan, was the host of the party. He was a large man "of commanding appearance" and exuding great energy. *History of Oakland County*, 87.
23. Dr. Olmstead Chamberlain (b. 1787, d. 1876), another prominent pio-

neer, emigrated to Oakland County in 1821 from Richmond, Vermont. M. Agnes Burton, "Appendix," 14 *MPHC*, 687.

24. An unnamed biographer attributed this tale to John Roberts, the brother of Robert E. Roberts. "Biographical Sketch of John Roberts," 223–24.

25. *History of Oakland County*, 70–71.

26. *TSCM* 5: 37.

27. Ross, 154–55; "Biographical Sketch of John Roberts," 223–24.

28. *Early Days*, 814–15.

29. Unless otherwise stated, biographical details are from *TSCM* 5: 30.

30. *(Pontiac, Mich.) Oakland Chronicle*, July 30, 1830.

31. *Chronology of Notable Events*, 277; Witherell, 221–25.

32. Thomas W. Palmer, 103.

33. *TSCM* 2: 485; *Detroit Gazette*, December 28, 1821. This occurred about one year after O'Keeffe nearly hanged the Frenchman.

34. "An Act concerning the Supreme Court of the Territory of Michigan," 6, *LTM* 2: 60, 61 (February 18, 1809) (granting original and exclusive jurisdiction to the Supreme Court in capital cases); see Farmer, 179.

35. "An Act to divide the Indiana Territory into two separate governments," *Stat.* 1: 309 (January 11, 1805).

36. "An Act concerning the supreme court of the territory of Michigan," sec. 1, *LTM* 1: 9 (July 24, 1805).

37. *Id.*, sec. 2.

38. "An Act in addition to an act entitled 'An Act to amend the ordinance and acts of Congress for the government of the territory of Michigan,' and for other purposes," sec. 6, *Stat.* 4: 80–81 (February 5, 1825) (mandating that at least two judges must preside at any session of the Michigan Supreme Court); "An Act to amend an act entitled 'An Act concerning the Supreme Court, Circuit, and County Courts of the Territory of Michigan, defining their jurisdiction and powers, and directing the pleadings and practices therein in certain cases," sec. 1, *LTM* 2: 692 (July 2, 1828) (all circuit courts held east of Lake Michigan "shall hereafter be held by the judges of the Supreme Court, or a majority of them). For a detailed description of Michigan's judicial system during the period from 1825 to 1836, see *TSCM*, 5: 1–21.

39. "An Act concerning the Supreme and county courts of the Territory of Michigan, defining their jurisdiction and powers, and directing the pleadings and practice therein, in certain cases," sec. 5, *LTM* 2: 264, 265 (April 21, 1825).

40. "An Act concerning the Supreme Court and County courts of the Territory of Michigan, defining their jurisdiction and powers, and directing the pleadings and practices therein in certain cases," sec. 4, *LTM* 1: 714, 715 (December 21, 1820).

41. Congress granted that jurisdiction to the superior courts of all territories in 1805. "An Act to extend jurisdiction in certain cases, to the Territorial Courts," *Stat.* 2: 338 (March 3, 1805). In practice, most of those cases involved seizures of ships and goods for failure to pay customs. If such a case was not tried before the court adjourned, often the parties had no choice but to wait until the next federal session of the court, a year later, while the goods and the ship rotted away.

42. "An Act to amend an act entitled 'An Act concerning the Supreme Court, Circuit, and County Courts of the Territory of Michigan, defining their jurisdiction and powers, and directing the pleadings and practices therein in certain cases,'" sec. 1, *LTM* 2: 692 (July 2, 1828).

43. Burgess-Jackson, 51–53.

44. Charles Lanman, 32–34 (William Woodbridge to Charles Lanman, December 12, 1822).

45. *TSCM* 5: xxvii. In 1823 Congress did authorize a fourth territorial judge to hold court in Prairie du Chien, Green Bay, and Mackinac and decide all cases arising west and north of Lake Michigan. However, that judge did not sit on the Supreme Court. *Stat.* 3: 722 (January 30, 1823).

46. Rau, 25.

47. *History of Wayne County*, 563.

48. Farmer, 94–95.

49. *Id.*, 133–34.

50. *Mich. Bios.*, s.v. Sibley, Solomon.

51. *TSCM*, 4:423–24.

52. *Mich. Bios.*, s.v. Woodbridge, William.

53. Charles Lanman, 43.

54. *Id.*, 149.

55. May, 127.

56. For Cass's and Sibley's political affiliations, see Rau. I realize that describing a person as a Whig in 1830 or before is technically inaccurate because that name did not attach to the heirs of the Federalists and of John Quincy Adams until a few years later. However, for our purposes, Whig is a useful shorthand for the proponents of that tradition.

57. Predictably, in 1832, after national partisanship had reached Detroit in the form of the Jackson administration, the sociable Sibley managed to keep his judgeship while the more politically contentious Woodbridge and Henry Chipman were ousted in favor of Jacksonians George Morell and Ross Wilkins.

58. *Chronology of Notable Events*, 146–47.

59. *Id.*

60. Farmer, 671–72.

61. *TSCM* 5: 30.

62. *Chronology of Notable Events*, 146–47.
63. Rau, 266.
64. *Id.*, 289.
65. *Id.*, 266.

CHAPTER 6

1. *Jour. A*, July 6, 1830 (trial begins); *NWJ*, July 21, 1830 ("The weather is too warm").
2. Farmer, 185.
3. *Story*, 274–75; Farmer, 185.
4. "An Act to provide for the adjustment of titles of land in the town of Detroit and Territory of Michigan, and for other purposes," sec. 2, *Stat.* 2: 399 (April 21, 1806).
5. "An Act concerning the town of Detroit," *LTM* 1: 283, 284 (September 13, 1806).
6. "An additional Act concerning the city of Detroit," sec. 2, *LTM* 1: 289, 290 (November 7, 1815).
7. Farmer, 474.
8. *Id.*, 475.
9. "An Act for the relief of Thomas Palmer and David M'Kinstry," *LTM* 2: 676 (June 23, 1828).
10. Farmer, 475; May, 121.
11. Farmer, 745–49.
12. Roberts, *Sketches*, 96.
13. *Early Days*, 865.
14. Unless otherwise noted, the details of this day's court proceedings are taken from *Jour. A*, July 6, 1830.
15. See "An Act concerning juries," *LTM* 1: 35 (August 17, 1805); "An Act concerning Grand and Petit Jurors," *LTM* 1: 490 (February 7, 1820); "An Act to amend an act entitled 'An Act concerning Grand and Petit Jurors,' and for other purposes," *LTM* 1: 789 (February 2, 1821); and "An Act concerning grand and petit jurors," *LTM* 2: 653 (May 30, 1828).
16. *Id.*
17. "An Act authorizing the election of a delegate from the Michigan territory to the Congress of the United States, and extending the right of suffrage to the citizens of said territory," sec. 2, *Stat.* 3: 482–83 (February 16, 1819).
18. "An Act concerning grand and petit jurors," sec. 1, 2, *LTM* 2: 653 (May 30, 1828).
19. *Id.*, sec. 4.

20. *NWJ*, January 27, 1830.

21. *NWJ*, April 17, 1830.

22. *Detroit Gazette*, January 3, 1823.

23. "An Act concerning grand and petit jurors," sec. 14, *LTM* 2: 653, 657 (May 30, 1828).

24. "An Act regulating general proceedings in criminal cases," sec. 13, *Idem*, 2: 459, 462 (April 12, 1827). In 1828 the Council revised the jury statute to provide that, in capital cases, the defendant was to be allowed "such number [of peremptory challenges] as is by the common law allowed." However, the Council did not delete the thirty-five-juror provision of the criminal procedure statute, and both provisions were included in the Legislative Council's compilation of Michigan laws in force that was published in 1833, indicating that the Council viewed the common law and thirty-five-challenge provisions to be the same. The Simmons defense used only thirty-four peremptory challenges. A handwritten list of jurors called on July 8, apparently made by Judge Woodbridge, shows that he was keeping track of the number of peremptory challenges made by each side, indicating that he was prepared to limit Stephen to thirty-five peremptory challenges. Roster of jury candidates in *United States v. Simmons*, Legal-Misc. Folder, Woodbridge Papers.

25. "An Act concerning grand and petit jurors," sec. 13, *LTM* 2: 653, 657 (May 30, 1828).

26. *United States v. John Reed*, TSCM 5: 330–37 (January 3, 1829).

27. *Id.*, 333–34.

28. The Democratic *Gazette* inflamed emotions about the decision by Whigs Woodbridge and Chipman to overturn the conviction in order to create a firestorm of controversy in Detroit. The *Gazette* pointed out that because the defendant had not used all of his peremptory challenges and that the court could have held that the defendant had waived any error.

29. See Appendix B, a summary of the jury selection.

30. *Story*, 290; Edwin Jerome, Sr., 17. In another article George Catlin said 134, which was closer to the actual number. Catlin, "Early Settlement in Eastern Michigan," 332.

31. *Jour. A*, July 6, 8, 12, 1830.

32. While sentencing Stephen, Judge Woodbridge recalled "the trouble that was occasioned, and the expense incurred by our efforts to secure you a Jury that had not *prejudged* your case." *NWJ*, August 11, 1830.

33. *TSCM* 5: liv (population of Wayne County in 1830 included 6,781 people, of whom only 3,679 were "free white males" of any age).

34. Except where noted, all details of this day's court proceedings are from *Jour. A*, July 6, 1830.

35. *Early Days*, 476.

36. Except where noted, all details of this day's court proceedings are from *Jour. A*, July 7, 1830.

37. Farmer, 672; Pap. in Box., 31.

38. *Detroit Gazette*, April 22, 1830. This last issue of the *Gazette* contained that description of the missing watch.

39. *(Pontiac, Mich.) Oakland Chronicle*, July 30, 1830.

40. Farmer, 491.

41. Pap. in Box., 30.

42. Except where noted, all details of this day's court proceedings are from *Jour. A*, July 8, 1830.

43. "An Act regulating general proceedings in criminal cases," sec. 23, *LTM* 2: 459, 463 (April 12, 1827).

44. Russell, 122, n. 20.

45. *Jour. A*, July 7, 1830; Pap. in Box., 180.

46. Pap. in Box., 30.

47. *Jour. A*, June 14, 1830.

48. *United States v. Abraham Salsbury*, Crim. Case No. 39, Docket, June Term, 1830 Folder, Woodbridge Papers.

49. *United States v. Thomas Driscoll*, Crim. Case No. 51, *Id*.

50. *United States v. William and David Hudson*, Crim. Case No. 49, *Id*.

51. *United States v. Francis Matevier*, Crim. Case No. 54, *Id*.

52. Except where noted, all details of this day's court proceedings are from *Jour. A*, July 12, 1830.

53. *NWJ*, August 11, 1830.

54. Farmer, 125; *Early Days*, 69, 715.

55. Invoice, Guy H. Leonard to Solomon Sibley, February 23, 1830, Folder 12, 1830 file, Solomon Sibley Papers, Burton Historical Collection, Detroit Public Library, Detroit, MI.

56. *United States v. Martin and Mary Socier*, notes, "Legal-Misc." Folder, Woodbridge Papers.

57. Pap. in Box, 180.

58. *Id*., 180; Peck, *Landsmen of Lenawee*, 129.

59. *NWJ*, July 21, 1830.

60. Colton, 1: 48.

61. *Id*., 1: 51.

62. George Catlin to Clarence Burton, January 9, 1931, Catlin Papers.

63. Except where noted, all details of this day's court proceedings are from *Jour. A*, July 13, 1830.

64. *Story*, 290.

65. Except where noted, all details of this day's court proceedings are from *Jour. A*, July 14, 1830.

66. *NWJ*, July 14, 1830.
67. *Jour. A*, July 15, 1830.
68. *Id.*, July 19, 1830.
69. *Id.*, July 21, 1830.
70. *Id.*, July 22, 1830.
71. *United States v. Stephen G. Simmons,* notes of authorities cited, U.S. Cases, "S-Misc." Folder, Woodbridge Papers.
72. 2 US (2 Dall.) 335 (1795).
73. *Clinton v. Englebrecht,* 80 U.S. (13 Wall.) 434, 447 (1871)(opinion by Chase, Chief Justice).
74. *Jour. A*, July 22, 1830.
75. *NWJ*, July 28, 1830; *(Monroe) Michigan Sentinel,* July 31, 1830.
76. Colton, 1: 48–53 (description of Stephen's sentencing hearing).
77. *Dictionary of American Biography,* s.v. Colton, Calvin. Colton's fame must have been relatively brief. In 1884, when an excerpt of his book was reprinted in *MPHC*, the author was identified as "Colton (Cotton)" [sic]. Colton, "Remarkable Instance of Capital Crime," 103. The editor of that volume of *MPHC* tried to tone down the emotionalism of the piece by deleting all of Colton's eight exclamation points. The quotations in the present text use Colton's original punctuation. Colton was busy while in Detroit. On July 29, 1830, he sent a several-hundred-word letter to the *New York Gazette* describing Detroit in very favorable terms. The letter, attributed to an anonymous minister, was reprinted in *NWJ* on September 1, 1830, and Colton included its contents in his book (Colton, 1: 41–47).
78. *NWJ*, August 11, 1830.
79. Although he did not say so explicitly, the tone of his comments suggests that Judge Woodbridge was more than a little annoyed that the other judges maneuvered him into pronouncing the death sentence alone.
80. *NWJ*, August 11, 1830.
81. *Id.*, January 27, 1830.
82. *Jour. A*, July 26, 1830; *NWJ*, September 22, 1830.
83. Colton, 1: 52. At the sentencing of Ke-wa-bish-kim in 1821, Judge James Witherell had expressed a similar sentiment: "And may the Great Spirit purify, pardon and receive your Soul." *Detroit Gazette,* December 28, 1821.

CHAPTER 7

1. "An Act concerning sheriffs," sec. 7, 8, *LTM* 2: 376, 378 (April 12, 1827).

2. Farmer, 565.

3. *Early Days*, 705. This version also appears in *Story*, 290, and in Jerome Sr., 18.

4. *Exec. Jour.*, 2: 9, September 10, 1830 ("On this 10th day of September, A.D. 1830, the resignation of Thomas G. Knapp, Sheriff of Wayne County, was received, accepted, and filed in this office"); for some reason, the *North-Western Journal* did not report Knapp's resignation until its September 29 edition, which also carried the story of the hanging. *NWJ*, September 29, 1830 ("Thomas S. Knapp has resigned the office of the Sheriff of this County. Benjamin Woodworth, the Coroner, is acting Sheriff"). That may be why Edwin Jerome, Sr., recalled, almost fifty years later, that Knapp resigned "[o]n the morning of the execution." Jerome Sr., 18.

5. All previous accounts have given Knapp's exercise of his conscience as the sole reason for his resignation. E.g., *Early Days*, 705; Jerome Sr., 18; *Story*, 290.

6. See, e.g., "An Act concerning costs and fees," sec. 3, *LTM* 1: 766, 768–773 (January 23, 1821); "An Act for the relief of the poor," sec. 4, *LTM* 2: 115, 116 (November 25, 1817).

7. "An Act to regulate the assessment and collection of Territorial taxes," sec. 4, 6, *LTM* 2: 298–99 (December 30, 1826).

8. "An Act concerning Sheriffs, Coroners, and Constables," sec. 1, *LTM* 1: 220 (November 3, 1815).

9. "An Act to divide the Indiana Territory into two separate governments," *Stat.* 2: 399 (January 11, 1805), which adopted the Northwest Ordinance by reference.

10. "An Act in addition to an act entitled 'An act to amend the ordinance and acts of Congress for the government of the territory of Michigan,' and for other purposes," sec. 3, *Stat.* 4: 80–81 (February 5, 1825).

11. *TSCM* 6: 427 (Sheldon's certificate of appointment is dated September 25, 1826).

12. "An Act to provide for the termination of the present session of the Legislative Council and for the annual commencement of future sessions of the Council," *LTM* 2: 747–48 (November 4, 1829) (current session of Council to end November 5, 1829).

13. *Detroit Gazette*, January 14, 1830.

14. *NWJ*, July 14, 1830.

15. *Exec. Jour.*, 1: 492, December 30, 1829.

16. "An Act to provide for the government of the Territory North-West of the River Ohio," sec. 2, *Stat* 1: 50, 52 (August 7, 1789) (in the absence of the Governor, the Secretary is "authorized and required to execute all the powers, and perform all the duties of the governor"); "An Act in

addition to an act, entitled 'An act to amend the ordinance and Acts of Congress for the government of the territory of Michigan' and for other purposes," Sec. 3, *Stat.* 4: 80(February 5, 1825) (power to make recess appointments).

17. "An Act concerning Sheriffs," sec. 4, *LTM* 2: 376 (April 12, 1827).

18. *Exec. Jour.*, 1: 492, January 5, 1830.

19. "An Act concerning Sheriffs," sec. 2, *LTM* 2: 376 (April 12, 1827).

20. *Detroit Gazette*, January 14, 1830.

21. "An Act in addition to an act, entitled 'An act to amend the ordinance and Acts of Congress for the government of the territory of Michigan' and for other purposes," sec. 3, *Stat.* 4:80 (February 5, 1825) (term of recess appointments).

22. *Exec. Jour.*, 1: 495, April 6, 1830.

23. *NWJ*, July 14, 1830.

24. *Id.*, July 21, 1830.

25. *Id.*, July 14, 1830. On January 28, 1831, Major Levi Cook, B. F. H. Witherell, and Henry Cole were members of a committee formed to thank the Council for opposing the 1829 and 1830 nominations of Thomas C. Sheldon for Sheriff. "Copies of Papers," 585.

26. "An Act concerning Sheriffs," sec. 4, *LTM* 2: 376 (April 12, 1827).

27. *NWJ*, September 29, 1830.

28. "An Act concerning Coroners," sec. 3, *LTM* 2: 565 (April 12, 1827).

29. E.g., *Story*, 290–91; Massie, 46–47; *Early Days*, 705.

30. *Exec. Jour.*, 2: 17 December 1, 1830.

31. *Detroit Courier*, January 20, 1831.

32. Roberts, *Detroit One Hundred Years Ago*, 88.

33. *Early Days*, 216.

34. *Id.*

35. Gilpin, 26.

36. "An addition to an Act concerning the Marshal of the Territory of Michigan," *LTM* 1: 215 (September 13, 1805); "An Act concerning Sheriffs, Coroners and Constables," *id.* 1: 220 (November 3, 1815).

37. E. Williams, 86.

38. MacCabe, 105; Farmer, 480. This location is now the entrance to the motor vehicle tunnel under the Detroit River between Detroit and Windsor, Ontario.

39. Farmer, 357.

40. Mackey, 108–09.

41. Larkin, 294.

42. Farmer, 215; *Early Days*, 705.

43. Farmer, 916.

44. Davenport to Wayne County, invoice for scaffold, September 20, 1830, Woodbridge Papers.

45. *Id.*; "An Act making certain appropriations," *LTM* 1: 249 (January 21, 1822). Sheriff Austin A. Wing received $176.55 for his services in the court and at the hanging of "a certain Indian," and Marshal Rowland was reimbursed $33.88 for erecting the gallows.

46. *Id.*, 47–48; Frank Anderson, 70–71.

47. *Detroit Gazette*, December 28, 1821.

48. *NWJ*, September 29, 1830; Farmer, 181.

49. *Wayne Prob.*, Case 440 (Claim of Levi Cook). Cook sold Stephen, between July 14 and September 23, 1830, one-and-three-quarters gallon of brandy and three-and-a-half pounds of tobacco.

50. "An Act to amend the ordinance and acts of Congress for the government of the territory of Michigan, and for other purposes," sec. 5, *Stat.* 3: 769, 770 (March 3, 1823): "the governor . . . shall have power to grant pardons for offences against the laws of said territory. . . ."

51. *Exec. Jour.*, 1: 471 (October 28, 1828) (in 1828 acting Governor James Witherell, one day after Governor Cass left the Territory, "respited" two Indians convicted of committing murder at Green Bay); *TSCM* 1: 51 (in 1807 Governor Hull pardoned Kiscakon, also known as "the Chippewa Rogue," because the defendant's father was an influential chief).

52. "An Act for Providing and Regulating Prisons," sec. 6, *LTM* 2: 384, 386 (April 12, 1827).

53. *NWJ*, September 29, 1830.

54. Comin, 27 (account of Parson Wells's life and ministry). His tenure in Detroit is also noted in MacCabe, 21–22; and in Farmer, 594–95.

55. *NWJ*, September 29, 1830.

56. *Id.*

57. *Id.*

58. *Wayne Prob.*, Case 440 (Last Will and Testament of Stephen G. Simmons). This will, in Henry Cole's handwriting and bearing Stephen's distinctive signature, was submitted to probate on January 17, 1831.

59. Pap. in Box., 180.

60. Farmer, 210.

61. *Early Days*, 706.

62. Farmer, 57–58 (list of city sextons and a description of the duties of their office, including burying all Protestant dead).

63. B. O. Williams, 549.

64. Nowlin, 50–51.

65. Thomas Palmer, 106.

66. *Mich. Bios.*, s.v. Cook, Levi; Burton, "Detroit in the Year 1832," 164–65; Farmer, 140.

67. *Jour. A*, July 8, 1830.

68. "First Presby.," 423 (Levi Cook was a Trustee of Detroit's Presbyterian Church).

69. Williams, 86.
70. Wilber, 2: 234.
71. See Appendix A.
72. *Chen. Rec.*, November 30, 1822.

CHAPTER 8

1. *Early Days*, 706.
2. *Id.*, 704.
3. "Great Gala Hanging."
4. Bishop, "Biographical Sketch," 477.
5. Osband, 444.
6. *NWJ*, September 29, 1830.
7. In 1830 Detroit had a population of 2,222. Woodford, *All Our Yesterdays*, 135.
8. According to the 1830 U.S. Census, there were 18,921 residents living in Wayne, Oakland, Monroe, and Washtenaw counties. Gilpin, 98.
9. Miller, 231–32.
10. *Exec. Jour.*, 2: 11, September 24, 1830 ("On this 24 Sep. 1830 His Excellency Lewis Cass left the seat of Government of the Territory on a visit to Ohio.").
11. "Great Gala Hanging."
12. *Id.*
13. "Scene of Detroit's Last Hanging in 1830," *Detroit News-Tribune,* December 22, 1900.
14. *NWJ*, September 29, 1830; Jerome Sr., 17–18; "Great Gala Hanging"; "Hanged in 1830"; *Early Days*, 705.
15. *Early Days*, 705.
16. Roberts, "Recollections," 567.
17. *City of Detroit*, 1156 (Eben Willcox, b. Detroit 1821; d. Detroit 1891).
18. Palmer described Witherell's home in 1830 as both a small yellow cottage (*Early Days*, 540) and a two-story dwelling (*Id.*, 705), located on the Campus Martius where the opera house stood in 1906 (*Id.*). The building that housed the Detroit Opera House in 1906 was on the eastern edge of the Campus Martius, according to photographs. Poremba, 118. Judging by the Soldiers and Sailors Monument, the only nineteenth-century structure still standing on the Campus Martius, the rear of Witherell's lot was probably no more than two hundred feet from the site of the scaffold. Friend Palmer was related to B. F. H. Witherell in two ways: Witherell's sister Mary was the mother of Palmer's cousin Thomas W. Palmer (who later, as Senator Palmer, donated the land for Palmer

Park), and Friend Palmer later married one of B. F. H. Witherell's daughters. *Early Days*, 92–93.

19. "Great Gala Hanging."
20. Farmer, 225.
21. Farmer, 317. According to Farmer, the City Guards were not organized until April 6, 1831.
22. *Early Days*, 705.
23. *Detroit Free Press*, January 31, 1879.
24. *Id.* The Senate voted to submit the petition to a committee for consideration. There is no evidence that the petition was ever acted on.
25. *NWJ*, September 29, 1830.
26. "Great Gala Hanging."
27. "Hanged in 1830."
28. *Wayne Prob.*, Case 440 (Claim of Levi Cook).
29. Watkins, 63.
30. Catlin to Clarence Burton, January 9, 1931, Catlin Papers.
31. *Wayne Prob.*, Case 440 (Account of Levi Cook).
32. Van Buren, "Pioneer Annals of Calhoun County," *MPHC* 5: 237, 244 (1882).
33. *Story*, 292–93: "[Simmons] sat looking over the throng of witnesses while the death warrant was read, and then arose and delivered an able address in which he confessed his faults, warned all in his hearing to beware of strong drink and said that he had hoped for the mercy of the court and of the Governor. Then in a strong baritone voice of excellent quality he sang a familiar hymn of the period . . ."
34. *The Hymn Tune Index,* Index Nos. SPLOLF2 and SPLOLF3, http://www.hti.music.uiuc.edu.
35. Jerome Sr., 11. Although Jerome gave this speech at the Society's 1877 annual meeting, it did not appear in print until 1880, when the proceedings of the 1877 annual meeting were published. Edwin Jerome, Sr., died in Detroit on June 21, 1880.
36. Masur, 26.
37. *Early Days*, 868; *Early Days in Detroit* is a chaotic, thousand-page compilation of newspaper articles, memorabilia, and odds and ends collected by Palmer over many years. The book was never edited or indexed properly because the author died just as that process was beginning, and his friends rushed the volume into print as a memorial to "the General." Thus, for example, although there is no entry for Stephen G. Simmons in the index, Palmer mentions him and the hanging in two different parts of the book.
38. "Hanged in 1830."
39. Jerome Jr., 426.

40. *TCSM* 5: xlii–xliii; Burgess-Jackson, 57–60.
41. *Detroit Gazette*, January 10, 1826.
42. Pap. in Box. 1–2.
43. *E.g.*, Jerome Sr., 17.
44. *NWJ*, August 11, 1830.
45. Appleby, 165. This phenomenon is discussed at length at *id.*, 161–93.
46. See Theodor Reik, *Myth and Guilt* (New York: George Braziller, Inc., 1957), 18–33. I thank Dr. Israel Woronoff for his insight on this issue.

CHAPTER 9

1. Banner, 91–92.
2. *Id.*, 99.
3. For a detailed exposition of the campaign in New York (and some details regarding Pennsylvania) during the end of the eighteenth and the first half of the nineteenth centuries, see Mackey, 36–166. The writings of individual reformers include Cesare Beccaria, *On Crimes and Punishment*, trans. David Young (Indianapolis: Hackett Pub. Co., 1986, first published 1764); Benjamin Rush, *Considerations on the injustice and impolicy of punishing murder by death* (Philadelphia, 1792); Samuel Whelpley, *Letters addressed to Caleb Strong* (New York, 1816); Edward Livingston, *Remarks on the Expediency of Abolishing the Punishment of Death* (Philadelphia, 1831).
4. Widder, 9.
5. See *Id.* 10; Henry Schoolcraft to George B. Porter, Superintendent, July 31, 1833, *Letters Received 1819–1835, Records of the Michigan Superintendency of Indian Affairs*, Microfilm Roll 33 (June-December 1833), Library of Michigan. The defendant was tried by the United States Attorney and was convicted under a federal statute, "An Act to provide for the punishment of crimes and offences committed within the Indian boundaries," *Stat.* 3: 383 (March 3, 1817). See Michilimackinac Circuit Ct. Docket Book, 1823–41, Michigan Supreme Court Papers, oversize vol. 22, p. 34, Bentley Historical Library.
6. Robert Stuart, Agent, American Fur Company, at Michilimackinac, to George B. Porter, Superintendent, August 1, 1833, *Letters Received 1819–1835, Records of the Michigan Superintendency of Indian Affairs*, Microfilm Roll 33 (June-December 1833), Library of Michigan.
7. *Oakland Chronicle* (Pontiac, MI), December 3, 1830.
8. *Messages of the Governors* 1: 64–65.
9. *Democratic Free Press* (Detroit), August 21, 1833; the same issue reprinted excerpts from Edward Livingston's *Report Made to the General*

Assembly of the State of Louisiana, on the Plan of a Penal Code for the said State (New Orleans, 1822). It is striking that this issue of the *Free Press*, published less than ten days before White Thunder was executed, does not mention his case.

10. "An Act relative to proceedings in criminal cases," sec. 2, *LTM* 3: 904 (March 4, 1831) (providing "that no person shall be punished for any offence [sic] by whipping").

11. "An Act for the punishment of Idle and Disorderly Persons," *LTM* 1: 588 (July 27, 1818).

12. See, generally, Dorr, "The Michigan Constitution."

13. *History of Oakland County,* 109, 168.

14. Dorr. *The Michigan Constitutional Convention,* 85.

15. *Id.,* 349.

16. *Id.*

17. *Democratic (Detroit) Free Press,* June 12, 1835.

18. Dorr, *The Michigan Constitutional Convention,* Appendix A, roll call 53, pp. 349–50.

19. Dorr, *The Michigan Constitutional Convention,* 451–52; *Michigan Sentinel* (Monroe), June 20, 1835.

20. *Democratic (Detroit) Free Press,* June 12, 1835.

21. "An Act providing for the preparing, digesting, and arranging a code of laws," *Michigan Public Acts of 1836* (March 8, 1836), 128.

22. *Senate Journal* (January 12, 1838), 47 [Cook proposal]

23. *Revised Statutes of the State of Michigan,* Part Fourth, title I, Ch. 3, 1 (1838).

24. *Id.,* Ch. 8, sec. 9.

25. *Id.,* Ch. 8, sec. 10.

26. E.g., Mackey, 115–19. That argument still has its adherents. See John D. Bessler, *Death in the Dark* (Boston: Northeastern University Press, 1997).

27. Neal, 111–15

28. *Id.,* 112–13

29. For a detailed study of the Fitzpatrick case, see Coffey. Although the existence of this case had been rumored among historians for decades, there was no proof until Professor Coffey and Dr. Morton tirelessly tracked down the facts from original sources.

30. Bishop, "Recollections." Although the title of this essay refers to "1838–39," the uprisings in Canada actually took place in 1837 and 1838. For a history, see *William Kilbern, The Firebrand: William Lyon McKenzie and the Rebellion in Upper Canada* (Toronto: Clarke Irwin, 1956).

31. Bishop, "Recollections"; *Early Days,* 113.

32. See Reid.

33. See *Michigan Biographies,* s.v. Anderson, Samuel F.; Littlejohn, Flavius.

34. *Michigan Western Statesman* (Marshall), April 28, 1846. For a perceptive analysis of possible patterns in, and reasons for, the 1843 and 1846 legislative voting on captial punishment, see Bennett.

35. *Democratic Free Press* (Detroit), January 30–February 10, 1843. January 30 (summary), February 3 (Littlejohn, Livermore, Purdy), February 4 (Bush), February 6 (Johnson, Vickery, Anderson), February 7 (Gage), February 9 (Littlejohn, Mottram), February 10 (Snow). Unfortunately, the paper did not print the speeches of O'Keefe and McLeod.

36. Banner, 113–14.

37. *House Journal* 194 (January 28, 1843).

38. *Id.* 210 (January 31 1843).

39. *Senate Journal* 158 (February 3, 1843) [adverse report]; *id.* 216 (February 7, 1843) [vote to strike all after the enacting clause].

40. *House Journal* 534 (March 9, 1843).

41. *Id.* 461 (March 7, 1843)

42. *Revised Statutes of the State of Michigan* (Detroit: Bagg and Harmon, 1846), introductory "Advertisement" by Sanford M. Green.

43. "An Act to provide for consolidating and revising the general laws of the State of Michigan," *Michigan Public Acts of 1844*, No. 26 (March 2, 1844).

44. *Id.* The legislature originally created a "council of revision" consisting of the commissioner and two judges to propose such changes as they agreed upon. However, the judges did not want to undertake the effort, and, a few days later, the act was amended to allow the commissioner to proceed alone. *Id.*, No. 93 (March 12, 1844).

45. *Senate Journal on the Revision*, 82 (April 25, 1846).

46. *Id.*, 86 (April 27, 1846).

47. *House Journal*, 514–15 (April 22, 1846).

48. *Id.*, 548 (April 29, 1846).

49. *Senate Journal on the Revision*, 91 (May 4, 1846).

50. The effective date set by the legislature for most parts of the new code. *Revised Statutes of the Sate of Michigan*, (Detroit: Bagg and Harmon, 1846), ch. 173, sec. 1

51. *Id.*, ch. 153, sec. 1. In fact, Michigan, like most other states, did retain capital punishment for treason against the state (*Id.*, ch. 152). However, the state treason statute was never used and was probably unconstitutional in any case.

52. *Detroit Weekly Advertiser*, February 23, 1847.

53. *Id.*, January 18, 1848. The speech was published as George Duffield, *The Divine Organic Law Ordained for the Human Race* (Detroit, 1848).

54. Pap. in Box, 46, 47.

55. Bingham, 101.

56. Lincoln, 1785; Wanger 768–69.
57. *Journal of the Constitutional Convention of 1867*, 645–46.
58. See returns in *Michigan Official Manual and Directory for 1931–32* (Lansing, 1932).
59. *House Journal*, 1066, 1715, 1914 (1952); *Senate Journal*, 1390 (1952).
60. See Mr. Wanger's own modest account of his victory, Wanger, 771–73.
61. Lincoln, 787.
62. See *Michigan Constitution of 1963*, Article XII.
63. Masur, 157.
64. See Bennett, 51–55.
65. Banner, 123–24.
66. Bennett, 51–55
67. Larkin, 294.
68. Masur, 26.
69. Wilber, 226–30.

CHAPTER 10

1. *History of Wayne County*, 563.
2. *Id.*, 560–61.
3. *TSCM* 5: 30–31.
4. Bald, 220, 225.
5. *Mich. Bios.*, s.v. Woodbridge, William; for an account of Woodbridge's political career, see Charles Lanman.
6. Assignment of bond, Henry S. Cole to George A. O'Keeffe, February 7, 1831, Case 1443, Box 20, Supreme Court of Michigan Collection.
7. *Id.*, Complaint, June 10, 1834.
8. *Id.*; *TSCM* 5: 147; *Memories of a Community*, 6.
9. Report of Master Charles Whipple, June 25, 1836, Case File 1443, Box 20, Supreme Court of Michigan Collection.
10. Recorded in Mortgage Book 4, page 290, Wayne County Records.
11. *Detroit Daily Free Press*, June 18, 1853. For a biographical sketch of George A. O'Keeffe, see Chardavoyne, 1581–83.
12. Burton, "Detroit in the Year 1832," 167.
13. J. Wilkie Moore, 414; *Mich. Bios.*, s.v. Cook, Levi.
14. *Wayne Prob.*, Case 440 (Petition of Levi Cook to act as sole executor).
15. *Id.* (Final account of Levi Cook, Executor).
16. *TSCM* 5: 29.
17. *Early Days*, 516.
18. Burton, *City of Detroit*, 1156.

19. *Detroit Courier*, January 20, 1831.
20. "An Act for the Relief of Benjamin Woodworth and for other purposes," *LTM* 3: 906 (March 4, 1831).
21. *Story*, 407.
22. Comin, 27.
23. *Id.*, 27.
24. Roberts, "Recollections," 568; *Early Days*, 170; *Story*, 301–2.
25. *Detroit Courier*, August 6, 1834 ("Died in Detroit, August 4, Mrs. Mary Ann S. Witherell, consort of B. F. H. Witherell, aged 28 years."); *id.*, September 3, 1834 (obituary of "Thomas S. Knapp, aged 35 years, one of the Aldermen of the City."); *Early Days*, 542. By contrast, during the first nine months of 1830, a period free from epidemics, Oakland County reported only six deaths, from all causes, from a population of 6,000. *(Pontiac, Mich.) Oakland Chronicle*, October 8, 1830.
26. *Mich. Bios.*, s.v. Witherell, Benjamin Franklin Hawkins.
27. *History of Wayne County*, 560–61.
28. George Catlin to Mary Lacey, June 13, 1924, Catlin Papers.
29. These details of Friend Palmer's life are compiled from an editorial footnote to Palmer, "Ferry Service between Detroit and Windsor," and from the editor's preface to *Early Days*.
30. Farmer, 71, 140.
31. *Id.*, 506, 705, 839.
32. *Dictionary of American Biography*, s.v. Colton, Calvin.
33. *Early Land Transfers* 6: 43.
34. *Id.*, 7: 19.
35. *Marriages in Washtenaw*, Book O, p. 136; *Id.*, p. 156.
36. *Wayne Prob.*, Case 503 (Letters of Appointment).
37. *Id.* (Butler Petition).
38. *TSCM* 6: 361.

Appendix A

1. *Early Land Transfers* 4: 208.
2. James Smith, 386.
3. *Chen. Rec.*, February 27, 1793.
4. *Id.*, May 17, 1815; *id.*, April 20, 1820.
5. *Id.*, April 20, 1820.
6. *Boston Transcript*, July 13, 1927, ref. 5836.
7. *TSCM* 6: 1443; *Wayne Prob.*, Case 440.
8. Abstract, 312–13.
9. *Chen. Rec.*, September 17, 1828.

10. *Id.*, October 1, 1828.
11. Pap. in Box., 180.
12. "An Act for the probate of wills, and the settlement of testate and intestate estates," sec. 16, *LTM* 2: 13, 16 (January 31, 1809).
13. *William St. Clair v. Stephen G. Simmons, Jour. A*, June 11, 1830.
14. James may have lived on his father's property near Ypsilanti. He received a U.S. patent for 160 acres of land in Washtenaw County on October 25, 1830, a month after his father's execution. Peck, *Washtenaw*, 135.
15. *Abstracts of Philadelphia Wills*, 3: 439.

bibliography

Primary Sources

I. Any research into the history of nineteenth-century Michigan must include the forty-volume compendium of memoirs, reminiscences, meeting reports, historical documents, obituaries, and other material known colloquially as the *Michigan Pioneer and Historical Collection* and cited here as *MPHC*. The titles of the individual volumes changed from year to year, as did the publishers. Some earlier volumes were printed in a second edition in the years following 1905, but others were not.

For example, Volume 1, which covered the society's annual meetings in 1876 and 1877, is entitled *Pioneer Collections: Report of the Pioneer Society of the State of Michigan Together with Reports of County, Town and District Pioneer Societies*, and was first published in 1878. Volume 8 is entitled *Collections of the Pioneer Society of the State of Michigan Together with Reports of County Pioneer Societies*, while Volumes 13 to 36 are entitled *Historical Collections: Collection and Researches Made by the Michigan Pioneer and Historical Society Including Reports of Officers and Papers Read at the Annual Meeting of [. . .]*. Some of the forty volumes were published by Robert Smith Printing Co. and the rest by Wynhook, Hallenbeck Crawford Co., both of Lansing, Michigan. Because not all of the volumes were reprinted, and because the publication dates of the first edition are not always given, I have cited the year or years covered by that volume instead of the year of publication.

II. The laws enacted by the various legislative authorities of the Territory of Michigan between 1805 and 1835 were compiled in several editions that included all public laws actually in force on the publication date (1805, 1816, 1820, 1827, and 1833). Unless otherwise noted, all citations to territorial laws are to the *Laws of the Territory of Michigan*, 4 vols. (Lansing: W. S. George and Co., 1871–84). This work, abbreviated as *LTM*, is a chronological compilation of all laws, public and private, enacted during Michigan's territorial period.

III. All citations to federal statutes are to the *Statutes at Large of the United States of America, 1789–1873*, 17 vols. (Washington, D.C., 1850–73). This work, abbreviated as *Stat.*, is a chronological compilation of all federal laws and treaties enacted during the stated period.

IV. Real estate transactions involving land in Chenango County, New York, recorded in the County Clerk's office in Norwich, are referred to by the date the deed was executed.

WORKS CITED

Abbott, Wilbur Cortez. *New York in the American Revolution*. New York: Charles Scribners' Sons, 1929. Reprint, Port Washington, NY: I. J. Friedman, 1962.

Abstract of the Last Will and Testament of John Simmons. *Collections of the New York Historical Society for the Year 1905* (1906): 312–13.

Abstracts of Philadelphia Wills. 11 vols. Philadelphia: Genealogical Society of Pennsylvania, 1999.

Anderson, Fannie. *Doctors under Three Flags*. Detroit: Wayne State University Press, 1951.

Anderson, Frank W. *Concise History of Capital Punishment in Canada*. Aldergrove, BC: Frontier Publishing, 1973.

"Annual Report of the Wayne County Chapter." *MPHC* 1 (1876–77): 338–517.

Appleby, Joyce. *Inheriting the Revolution: The First Generation of Americans*. New York: Belknap Press, 2000.

Bald, F. Clever. *Michigan in Four Centuries*. Rev. ed. New York: Harper and Row, 1961.

Banner, Stuart. *The Death Penalty: An American History*. Cambridge, MA: Harvard University Press, 2002.

Barck, Oscar Theodore. *New York City during the War of Independence, with Special Reference to the Period of British Occupation*. New York: Columbia University Press, 1931.

Barfknecht, Gary W. *Murder, Michigan*. Davison, MI: Friede Publications, 1983.

Bayles, W. Harrison. *Old Taverns of New York*. New York: Frank Allaben Genealogical Co., 1915.

Bennett, Edward W. "The Reasons for Michigan's Abolition of Capital Punishment." *Michigan History Magazine* 62 (November-December 1978): 42–55.

"Big Steve Made His Mark on the Day of the Hanging," *Detroit Free Press* (March 20, 1960).

Bingham, H. H. "The Abolishment of the Death Penalty: History of the Substitution of Solitary Imprisonment for the Death Penalty in the State of Michigan and the Comparative Results." *MPHC* 3 (1879–80): 99–102.

"Biographical Sketch of John Roberts, Esq., of Detroit." *MPHC* 3 (1879–80): 222–25.

Bishop, Levi. "Biographical Sketch of General Lawson Alexander Van Akin." *MPHC* 6 (1883): 476–78.

———. "Recollections of the 'Patriot War' of 1838–39." *MPHC* 12 (1889): 414.

Blois, John T. *Gazetteer of the State of Michigan*. Detroit, 1838. Reprint, New York: Arno Press-NY Times, 1975.

Blume, William Wirt. "Criminal Procedure on the American Frontier: A Study of the Statutes and Court Records of Michigan Territory 1805–1825." *Michigan Law Review* 57 (1958): 195–256.

———. "Legislation on the American Frontier: Adoption of Laws by Governor and Judges—Northwest Territory 1788–1798; Indiana Territory 1800–1804; Michigan Territory 1805–1823." *Michigan Law Review* 60 (1962): 317.

———. "Territorial Courts and Law: Unifying Factors in the Development of American Legal Institutions." *Michigan Law Review* 61 (1962): 39 (Part I); 467 (Part II).

Buley, R. Carlyle. *The Old Northwest: Pioneer Period, 1815–1840*. 2 vols. Bloomington, IN: Indiana University Press, 1950.

Burbey, Louis H. "History of Executions in What Is Now the State of Michigan." *Michigan History* 22 (1938): 443–57.

Burgess-Jackson, Keith. "Violence on the Michigan Frontier: The Incidence of

Sporadic Assault in Michigan Territory, 1817–1830," *Detroit in Perspective* 7, no. 1 (Spring 1983): 46–74.

Burns, Ric, and James Sanders. *New York, An Illustrated History*. New York: Knopf, 1999.

Burton Abstract and Title Co. Abstract of Simmons' Tavern Property. Archives. City of Wayne Historical Museum, Wayne, MI.

Burton, Clarence M. Papers in Boxes in Attic of City Hall. *1819–72 Court and Other Records Copied from Original Files. County Building*. Detroit: Burton Historical Collection, Detroit Public Library, 1910–11.

———. "Detroit in the Year 1832." MPHC 28 (1897–98): 163–71.

Burton, M. Agnes, "Appendix, Vol. XIV." MPHC 14 (1889): 679–90.

Catlin, George B. *The Story of Detroit*. 2nd ed. Detroit: Detroit News, 1926.

———. "Early Settlement in Eastern Michigan." *Michigan History Magazine* 26 (1942): 319.

———. Papers. Burton Historical Collection. Detroit Public Library, Detroit, MI.

Chardavoyne, David G. "George A. O'Keeffe: Pioneer Irish-American Lawyer." *Michigan Bar Journal* 79 (November 2000): 1581.

Chronology of Notable Events in the History of the Northwest Territory and Wayne County. Edited by Frederick Carlisle. Detroit: Wayne County Historical Pioneer Society, 1890.

City of Detroit Michigan: 1701–1922. Edited by Clarence M. Burton. 4 vols. Detroit and Chicago: S. J. Clarke Publishing Co., 1922.

Clark, Hiram C. *History of Chenango County*. Norwich, NY: Thompson and Pratt, 1850.

Clary, David A., and Joseph W. A. Whitehorne. *The Inspectors General of the United States Army, 1777–1903*. Washington, DC: United States Army, 1987.

Coffey, Thomas L. and Jerry L. Morton. "Trial, Error, and the Abolition of the Death Penalty." *Journal of Contemporary Criminal Justice* 5 (1989): 248–255.

Cohen, Patricia Cline. *A Calculating People: The Spread of Numeracy in Early America*. New York: Routledge, 1999.

Colburn, Harvey C. *The Story of Ypsilanti*. Ypsilanti, MI: [n.p.], [1923?]. Reprint, Ypsilanti, MI: Ypsilanti Bicentennial Commission, 1976.

Colton, Calvin. *Tour of the American Lakes, and among the Indians of the Northwest Territory, in 1830; disclosing the character and prospects of the Indian race*. 2 vols. London: F. Westley and A. H. Davis, 1833. Reprint, Port Washington, NY: Kennikat Press, 1972. An excerpt from this book was published as "Remarkable Instance of Capital Crime: Account of the Last Case of Capital Punishment in Michigan, from Colton's (Cotton's) 'Tour of the Lakes in 1830,' " MPHC 6 (1883): 103–5.

Comin, John. *History of the Presbyterian Church in Michigan*. Ann Arbor, MI: Ann Arbor Press, 1950.

"Copies of Papers in the Possession of the Historical Society, at Detroit." *MPHC* 12 (1887): 351–662.

Corlew, Robert E. *Tennessee: A Short History*. 2nd ed. Knoxville, TN: University of Tennessee Press, 1981.

Crawford, Rev. Riley C. "Address to the Pioneers of Oakland County, 1883." *MPHC* 14 (1889): 585–602.

Dain, Floyd R. *Detroit and the Western Movement*. Detroit: Wayne University Press [sic], 1951.

Darby, William. *A Tour from the City of New York, to Detroit, In the Michigan Territory, Made Between the 2d of May and the 22d of September, 1818*. New York: [n.p.], 1819. Reprint, Chicago: Quadrangle Books-Americana Classics, 1962.

Delavigne, Theodore, "Michigan Never Paid the Hangman's Piper," *Detroit Free Press* (February 24, 1929).

"Detroit Young Men's Temperance Society." *MPHC* 12 (1887): 457–61.

Dewey, Francis Asbury. "Some Sketches of Long Ago, Reminiscences of Francis Asbury Dewey." *MPHC* 14 (1889): 528–31.

Digested Summary and Alphabetical List of Private Claims Which have been Presented to the House of Representatives. Misc. Docs., unnumbered, series 653–655. Washington, DC: U.S. House of Representatives, 1853. Reprint, Baltimore, MD: Genealogical Publishing Co., 1970.

Dorr, Harold Mcvicar. *The Michigan Constitutional Convention of 1835–36, the Debates and Minutes*. Ann Arbor, MI: University of Michigan Press, 1940.

———. "The Michigan Constitution of 1835," *Papers of the Michigan Academy of Science, Art, and Letters* 19 (1933): 451.

Duffield, Rev. George. *The Divine Organic Law Ordained for the Human Race* (Detroit: Garrett and Geiger, 1848).

Dunbar, Willis F., and George S. May. *Michigan: A History of the Wolverine State*. Rev. ed. Grand Rapids, MI: Wm. B. Eerdmans Publishing Co., 1980.

Early Land Transfers, Detroit and Wayne County, Michigan. 53 vols. Michigan Works Progress Administration, Vital Records Project. Detroit: Louise St. Clair Chapter, D.A.R., 1936—1940.

Ellis, Edward Robb. *The Epic of New York City*. New York: Kondansha International, 1966.

Executive Journals of the Territory of Michigan. Michigan State Archives, Lansing, MI.

Farmer, Silas. *History of Detroit, Wayne County and Early Michigan: A Chronological Encyclopedia of the Past*. 3rd ed. 2 vols. in 1. Detroit: Silas Farmer and Co., 1890. Reprint, Detroit: Gale Research Co., 1969.

Farrand, B. C. "Early Days in Desmond and Vicinity, from Sources Written and Unwritten." MPHC 13 (1888): 334–42.

Fenn, Elizabeth A. Pox Americana, the Great Smallpox Epidemic of 1775–82. New York: Hill and Wang, 2001.

Filler, Louis. "Movements to Abolish the Death Penalty in the United States." Annals of the American Academy of Politics and Social Science 284 (1952): 124–37.

"First Presbyterian Church in Detroit." MPHC 1 (1876–77): 417–29.

Fleming, Thomas. Duel: Alexander Hamilton, Aaron Burr and the Future of America. New York: Basic Books, 1999.

Friedrich, Otto. Olympia: Paris in the Age of Manet. New York: Harper Collins, 1992.

Fuller, George Newman. Economic and Social Beginnings of Michigan. Lansing, MI: Wynkoop Hallenbeck Crawford Co., 1916.

General Index to Compiled Military Service Records of Revolutionary War Soldiers. Washington, DC: National Archives Microfilm Publications, 1972.

Gilpin, Alec R. The Territory of Michigan (1805–1837). Lansing, MI: Michigan State University Press, 1970.

Hamersly, Thomas H. Complete Regular Army Register of the United States for One Hundred Years (1779 to 1879). 3rd ed. Washington, DC: T. H. S. Hamersly, 1881.

"Hanged in 1830," Detroit News-Tribune (December 22, 1900), Burton Scrapbook No. 8, Burton Historical Collection. Detroit Public Library, Detroit, MI.

Hawley, Mary. "The History of Wayne." The Wayne Dispatch [n.d.], 1924.

Heitman, Francis B. Historical Register and Dictionary of the United States Army. 2 vols. Washington, DC: GPO, 1903. Reprint, Urbana: University of Illinois Press, 1965.

Hoch, Henry George. "First and Last Show in 1830 Proved a Flop." Detroit News (July 31, 1938).

Holmes, Oliver W., Jr. The Common Law. Boston: Little Brown, 1881.

Hoyt, Dr. James M. "History of the Town of Commerce." MPHC 14 (1889): 421.

Humphrey, John T., Pennsylvania Births: Philadelphia County, 1766–1780. Washington, DC: Humphrey Publications, 1995.

Hyde, John. Historical Sketches of Old New Berlin. New Berlin, NY, 1876. Reprint, New Berlin, NY: Unadilla Valley Historical Society, 1907.

Jerome, Edwin, Jr. "Obituary Report Prepared by Edwin Jerome for the Year Ending February 4, 1880." MPHC 4 (1881): 422–27.

Jerome, Edwin, Sr., "The Jerome Family," MPHC 2 (1878): 11–19.

Jones, Thomas L. "The Last Person Michigan Executed." Michigan Monthly Magazine (March 1996): 16.

Journal A. Wayne County Circuit Court Collection. Bentley Historical Library. University of Michigan, Ann Arbor, MI.

Journal of Ferry and Tavern Licenses, 1820–1829. Wayne County Court Files and Papers. Burton Historical Collection. Detroit Public Library, Detroit, MI.

Keen, Richard A. *Michigan Weather.* Helena, MT: American and World Geographic Publishing, 1993.

Lanman, Charles. *The Life of William Woodbridge.* Washington, DC: Blanchard and Mohun, 1867.

Lanman, James H. *History of Michigan from Its Earliest Colonization to the Present Time.* New York: Harper, 1841.

Larkin, Jack. *The Reshaping of Everyday Life.* New York: Harper Perennial, 1989.

Laurence, John. *A History of Capital Punishment: With Special Reference to Capital Punishment in Great Britain.* London: Sampson Low, Marston and Co., [1930?].

Leake, Paul. *History of Detroit.* Detroit: Lewis Publishing Co., 1912.

Lincoln, James H. "The Everlasting Controversy: Michigan and the Death Penalty." *Wayne Law Review* 33 (1987): 1765–90.

Lippincott, Horace Mather. *Early Philadelphia: Its People, Life, and Progress.* Philadelphia: J. B. Lippincott, 1917.

MacCabe, Julius P. Bolivar. *Directory of the City of Detroit with its Environs and Register of Michigan for the Year 1837.* Detroit: William Harsha, 1837. Reprint, Detroit: R. L. Polk and Co., 1937.

Mackey, Philip English. *Hanging in the Balance: The Anti-Capital Punishment Movement in New York State, 1776–1861.* New York: Garland Publishing, Inc., 1982.

Marriage and Death Notices from the New York Weekly Museum, 1789–1796. Compiled by Consuelo Furman and Robert Furman. New York: [n.p.], 1950.

Marriages, 1827–1857, in Washtenaw County, Michigan. Ann Arbor, MI: Sarah Caswell Angell Chapter, D.A.R., 1961.

Martin, John Hill. *Martin's Bench and Bar of Philadelphia.* Philadelphia: Rees Welsh and Co., 1883.

Massie, Larry B. *Voyages into Michigan's Past.* Marquette, MI: Avery Color Studios, 1988.

Masur, Louis P. *Rites of Execution: Capital Punishment and the Transformation of American Culture, 1776–1865.* New York: Oxford University Press, 1991.

Mather, Frederic G. *The Refugees of 1776 from Long Island to Connecticut.* Albany, NY: J. B. Lyon Co., 1913.

May, George S. *Pictorial History of Michigan.* 2 vols. Grand Rapids, MI: Eerdmans Publishing, 1967–69.

McCullough, David. *John Adams*. New York: Simon and Schuster, 2001.

Messages of the Governors of Michigan. 4 vols. Edited by George Newman Fuller. Lansing, MI: Michigan Historical Commission, 1925–27.

Michigan Biographies: Early History of Michigan with Biographies of State Officers, Members of Congress, Judges and Legislators. 2 vols. Lansing, MI: Thorp and Godfroy, 1888. Reprint, 2 vols. in 1, Lansing: Michigan Historical Commission, 1924.

Miller, Albert. "Pioneer Sketches." MPHC 7 (1884): 229–62.

Moore, J. Wilkie. "Michigan under the First, and under the Second Harrison." MPHC 14 (1889): 409–18.

Moore, Julia Gatlin. *History of the Dearborn Area, 1709–1940*. 2 vols. [n.p.], [1920?].

Moore, Lucy. *The Thieves Opera*. San Diego: Harvest-Harcourt, 1998.

"Muster Rolls of Troop of Light Dragoons Van Rensselear." Muster Rolls of Regular Army Organizations, 1784–10/31/1912, RG-94. Records of the Adjutant General's Office, PI-17, Entry 53, Box 118–A. National Archives of the United States, Washington, DC.

New York Genealogical and Biographical Record. 132 vols. New York: New York Genealogical and Biographical Society, 1870–2001.

Norris, Maria W. "Biographical Notes and Incidents in the Pioneer Life of Mrs. R. B. Norris." MPHC 2 (1878): 504–21.

Nowlin, William. *The Bark Covered House, or Back in the Woods Again*. Detroit: [n.p.], 1876. Reprint, Dearborn, MI: Dearborn Historical Commission, 1959.

Osband, Melvin D. "My Recollections of Pioneers and Pioneer Life in Nankin." MPHC 14 (1889): 431–83.

Palmer, Friend. *Early Days in Detroit*. Detroit: Hunt and June, 1906.

———. "Ferry Service between Detroit and Windsor." MPHC 32 (1902): 463–67.

———. Papers. "Great Gala Hanging, Execution of Simmons with Band Accompaniment," *Detroit Evening Journal* ([n.d.], 1885). Scrapbook No. 7, pp. 97–98. Burton Historical Collection. Detroit Public Library, Detroit, MI.

Palmer, Thomas W. "Sketch of the Life and Times of James Witherell." MPHC 4–10 (1881): 103–15.

Peck, Paul R. *Landsmen of Lenawee County*. Clark Lake, MI: Liberty Town Press, 1981.

———. *Landsmen of Washtenaw County: An Atlas and Plat of the First Landowners of Washtenaw County, Michigan*. Clark Lake, MI: Liberty Town Press, 1986.

———. *Landsmen of Wayne County: An Atlas and Plat of the First Landowners of Wayne County, Michigan*. Clark Lake, MI: Liberty Town Press, 1985.

Pippinger, Wesley E. *District of Columbia Probate Records*. Westminster, MD: Family Line Publications, 1996.

Population Schedules of the Fifth Census of the United States, 1830. Washington, DC: National Archives and Record Service, GSA, 1959.

Population Schedules of the Fourth Census of the United States, 1820. Washington, DC: National Archives and Record Service, GSA, 1959.

Population Schedules of the Second Census of the United States, 1800. Washington, DC: National Archives and Record Service, GSA, 1959.

Population Schedules of the Third Census of the United States, 1810. Washington, DC: National Archives and Record Service, GSA, 1959.

Poremba, David Lee. *Images of America, Detroit 1860–1899*. Charleston, SC: Arcadia Publishing, 1998.

Post, Albert. "Michigan Abolishes Capital Punishment." *Michigan History* 29 (1945): 44–50.

Public Papers of George Clinton, First Governor of New York. 10 vols. Albany, NY: State of New York, 1899–1914.

Quaife, M. M. "Capital Punishment in Detroit." *Burton Historical Collection Leaflets*. Vol. 4, No. 3 (January 1926): 33.

———, and Sidney Glazer. *Michigan: From Primitive Wilderness to Industrial Commonwealth*. New York: Prentice-Hall, 1948.

Rau, Louise. "Solomon Sibley: The Public Servant." Ms., Burton Historical Collection. Detroit Public Library, Detroit, c. 1950.

Reid, Edwin C. "Death of the Venerable Judge Littlejohn." *MPHC* 3 (1880): 310.

Riddell, William Renwick. *Michigan under British Rule: Law and Courts, 1760–1796*. Lansing, MI: Michigan Historical Commission, 1926.

Risch, Erna. *Quartermaster Support of the Army, a History of the Corps, 1775–1939*. *Washington, DC*: U.S. Army Center of Military History, 1939.

Roberts, Robert Ellis. *Detroit One Hundred Years Ago*. Detroit: [n.p.], 1883.

———. "Recollections of Robert E. Roberts. *MPHC* 2 (1878): 567–73.

———. *Sketches of the City of Detroit, State of Michigan: Past and Present*. Detroit: [n.p.], 1855.

Roberts, Snyder E. *Roots of Roane County, Tennessee, 1792–*. Rockwood, TN: Roane County Publishing Co., 1981.

Ross, Robert Budd. *The Early Bench and Bar of Detroit: from 1805 to the end of 1850*. Detroit: Richard P. Joy and Clarence M. Burton, 1907.

Russell, D. V. *Michigan Censuses for 1710 to 1830*. Detroit: Detroit Society for Genealogical Research, 1982.

Scott, Kenneth. *Rivington's New York Newspaper: Excerpts from a Loyalist Press, 1773–1783*. New York: New York Historical Society, 1973.

————, and Kristin L. Gibbons. *New York Magazine Marriages and Deaths, 1790–1797*. New Orleans, LA: Polyanthos, 1975.

Smith, James Hadden. *History of Chenango and Madison Counties, New York*. Syracuse, NY: D. Mason and Co., 1880.

Smith, Thomas Edward Vermilye. *The City of New York in the Year of Washington's Inauguration, 1789*. New York: Anson D. F. Randolph and Co., 1889.

Stark, George W. *City of Destiny: The Story of Detroit*. Detroit: Arnold-Powers, 1943.

Supreme Court of Michigan Collection. Bentley Historical Library. University of Michigan. Ann Arbor, MI.

Taylor, Alan. *William Cooper's Town*. New York: Random House, 1995.

Taylor, George. "First Visit to Michigan, Some Incidents Connected with Early Methodism in Michigan." MPHC 6 (1883): 15–17.

Taylor, Isaac. *History of the Transmission of Ancient Books to Modern Times Together with the Process of Historical Proof*. Liverpool: Edward Howell, 1879.

Transactions of the Supreme Court of Michigan, 1805–1846. Edited by William Wirt Blume. 6 vols. Ann Arbor, MI: University of Michigan Press, 1935–40.

Tucker, Gideon J. *Names of Persons for Whom Marriage Licenses were Issued by the Secretary of the Province of New York previous to 1784*. Albany, NY: Weed Parsons and Co., 1860. Reprint, Baltimore: Genealogical Publishing Co., 1968.

Van Buren, A. D. P. "Dean Isaac Mason's Early Recollections of Michigan." MPHC 5 (1882): 397–402.

————. "Pioneer Annals." MPHC 5 (1882): 237–59.

————. "The Fever and Ague—'Michigan Rash'—Mosquitoes—The Old Pioneers' Foes." MPHC 5 (1882): 300–4.

Villard, Oswald Garrison. "The Early History of Wall Street, 1653–1789." In *Historic New York: Being the First Series of the Half Moon Papers*, edited by Maud Wilder Goodwin, Alice Carrington Royce, and Ruth Putnam. New York: G. P. Putnam's Sons, 1897–99.

Wanger, Eugene G. "Historical Reflections on Michigan's Abolition of the Death Penalty." *Thomas M. Cooley Law Review* 13 (1996): 755–74.

Washington, George. *Writings of George Washington*. Edited by Worthington C. Ford. 14 vols. New York, 1889–93.

Watkins, L. D. "Seventy Years of Michigan." MPHC 30 (1905): 63–68.

Wayne Centennial Committee, Inc. *The Memories of a Community, Wayne Memorial Centennial*. Wayne, MI: Dispatch Publications, 1969.

Wayne County Circuit Court Collection, Burton Historical Collection. Detroit Public Library, Detroit, MI.

Wayne County Circuit Court Collection, Michigan State Archives. Lansing, MI.

Wayne County Circuit Court Collection. Bentley Historical Library. University of Michigan, Ann Arbor, MI.

Wayne County Probate Court Collection, Michigan State Archives. Lansing, MI.

Weigley, Russell F. *History of the United States Army*. New York: Macmillan, 1967.

White, Virgil D. *Genealogical Abstracts of Revolutionary War Pension Files*. Waynesboro, TN: National Historical Publishing Co., 1992.

Widder, Keith R. "Justice at Mackinac." *Mackinac History* 2, no. 2 (1974): 1–12.

Wilber, Floyd A. *Early Glimpses of the New Berlin Area and Related Areas Nearby*. 2 vols. New Berlin, NY: [n.p.], 1967.

Williams, B. O. "My Recollections of the Early Schools of Detroit That I Attended from the Year 1816 to 1819." *MPHC* 5 (1882): 547–50.

Williams, Ephraim S. "Detroit Three Score Years Ago." *MPHC* 10 (1886): 84–87.

Wilson, Thomas B. *Inhabitants of New York 1774–1776*. Baltimore: Genealogical Publishing Co., 1993. [includes reprint of *Calendar of Historical Manuscripts Relating to the War of Revolution*. Albany, 1868].

Winder, John. Papers. Bentley Historical Library, University of Michigan. Ann Arbor, MI.

Witherell, Peter C., and Edwin R. Witherell. *History and Genealogy of the Witherell/Wetherell/Witherill Family of New England*. Baltimore: Gateway Press, 1976.

Woodbridge, William. Papers. Burton Historical Collection. Detroit Public Library, Detroit, MI.

Woodford, Frank B. *Lewis Cass: The Last Jeffersonian*. New Brunswick, NJ: Rutgers University Press, 1950. Reprint, New York: Octagon Books, 1973.
———, and Arthur Woodford. *All Our Yesterdays: A Brief History of Detroit*. Detroit: Wayne State University Press, 1969.

index

Titles in the Great Lakes Books Series

Deep Woods Frontier: A History of Logging in Northern Michigan, by Theodore J. Karamanski, 1989

Orvie, The Dictator of Dearborn, by David L. Good, 1989

Seasons of Grace: A History of the Catholic Archdiocese of Detroit, by Leslie Woodcock Tentler, 1990

The Pottery of John Foster: Form and Meaning, by Gordon and Elizabeth Orear, 1990

The Diary of Bishop Frederic Baraga: First Bishop of Marquette, Michigan, edited by Regis M. Walling and Rev. N. Daniel Rupp, 1990

Walnut Pickles and Watermelon Cake: A Century of Michigan Cooking, by Larry B. Massie and Priscilla Massie, 1990

The Making of Michigan, 1820–1860: A Pioneer Anthology, edited by Justin L. Kestenbaum, 1990

America's Favorite Homes: A Guide to Popular Early Twentieth-Century Homes, by Robert Schweitzer and Michael W. R. Davis, 1990

Beyond the Model T: The Other Ventures of Henry Ford, by Ford R. Bryan, 1990

Life after the Line, by Josie Kearns, 1990

Michigan Lumbertowns: Lumbermen and Laborers in Saginaw, Bay City, and Muskegon, 1870–1905, by Jeremy W. Kilar, 1990

Detroit Kids Catalog: The Hometown Tourist, by Ellyce Field, 1990

Waiting for the News, by Leo Litwak, 1990 (reprint)

Detroit Perspectives, edited by Wilma Wood Henrickson, 1991

Life on the Great Lakes: A Wheelsman's Story, by Fred W. Dutton, edited by William Donohue Ellis, 1991

Copper Country Journal: The Diary of Schoolmaster Henry Hobart, 1863–1864, by Henry Hobart, edited by Philip P. Mason, 1991

John Jacob Astor: Business and Finance in the Early Republic, by John Denis Haeger, 1991

Survival and Regeneration: Detroit's American Indian Community, by Edmund J. Danziger, Jr., 1991

Steamboats and Sailors of the Great Lakes, by Mark L. Thompson, 1991

Cobb Would Have Caught It: The Golden Age of Baseball in Detroit, by Richard Bak, 1991

Michigan in Literature, by Clarence Andrews, 1992

Under the Influence of Water: Poems, Essays, and Stories, by Michael Delp, 1992

The Country Kitchen, by Della T. Lutes, 1992 (reprint)

The Making of a Mining District: Keweenaw Native Copper 1500–1870, by David J. Krause, 1992

Kids Catalog of Michigan Adventures, by Ellyce Field, 1993

Henry's Lieutenants, by Ford R. Bryan, 1993

Historic Highway Bridges of Michigan, by Charles K. Hyde, 1993

Lake Erie and Lake St. Clair Handbook, by Stanley J. Bolsenga and Charles E. Herndendorf, 1993

Queen of the Lakes, by Mark Thompson, 1994

Iron Fleet: The Great Lakes in World War II, by George J. Joachim, 1994

Turkey Stearnes and the Detroit Stars: The Negro Leagues in Detroit, 1919–1933, by Richard Bak, 1994

Pontiac and the Indian Uprising, by Howard H. Peckham, 1994 (reprint)

Charting the Inland Seas: A History of the U.S. Lake Survey, by Arthur M. Woodford, 1994 (reprint)

Ojibwa Narratives of Charles and Charlotte Kawbawgam and Jacques LePique, 1893–1895. Recorded with Notes by Homer H. Kidder, edited by Arthur P. Bourgeois, 1994, co-published with the Marquette County Historical Society

Strangers and Sojourners: A History of Michigan's Keweenaw Peninsula, by Arthur W. Thurner, 1994

Win Some, Lose Some: G. Mennen Williams and the New Democrats, by Helen Washburn Berthelot, 1995

Sarkis, by Gordon and Elizabeth Orear, 1995

The Northern Lights: Lighthouses of the Upper Great Lakes, by Charles K. Hyde, 1995 (reprint)

Kids Catalog of Michigan Adventures, second edition, by Ellyce Field, 1995

Rumrunning and the Roaring Twenties: Prohibition on the Michigan-Ontario Waterway, by Philip P. Mason, 1995

In the Wilderness with the Red Indians, by E. R. Baierlein, translated by Anita Z. Boldt, edited by Harold W. Moll, 1996

Elmwood Endures: History of a Detroit Cemetery, by Michael Franck, 1996

Master of Precision: Henry M. Leland, by Mrs. Wilfred C. Leland with Minnie Dubbs Millbrook, 1996 (reprint)

Haul-Out: New and Selected Poems, by Stephen Tudor, 1996

Kids Catalog of Michigan Adventures, third edition, by Ellyce Field, 1997

Beyond the Model T: The Other Ventures of Henry Ford, revised edition, by Ford R. Bryan, 1997

Young Henry Ford: A Picture History of the First Forty Years, by Sidney Olson, 1997 (reprint)

The Coast of Nowhere: Meditations on Rivers, Lakes and Streams, by Michael Delp, 1997

From Saginaw Valley to Tin Pan Alley: Saginaw's Contribution to American Popular Music, 1890–1955, by R. Grant Smith, 1998

The Long Winter Ends, by Newton G. Thomas, 1998 (reprint)

Bridging the River of Hatred: The Pioneering Efforts of Detroit Police Commissioner George Edwards, by Mary M. Stolberg, 1998

Toast of the Town: The Life and Times of Sunnie Wilson, by Sunnie Wilson with John Cohassey, 1998

These Men Have Seen Hard Service: The First Michigan Sharpshooters in the Civil War, by Raymond J. Herek, 1998

A Place for Summer: One Hundred Years at Michigan and Trumbull, by Richard Bak, 1998

Early Midwestern Travel Narratives: An Annotated Bibliography, 1634–1850, by Robert R. Hubach, 1998 (reprint)

All-American Anarchist: Joseph A. Labadie and the Labor Movement, by Carlotta R. Anderson, 1998

Michigan in the Novel, 1816–1996: An Annotated Bibliography, by Robert Beasecker, 1998

"Time by Moments Steals Away": The 1848 Journal of Ruth Douglass, by Robert L. Root, Jr., 1998

The Detroit Tigers: A Pictorial Celebration of the Greatest Players and Moments in Tigers' History, updated edition, by William M. Anderson, 1999

Father Abraham's Children: Michigan Episodes in the Civil War, by Frank B. Woodford, 1999 (reprint)

Letter from Washington, 1863–1865, by Lois Bryan Adams, edited and with an introduction by Evelyn Leasher, 1999

Wonderful Power: The Story of Ancient Copper Working in the Lake Superior Basin, by Susan R. Martin, 1999

A Sailor's Logbook: A Season aboard Great Lakes Freighters, by Mark L. Thompson, 1999

Huron: The Seasons of a Great Lake, by Napier Shelton, 1999

Tin Stackers: The History of the Pittsburgh Steamship Company, by Al Miller, 1999

Art in Detroit Public Places, revised edition, text by Dennis Nawrocki, photographs by David Clements, 1999

Brewed in Detroit: Breweries and Beers Since 1830, by Peter H. Blum, 1999

Detroit Kids Catalog: A Family Guide for the 21st Century, by Ellyce Field, 2000

"Expanding the Frontiers of Civil Rights": Michigan, 1948–1968, by Sidney Fine, 2000

Graveyard of the Lakes, by Mark L. Thompson, 2000

Enterprising Images: The Goodridge Brothers, African American Photographers, 1847–1922, by John Vincent Jezierski, 2000

New Poems from the Third Coast: Contemporary Michigan Poetry, edited by Michael Delp, Conrad Hilberry, and Josie Kearns, 2000

Arab Detroit: From Margin to Mainstream, edited by Nabeel Abraham and Andrew Shryock, 2000

The Sandstone Architecture of the Lake Superior Region, by Kathryn Bishop Eckert, 2000

Looking Beyond Race: The Life of Otis Milton Smith, by Otis Milton Smith and Mary M. Stolberg, 2000

Mail by the Pail, by Colin Bergel, illustrated by Mark Koenig, 2000

Great Lakes Journey: A New Look at America's Freshwater Coast, by William Ashworth, 2000

A Life in the Balance: The Memoirs of Stanley J. Winkelman, by Stanley J. Winkelman, 2000

Schooner Passage: Sailing Ships and the Lake Michigan Frontier, by Theodore J. Karamanski, 2000

The Outdoor Museum: The Magic of Michigan's Marshall M. Fredericks, by Marcy Heller Fisher, illustrated by Christine Collins Woomer, 2001

Detroit in Its World Setting: A Three Hundred Year Chronology, 1701–2001, edited by David Lee Poremba, 2001

Frontier Metropolis: Picturing Early Detroit, 1701–1838, by Brian Leigh Dunnigan, 2001

Michigan Remembered: Photographs from the Farm Security Administration and the Office of War Information, 1936–1943, edited by Constance B. Schulz, with Introductory Essays by Constance B. Schulz and William H. Mulligan, Jr., 2001

This Is Detroit, 1701–2001, by Arthur M. Woodford, 2001

History of the Finns in Michigan, by Armas K. E. Holmio, translated by Ellen M. Ryynanen, 2001

Angels in the Architecture: A Photographic Elegy to an American Asylum, by Heidi Johnson, 2001

Uppermost Canada: The Western District and the Detroit Frontier, 1800–1850, by R. Alan Douglas, 2001

Windjammers: Songs of the Great Lakes Sailors, by Ivan H. Walton with Joe Grimm, 2002

Detroit Tigers Lists and More: Runs, Hits, and Eras, by Mark Pattison and David Raglin, 2002

The Iron Hunter, by Chase S. Osborn, 2002 (reprint)

Independent Man: The Life of Senator James Couzens, by Harry Barnard, 2002 (reprint)

Riding the Roller Coaster: A History of the Chrysler Corporation, by Charles K. Hyde, 2003

Michigan's Early Military Forces: A Roster and History of Troops Activated prior to the American Civil War, rosters compiled by Le Roy Barnett with histories by Roger Rosentreter, 2003

Beyond the Windswept Dunes: The Story of Maritime Muskegon, by Elizabeth Sherman, 2003

The French Canadians of Michigan: Their Contribution to the Development of the Saginaw Valley and the Keweenaw Peninsula, 1840–1914, by Jean Lamarre, 2003

Fired Magic: Detroit's Pewabic Pottery Treasures, by Marcy Heller Fisher, illustrated by Marjorie Hecht Simon, 2003

A Hanging in Detroit: Stephen Gifford Simmons and the Last Execution under Michigan Law, by David G. Chardavoyne, 2003

For an updated listing of books in this series, please visit our Web site at http://wsupress.wayne.edu